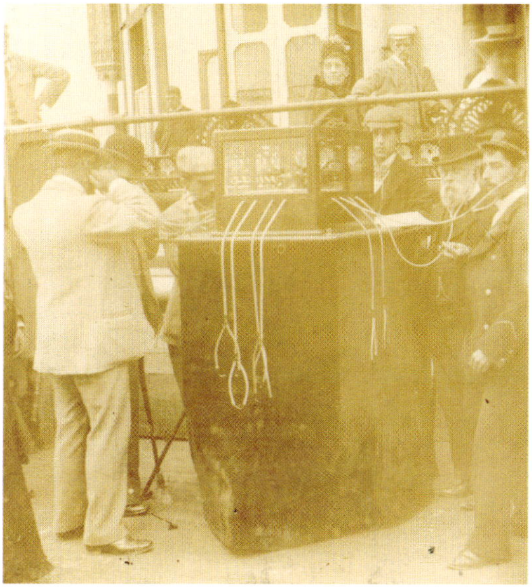

steve roden, dust-to-digital, 2011

i listen to the wind that obliterates my traces.
the wind that resembles nothing,
understands nothing nor cares what it does,
but is so lovely to listen to.
the soft wind,
soft like oblivion.

when the new morning breaks
i shall wander further,
in the windless dawn begin my wandering afresh
with my very first step
in the wonderfully untouched sand.

par lagerkvist, *aftonland*

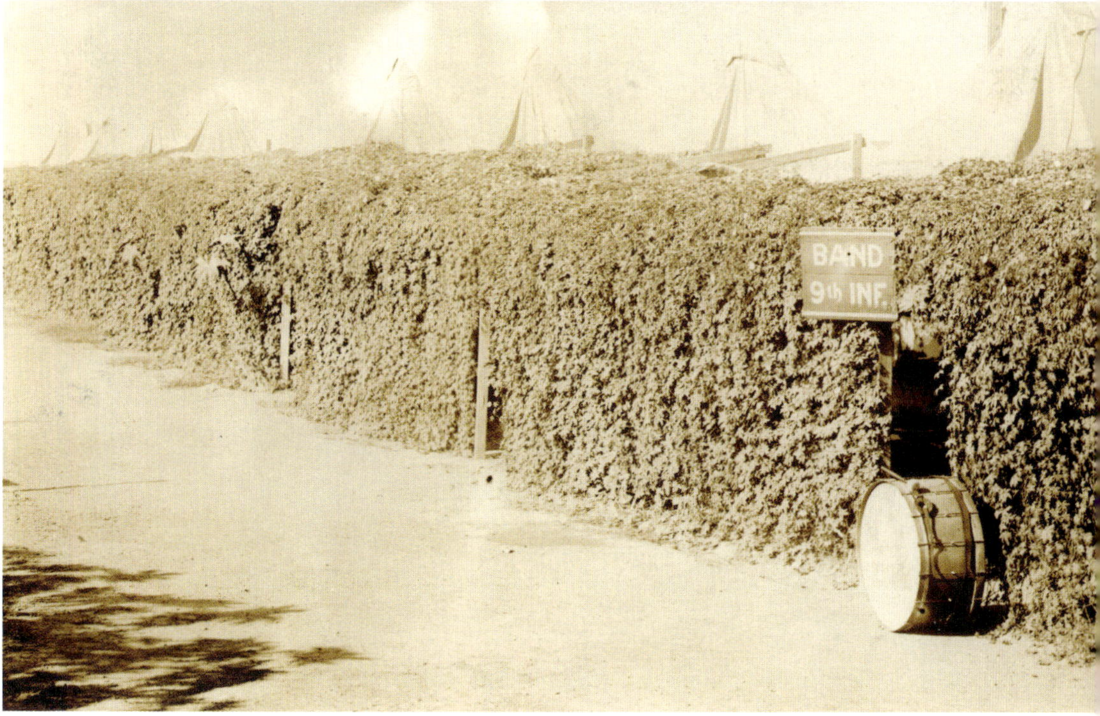
BAND
9th INF.

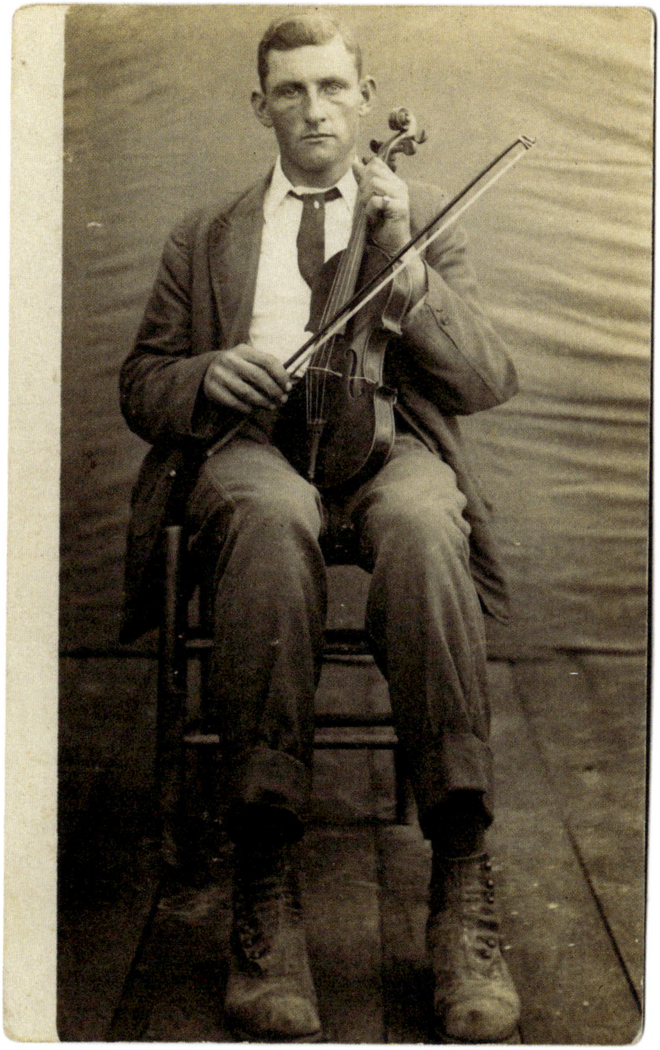

Mr. GEORGE G. DeMOSS

Playing two cornets at once., Soprano on one and alto on the other.

walking alone, stumbling over stones, i happened upon a dust-covered disc of bradley kincaid's recording of *froggie went a-courting*. it wasn't something i was looking for, nor did the record seem to want me to pick it up, but there we were, confronted with each other and zero expectations. as i stood thinking that the performance embedded within this disc would be relatively insignificant, the record stared silently back, knowing full well that i was unworthy of the remarkable presence hidden beneath its unremarkable and very scratched surface. for some reason i decided to take it home, and once i set the needle down upon its outermost grooves i was smitten.

it wasn't kincaid's usual affectations that began to work on my insides but how, for the first time, he'd managed to get out of the way of his own fragile singing and wonderfully awkward sense of time. he let the song breathe, injecting it with a rare essence of authenticity, feeling closer to the vulnerability of a beginner than the polish of a recording star. *froggie went a-courting* seems something of an aberration within kincaid's vast and mediocre discography, sounding more like music captured than performed. while there are no individual elements that stand out, all of the recording's seemingly unremarkable bits coalesce into a single "voice," setting the listener gently down upon a path that slowly moves from the mundane towards the utterly sublime.

kincaid's recording is not my favorite here, but more than any of
the others i have gathered it feels like a perfect anchor for this
whole project: a weighted presence of connective tissue, binding all
of the lookings, readings and listenings, to a common "mood core."
and so kincaid's *froggie went a-courting* has unwittingly become the
foundation of what i've brought together; positioning itself in
my mind as a kind of measuring stick of emotion even though
i am unable to articulate why the recording truly moves me.

certainly, goose bumps are a foregone conclusion when listening to voices like skip james or blind willie johnson; but sometimes a seemingly ordinary record will also direct goose bumps to knock upon your "soul door." it is my inability to understand or reconcile this latter form of goose bumps that allows certain ordinary things to reek of an entirely different kind of magic: a mysterious feeling that is devoid of any suggestion of logic or understanding towards the power of its source.

> *the first came in was a little white moth,*
>   *mmmm hmmm...*
> *the first came in was a little white moth,*
> *and she spread on the tablecloth,*
>   *mmmm hmmm...*
>
>   bradley kincaid,
>   *froggie went a-courting,*
>   supertone record, 1928

as i sit listening in full communion with kincaid's fragile-voiced *froggie*, i notice in the line about the moth and the tablecloth, he sings "she spread on the tablecloth" instead of the more common lyric "she spread out the tablecloth." in this subtle shift of two tiny words, i wonder if kincaid knew that the song's moth would be transformed. unlike the multitude of moths who had "spread out the tablecloth" before her, kincaid's moth is a stilled presence "spread on the tablecloth" like a statue... and i believe that in her stillness, she might also be listening.

he practices a cult with the moths and butterflies that fly into his room at night. he speaks to them for hours. he calls them his little soul animals [seelentierchen] and tells them about his suffering...

                    phillipe-alain michaud,
                    aby warburg and the image
                    in motion

i see kincaid's moth as a stone with wings, and through the singer's sleight-of-hand (or mind, or mouth), the tablecloth's landscape continues to evolve in my mind's eye until it is covered with static wing-spread moths—all of them listeners, patient in the service of wedding guests needing to unburden themselves before the feast and dance can take place. while the frog travels across the pond, about to be eaten by a snake, everyone else—miss mousey, uncle rat, the weasel and the bumble bee—is seated in their respective chairs "way down yonder in a hollow tree," each facing their own silent moth to softly tell their troubles to.

within this hollow tree, i see the wedding supper-table spread with gathered listeners, and i am fairly certain that a few of these "*seelentierchen*" have had their insides already filled; not just with dogwood soup and catnip tea, but with the sufferings of aby warburg. if there was ever a precedent to harry smith's intuitive connection of american music recordings with robert fludd's alchemical diagrams of the 1600's, it would be warburg's unfinished masterpiece, the "mnemosyne atlas." this compendium of over 2000 images pinned to 79 panels attempted to archive the consistency of various universal physical gestures and expressions throughout history, connecting such imagery as botticelli's 1485 painting the birth of venus, a 1920's cologne ad and medieval zodiac diagrams.

in this light, how can one ignore the fact that warburg died a year after kincaid recorded this song? it is, of course, unlikely that warburg heard kincaid's recording, but his obsession with native american rituals did have him traveling in the mid-1890's from europe to the american west. there, during his journey through the arizona desert, where he was photographed numerous times wearing a cowboy hat, he certainly could've heard *froggie went a-courting* played by some anonymous musician, or guide, while sitting around an evening's campfire.

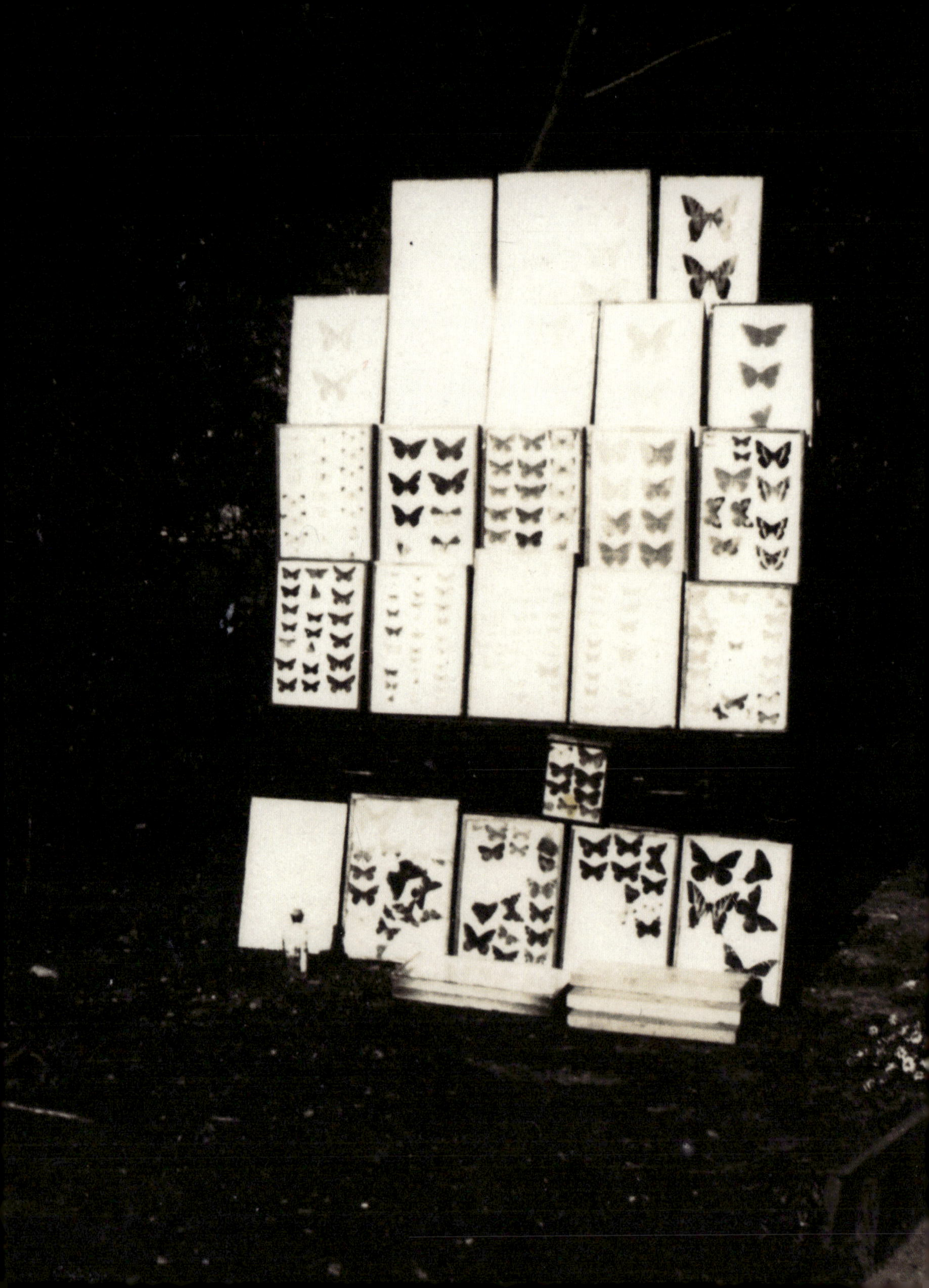

like a group of butterflies arranged and pinned within a broad display case my own vision of kincaid's moth laid out on the tablecloth expands exponentially, resembling an array of things that i have often spread out myself, although usually upon the floor. it is no stretch to perceive a mass of particularly treasured objects upon a table as a collection; and it is only a minutely larger stretch to see that these gathered things, too, are listening. for who among us who *is* a collector, has not at one time or another sat in the throes of loneliness, melancholy or suffering, and held a communion of sorts with a record or two: *one sits alone, listening in a darkened room, as the music floats, notes like a mass of moths, directed towards ears, as if a brightly lit pair of light bulbs in the night.* as a group of favorite sounds enter us they move quickly to our souls and our insides are mended a little... even if it is only for an evening.

Papa and his only true friends.

proof of the universal nature of the collector's deeper feelings towards what he or she has gathered, can be seen in the numerous photographs i have found of a single person surrounded by an assortment of musical instruments. one recent acquisition pictures a man sitting on a piano stool, surrounded by a guitar, banjo, piano, sheet music, some pennants and a phonograph horn—which he seems to be staring vacantly into as if he were listening. at the bottom of the photograph, the sitter has written: "papa and his only true friends," and on the back: "myself and my only friends." his message twice written is clear—inanimate objects can also be seen by their gatherer as *seelentierchen*."

perhaps it is only a coincidence, but just about the time this photograph was taken, walter benjamin was working on his famous essay about owning and collecting books—writing that it is not the books that come alive in the collector, but the collector who begins to come alive within the objects he or she has collected. this photograph of "papa" and his "only true friends" exists as evidence of benjamin's truth.

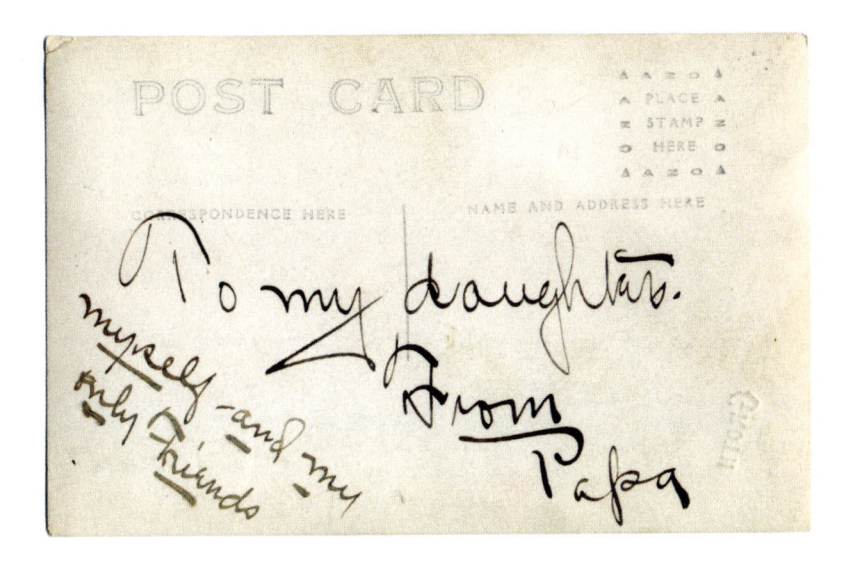

> *if you have this love of inconsiderable things and seek quite simply, as one who serves, to win the confidence of what seems poor: then everything will become easier, more coherent and somehow more conciliatory for you, not in your intellect, perhaps, which lags marveling behind, but in your inmost consciousness, waking and cognizance.*
>
> rainer maria rilke,
> *letters to a young poet*

of course, i too have sat alone many a night amongst a pile of books, a stack of records or a box of old photographs: conversing, organizing, arranging, connecting, disconnecting and listening to the voices of these *inconsiderable things.* in such moments i begin to form a world, seeing (or hearing) each thing shift from an individual star towards part of a larger constellation. when new paths between things are revealed, new images are formed, and the relationship of single objects to each other becomes more complex, more overwhelming and less defined.

as long as one is able to interpret and re-interpret the relationship between the objects on the table, the collection remains alive in *one's inmost consciousness,* enabling the collector to make deeper intuitive connections that leave the intellect *to lag marveling behind*. a collection should not have to conform to some overbearing logical and finite sense of completion, as much as it should have the potential to exist in a state of flux and evolution. a collection guided by openness is not afraid of imperfection, for an imperfect collection necessitates deeper questions than one which simply attempts to complete a checklist.

certainly one must have a determined criteria for addition and inclusion, but that criteria should also be shifting and changing as old rules are allowed to be broken and new rules are allowed to be born. previously unsought discoveries should have permission to shift things, allowing the collection to be a conversation whose guiding principles can be built up and taken apart in the service of both expansion and contraction (as well as rigor, focus, obsession, passion and vision). building a collection should be a personal endeavor, where value is determined by the gatherer rather than the marketplace.

the painter arthur dove once said that everything an artist makes is a self-portrait, and i tend to think that most collections reflect a similar view. the best collections and the most visionary collectors bring objects together that do not necessarily seem comfortable with each other at first glance, yet upon deeper inspection these seemingly disparate parts reveal a consistency of thought rather than a consistency of form. such cases have the potential to reveal the complex inner workings of the gatherer.

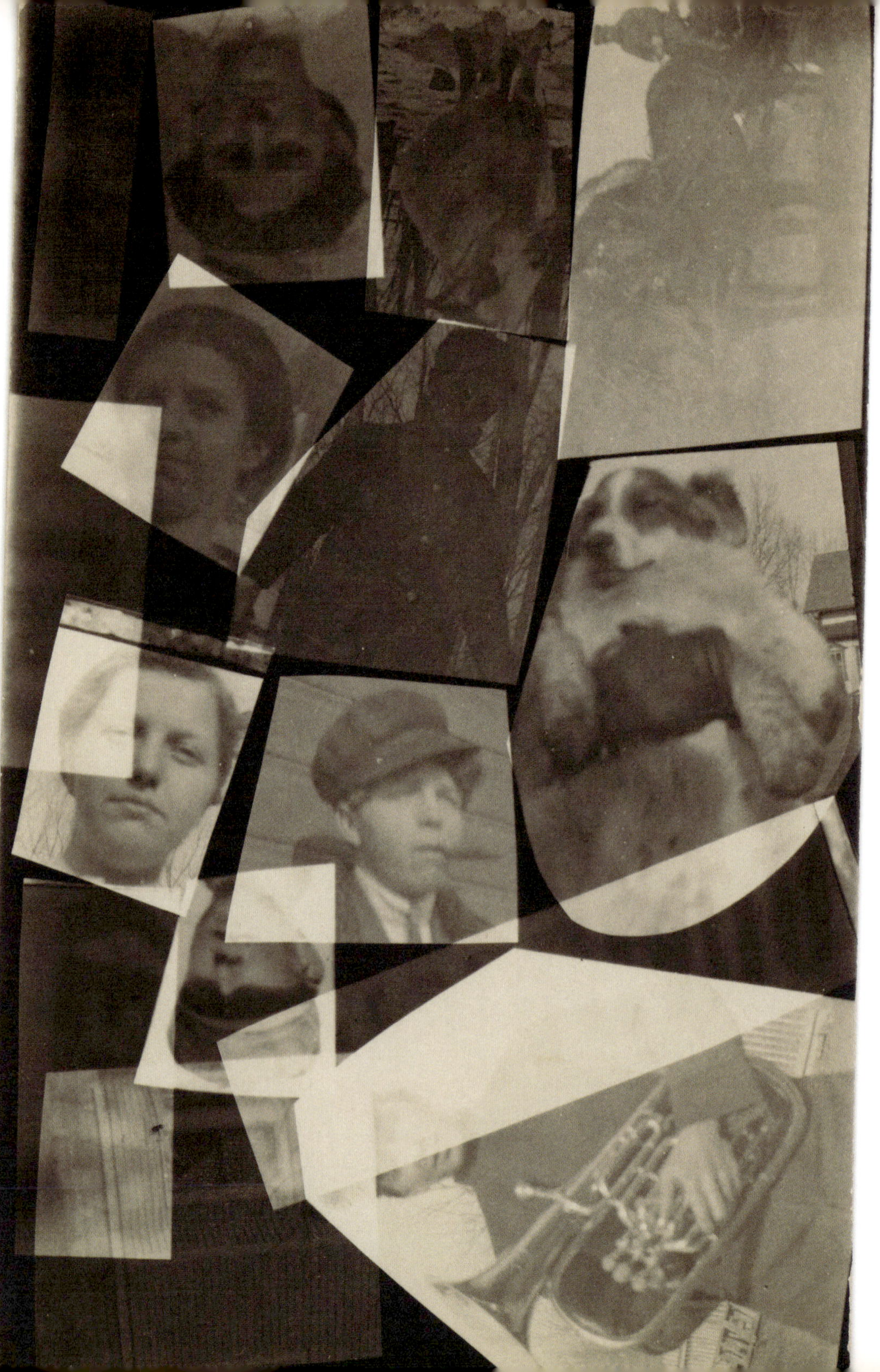

> *over the light bulbs there's all these dead moth wings...
> and i hate that... such a sadness... there must surely be
> something to do with that... i tenderly pick them out
> and i start pasting them to a strip of film... in one way
> you could say it is... a kind of madness to give them life
> again to animate them again... to engage with it in some
> way that makes of it something.*
>
> stan brakhage,
audio from *by brakhage:*
an anthology

as i travel down this road of collections, troubles and moths i feel the magnetic pull of my favorite culmination of all three: stan brakhage's film *mothlight*. in the audio commentary found on criterion's dvd anthology of his films, brakhage speaks of collecting dead moth wings, slowly fixing them upon the surface of clear 16mm film, and sending them through a projector so that these stones with wings are somehow able to fly again. as the light from the projector blasts through the thin fragile wing and film surfaces, the bulb seems a full moon or a sun. from the darkness of death and night, these stilled bits of lost life are suddenly thrust into an artificial brightness of day, hovering around a glow as if all is suddenly as it was before. as they are re-introduced to the land of the moving, the moth's wings move in jitters and shifts with a heightened sense of speed, so "lifefull" they seem as if they might burst.

the acquisition of an old book is its rebirth

walter benjamin,
illuminations

brakhage's tender arrangement of dead moths—who in the manner of frankenstein's monster have been brought back to life through human hands—evokes walter benjamin's description of a book collector meditatively unpacking a collection that has been in storage. obviously, there is a connection between benjamin's suggestion that a collector can breathe new life into an old book and brakhage's delicate and intimate game of pick-up-sticks with a cluster of lifeless moth parts. for those of us who gather old records, photographs, books and such from garage sales, flea markets and even the virtual closets of ebay, we too are in the business of rebirth... giving new life to objects that might otherwise remain entirely forgotten in the perpetual darkness of cardboard boxes, attics, basements or storage spaces.

like the great first gatherer of old records and paper airplanes (not to mention hand-painted russian eggs and string figures...), harry smith was not only a forefather to those of us who collect recordings of early american music, but also one of the first to give relevance (and love) back to a series of humble objects on the verge of obsolescence. just as brakhage gave dead moths the flickering of life, so do we who listen to forgotten musics in their original form give new life to voices lying dormant within the tiny confines of dust filled grooves. as the record begins to spin, i watch its scarred surface move in a circular whirl. its visible history of handling—scratches, digs, cracks and chips—as well as the spinning colors of its label, confuses my eyes like marcel duchamp's rotoreliefs and brion gysin's dream machine. immersed in silent wonder, i breathe myself into the spinning object and set the needle down upon its surface. i close my eyes, waiting for silenced voices to sing again as the needle begins to trace a pattern of concentric circles. as the music becomes audible, i am immersed in distant voices singing through both space and time, and in the words of alfred g. karnes, i have found myself within "a portal, there to dwell with the immortal."

between the covers of this book you will see, read and hear a collision of gathered forgottens: the homespun, the modern, the amateur, the master, the professional, the hobbyist, the hillbilly, the city slicker, the self-taught, the academically inclined, the private, the showman, the natural, the cultural, the nobel prize winner, the backwoods wanderer, the primal, the translated, the literal, the abstract, the complete, the fragmented, the studio recording, the field recording, the home recording, the manipulated, the documentary, the angular, the soft, the clean, the dirty, the perfect, the broken, the precise, the awkward, the blind, the gazing, the ethereal, the actual, the focused, the blurred, the scratched, the stained, the anonymous, the famous, the stylist, the authentic, the humble, the big-headed, the lyrical, the grunting, the patient, the rushed, the loudly, the hushed, the loved, the hated, the melancholy, the joyous, the smitten, the numbed, the cityscape, the landscape, the shouted, the whispered...

many of these things speak in a voice not unlike kincaid's rendering of *froggie went a-courting*, and all of them seem comfortable residing beneath a banner wrought from a line of a poem by par lagerkvist that hums: "i listen to the wind that obliterates my traces." the fact that these words, written by a swedish nobel prize laureate, could easily be a lyric sung by carl t. sprague or emery glen was a big part of my decision to bring such things together.

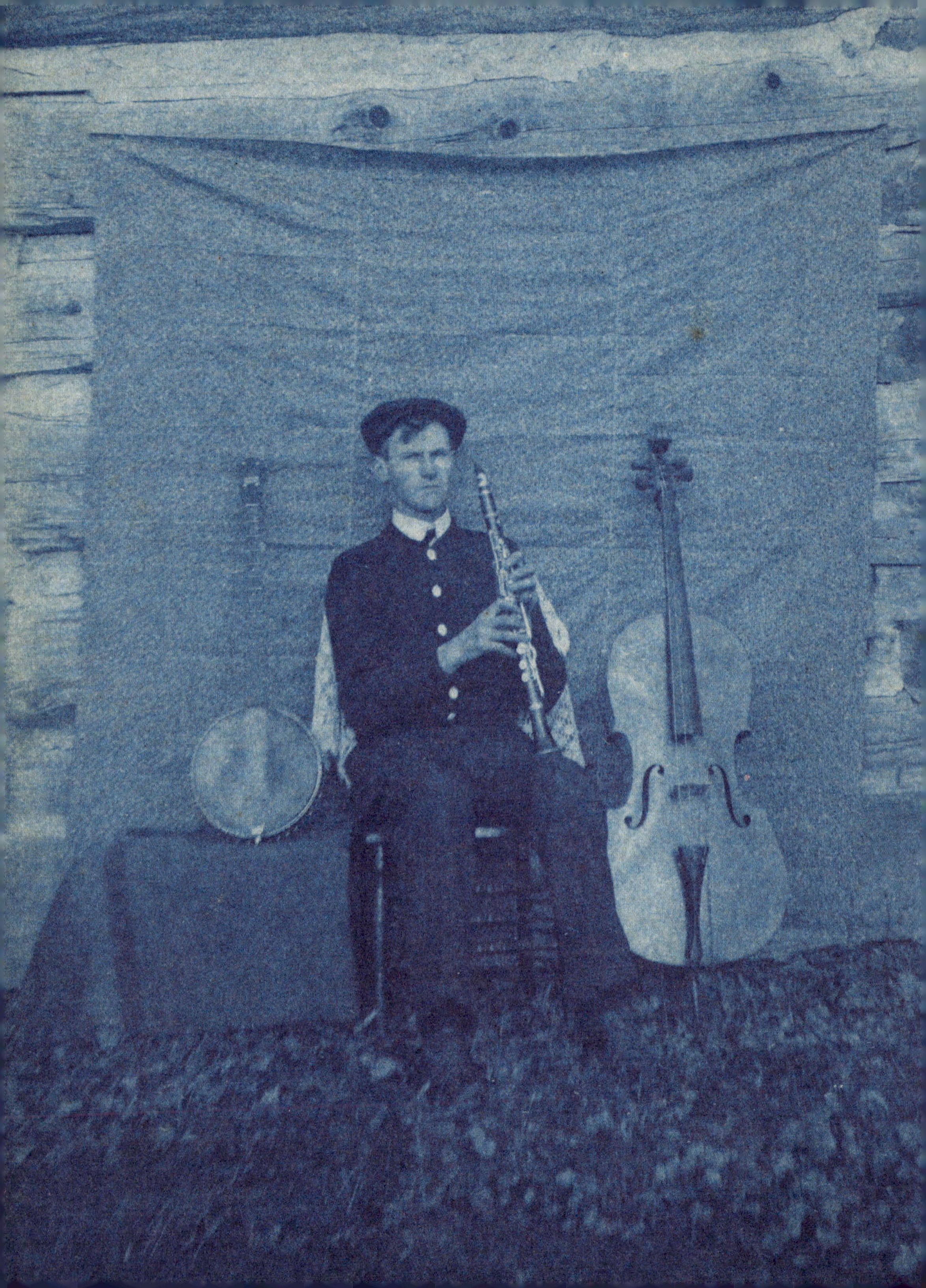

in the mid 1930's, chicago radio star grandpa jones spoke of the power of bradley kincaid's music saying, "you've got to really listen to [kincaid's songs] because they are slow and tell a story." jones was not only suggesting the use of patient ears, but of the importance of directing one's "listening focus" beyond a song's words. i don't know if jones ever read much rilke, but the notion that kincaid's pathos could be found in his articulations, pauses, rhythms and timbres—rather than his words—certainly seems to jibe with rilke's concept of "inconsiderable things." of course, several of the songs and images here *do* have the blatant power of blind willie johnson and skip james; but most of them work their magic through decidedly subtler voices, and jones's suggestion of the rewards of patient listening (and looking) applies to nearly everything here.

while i have no idea whether i have been able to give any of these recordings, quotations and photographs new life by bringing them together, my hope is that these visual and audible stepping stones offer you a multiplicity of connections, paths, left turns, revisits and wanderings. perhaps you can form your own constellations, and if nothing else, i have certainly gathered together a hell of a lot more things you can tell your troubles to....

—steve roden, 2011

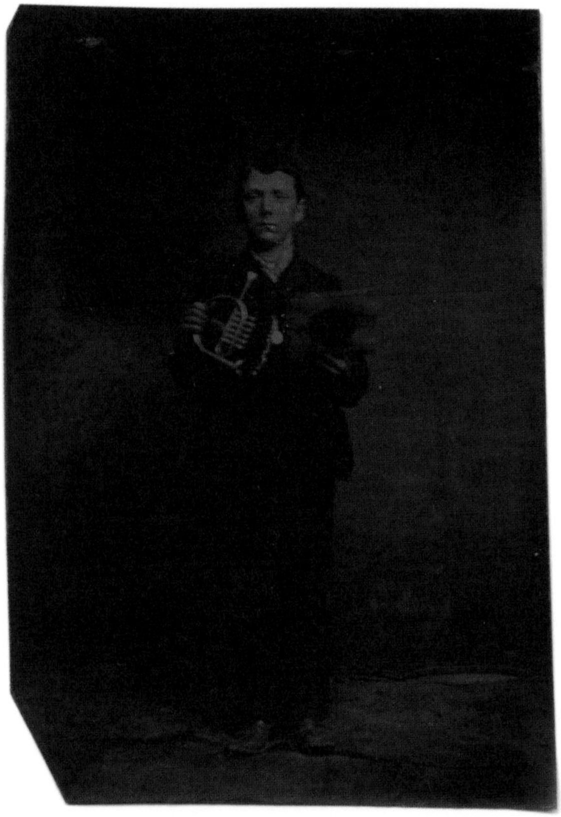

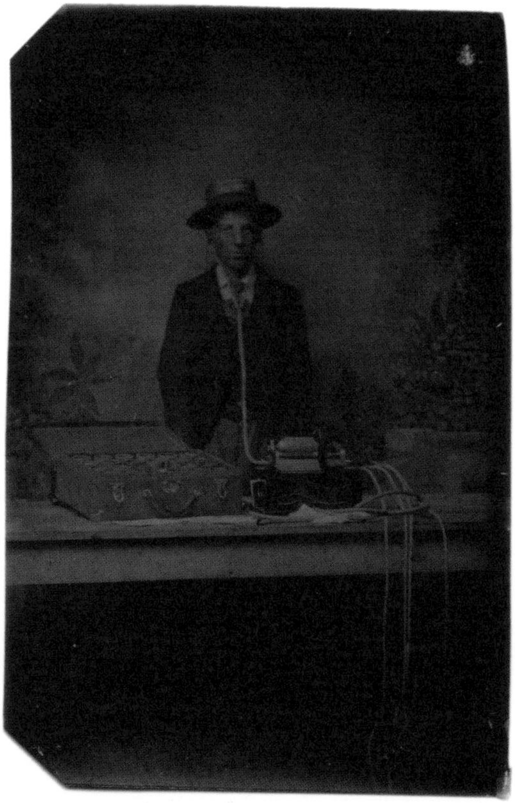

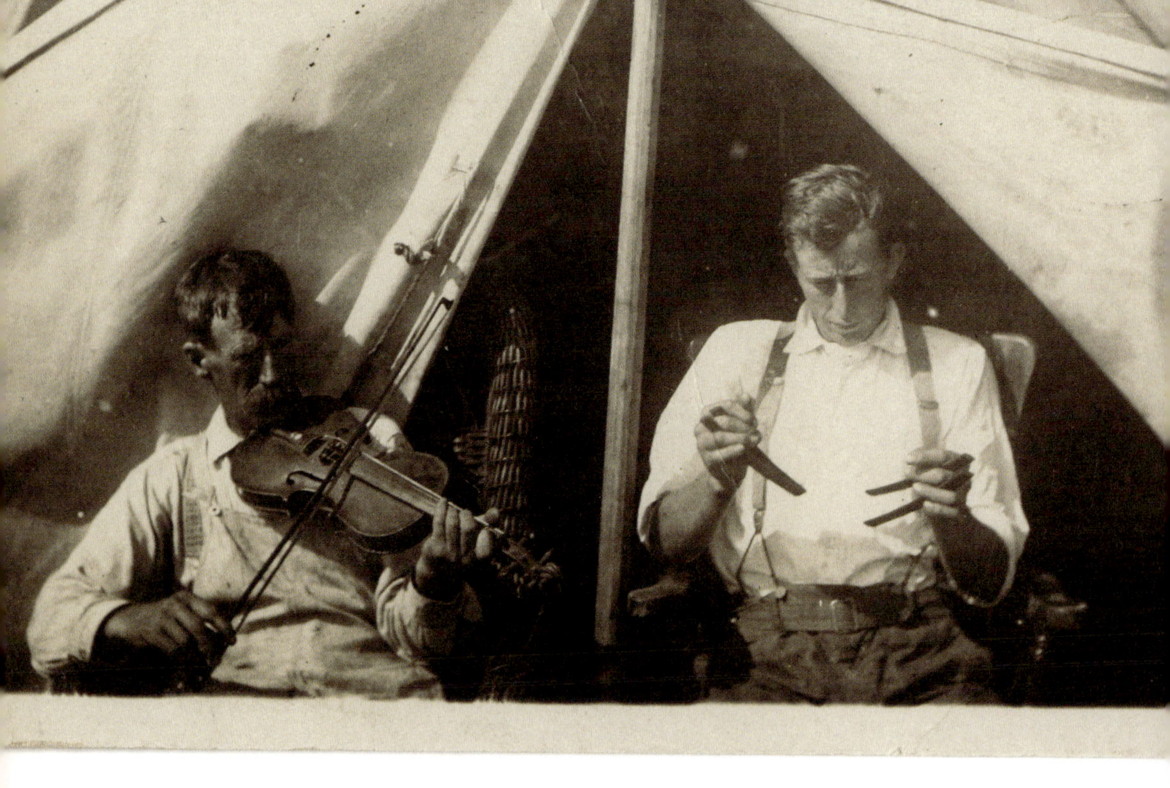

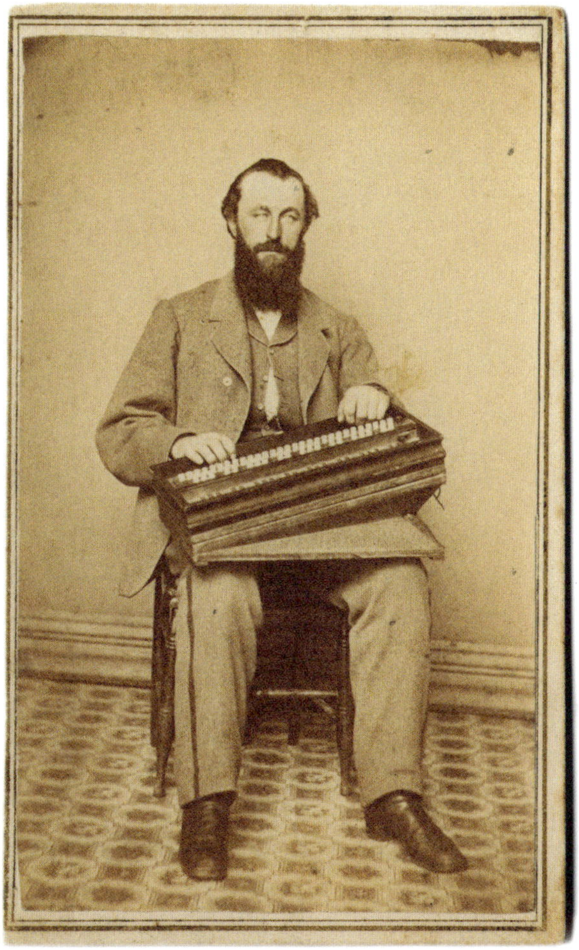

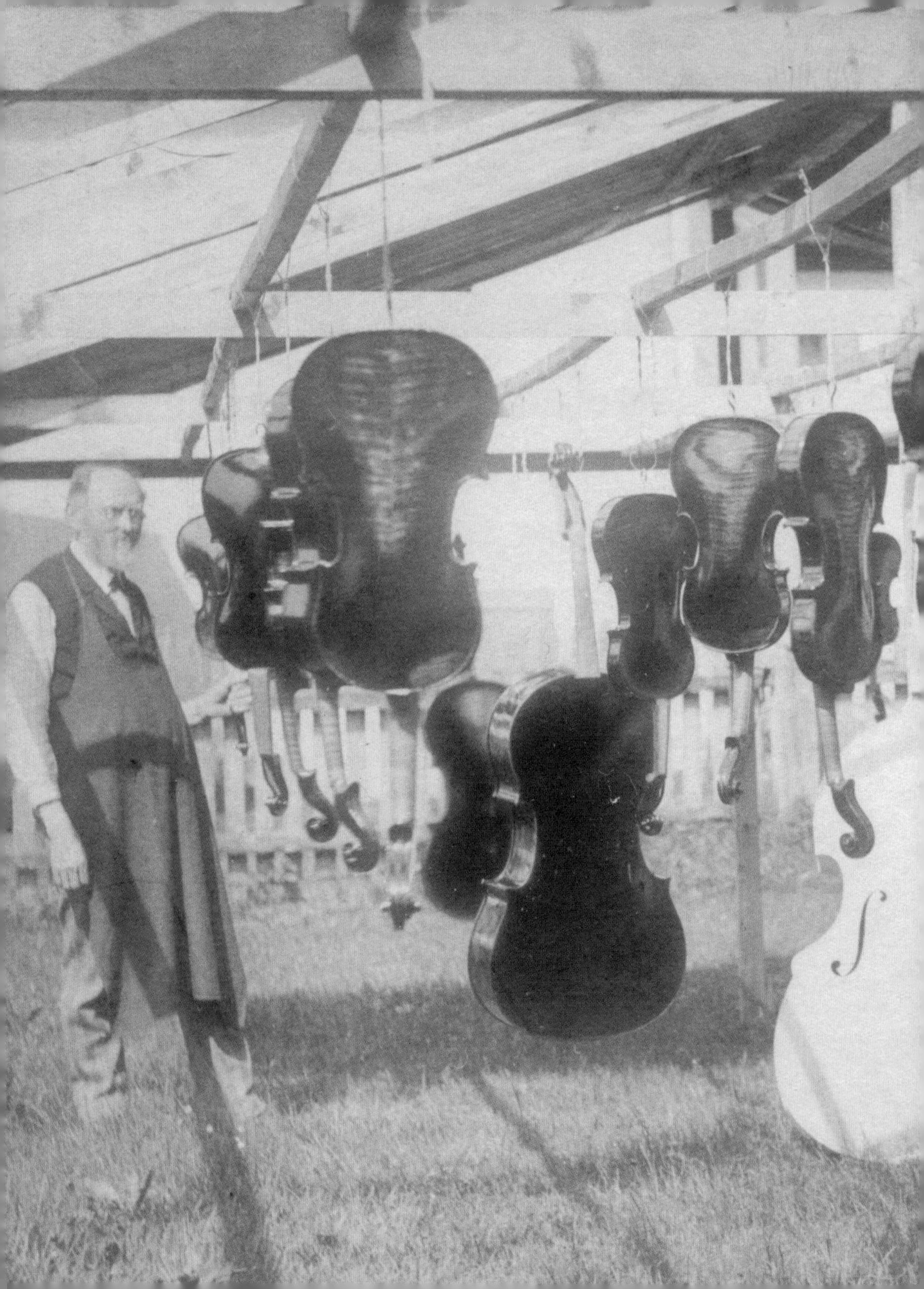

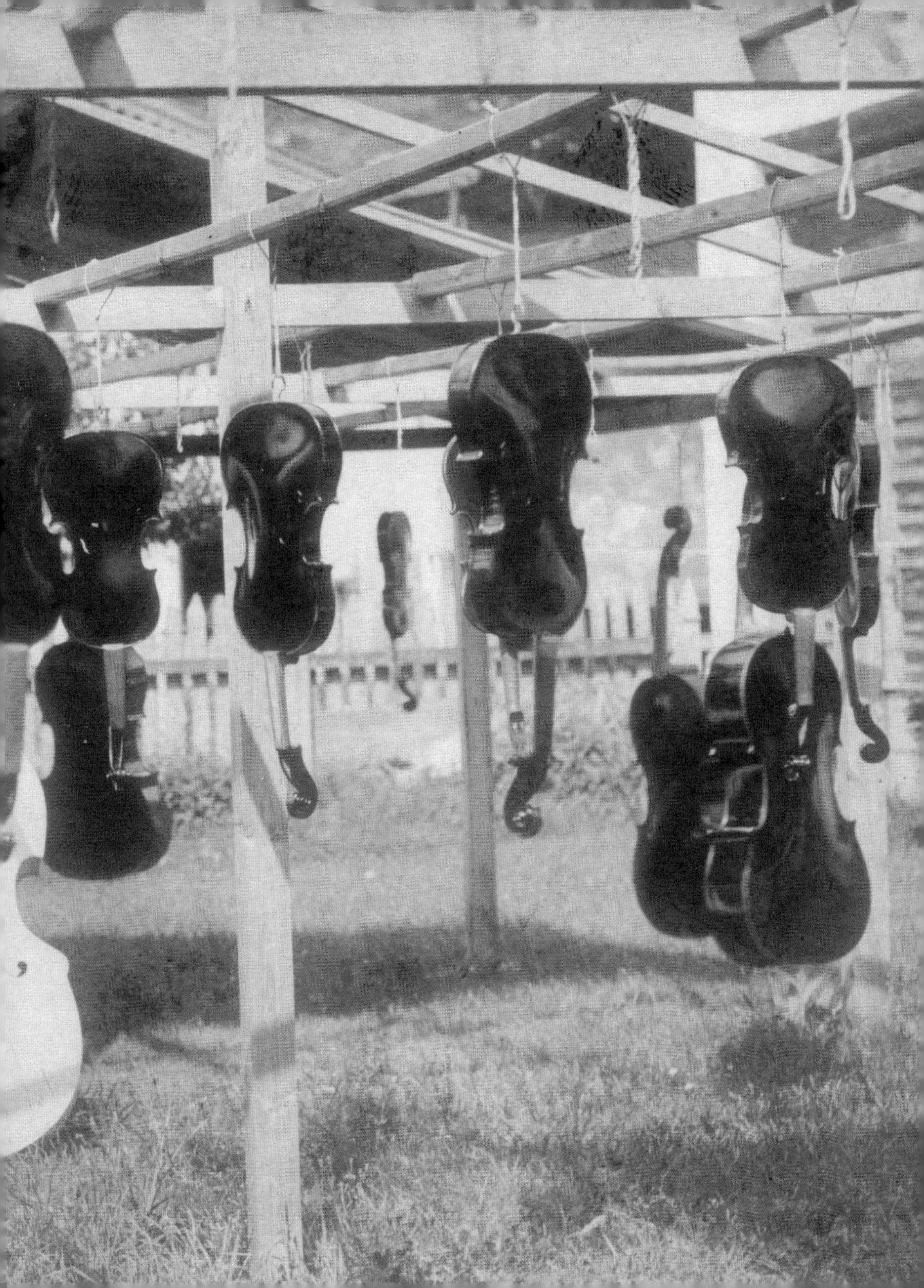

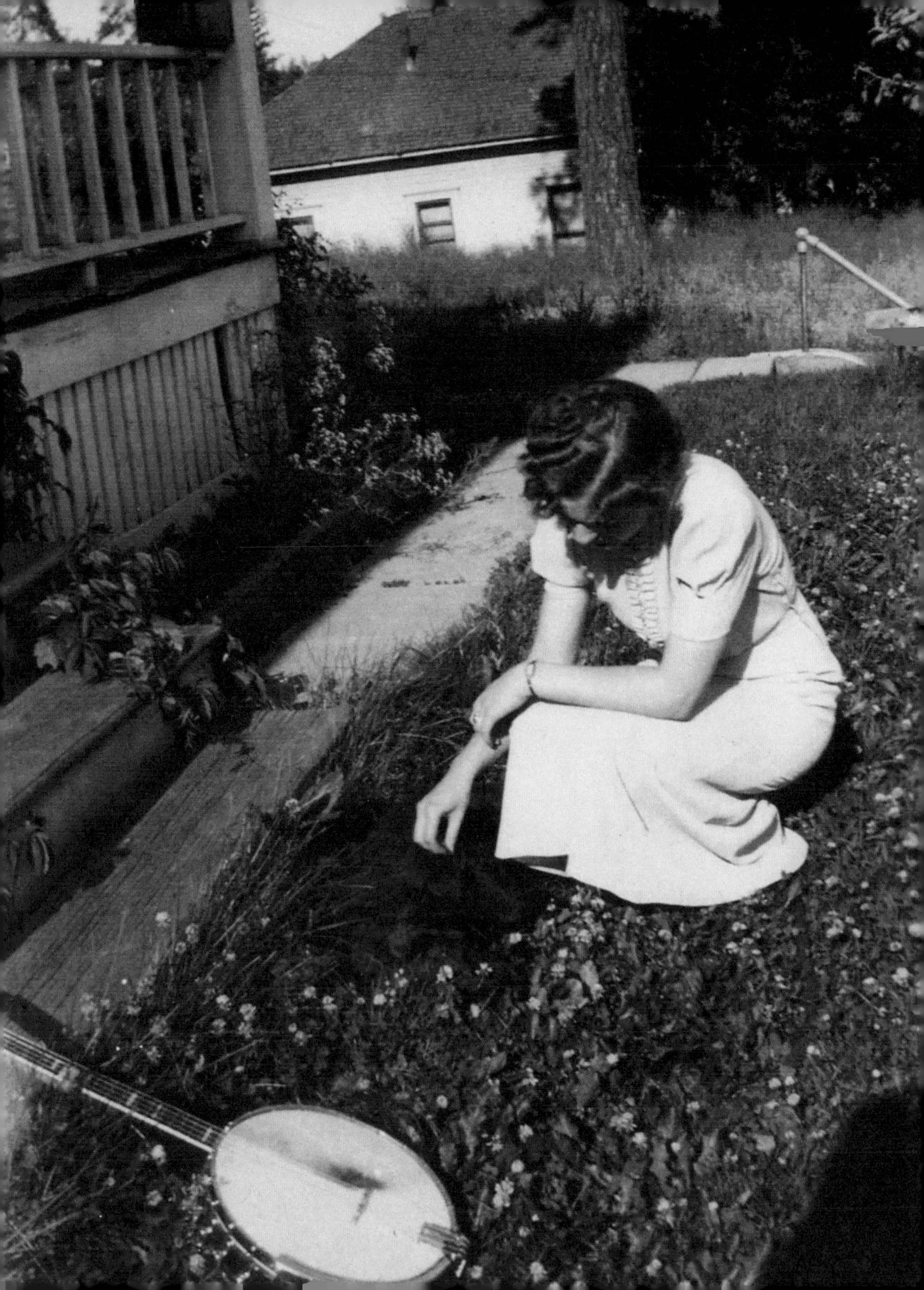

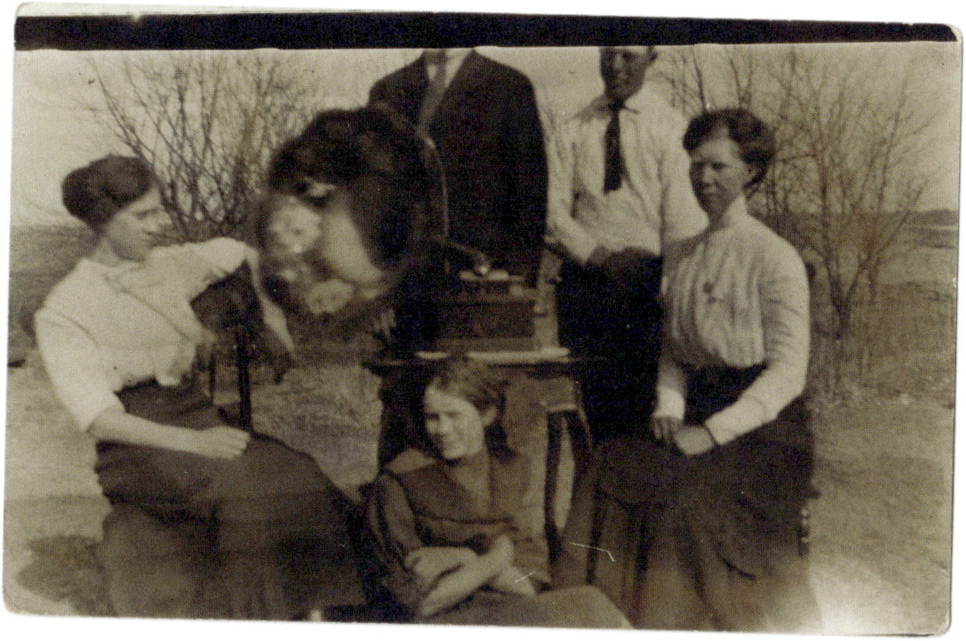

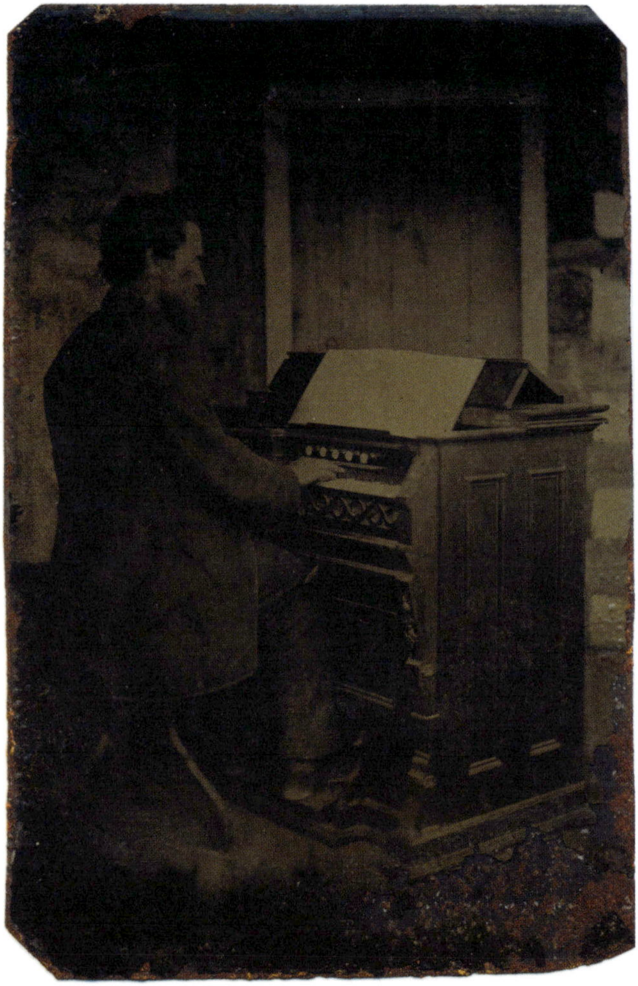

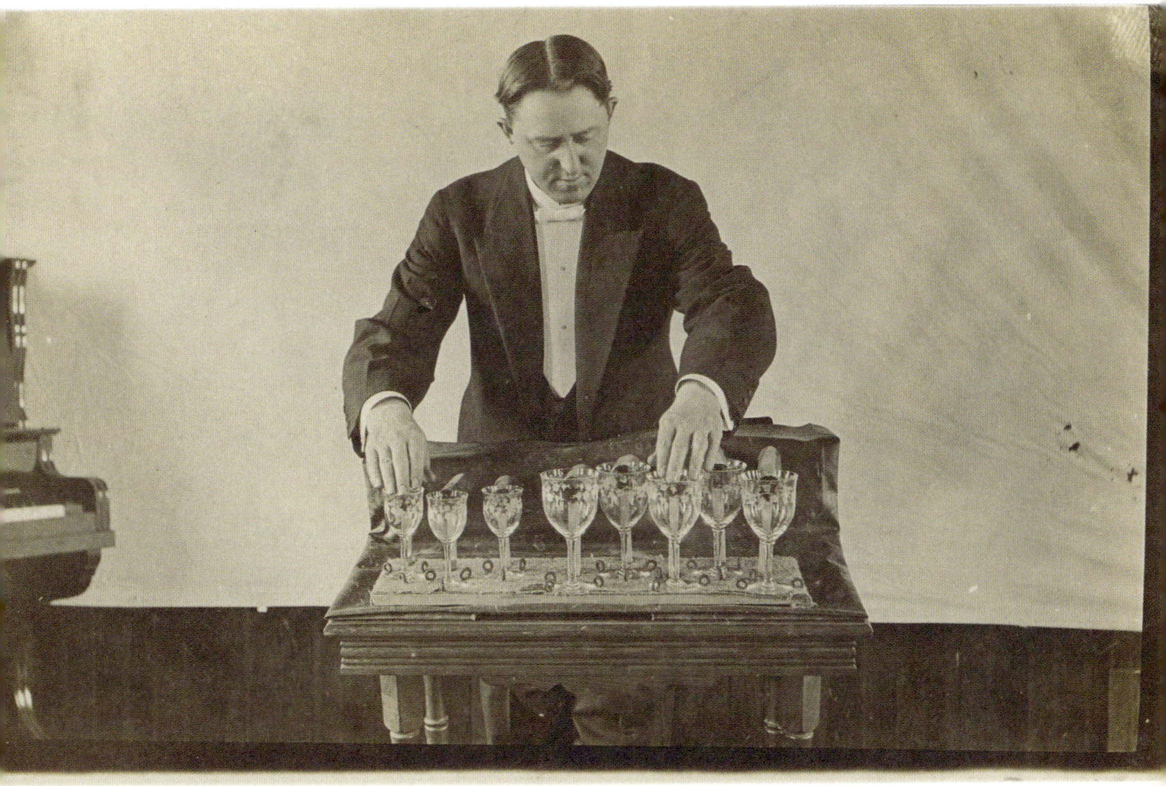

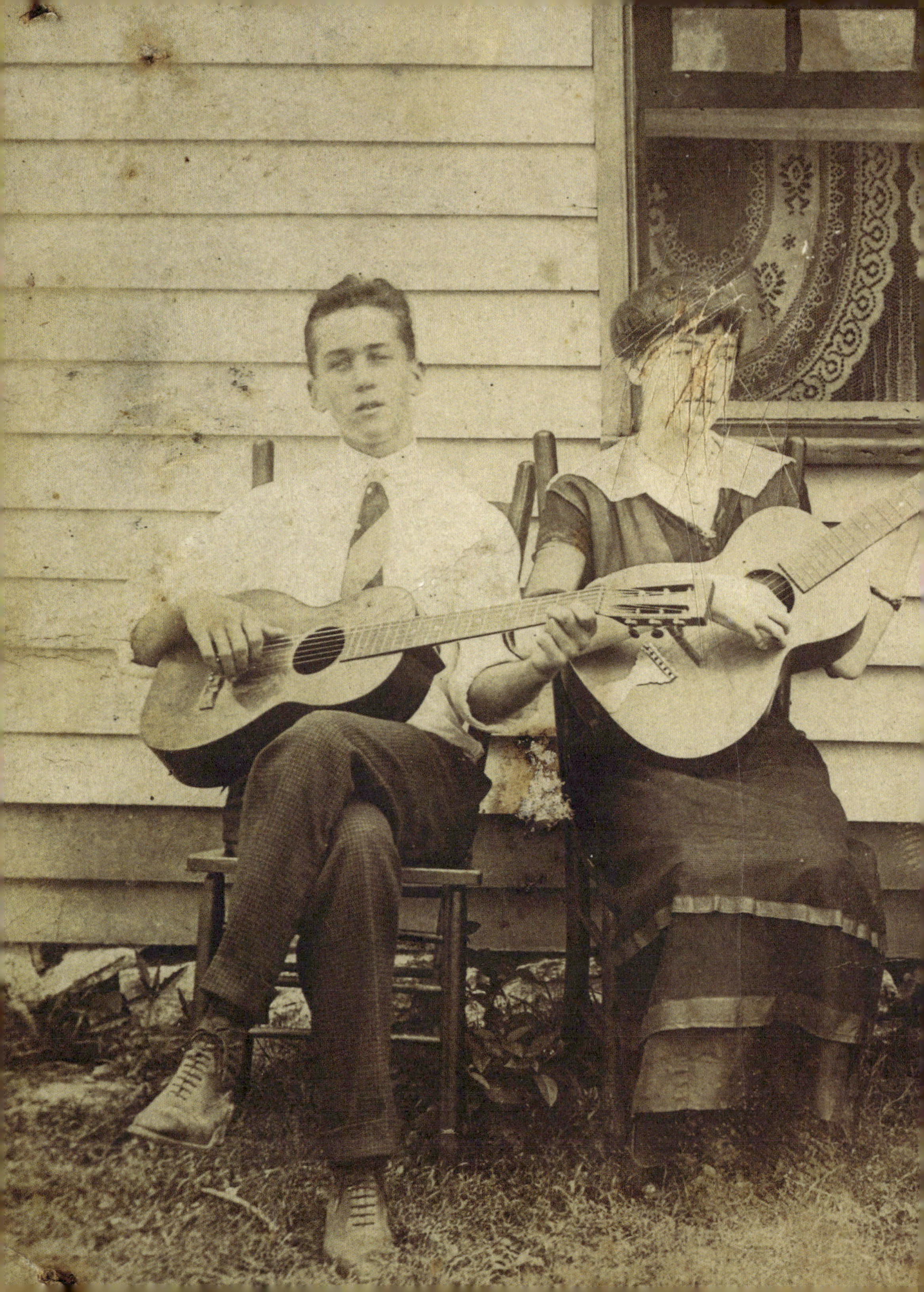

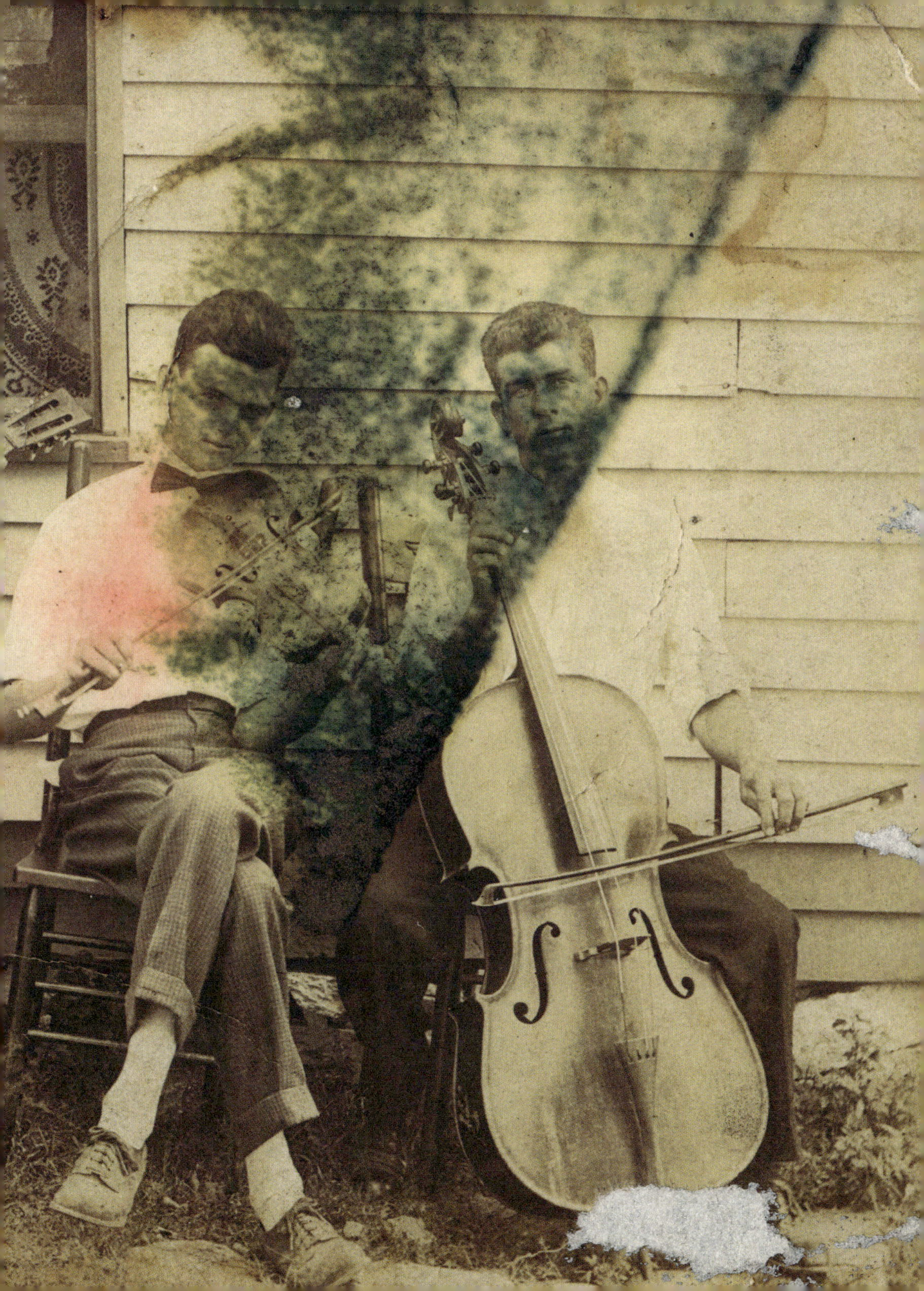

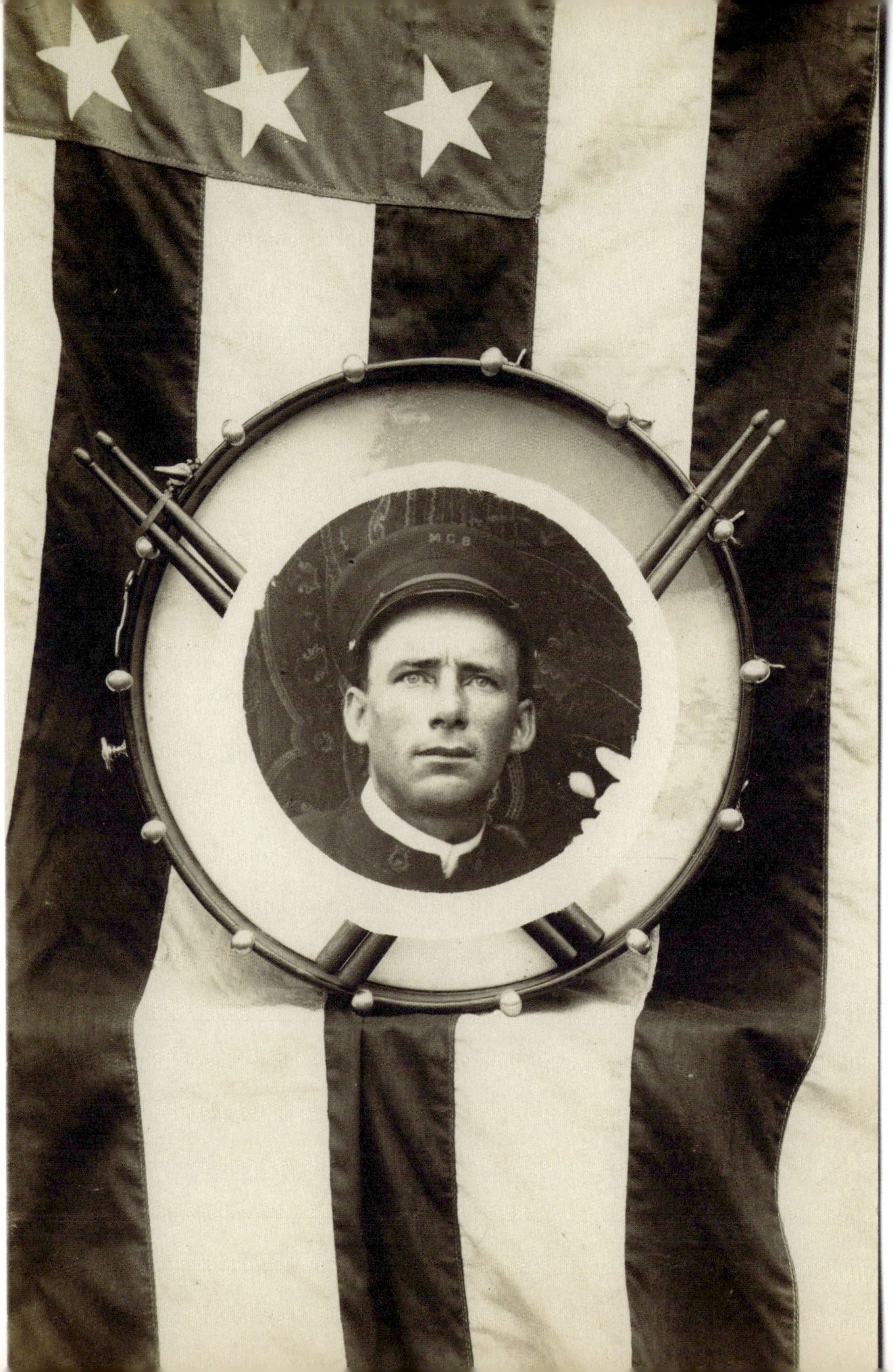
MCB

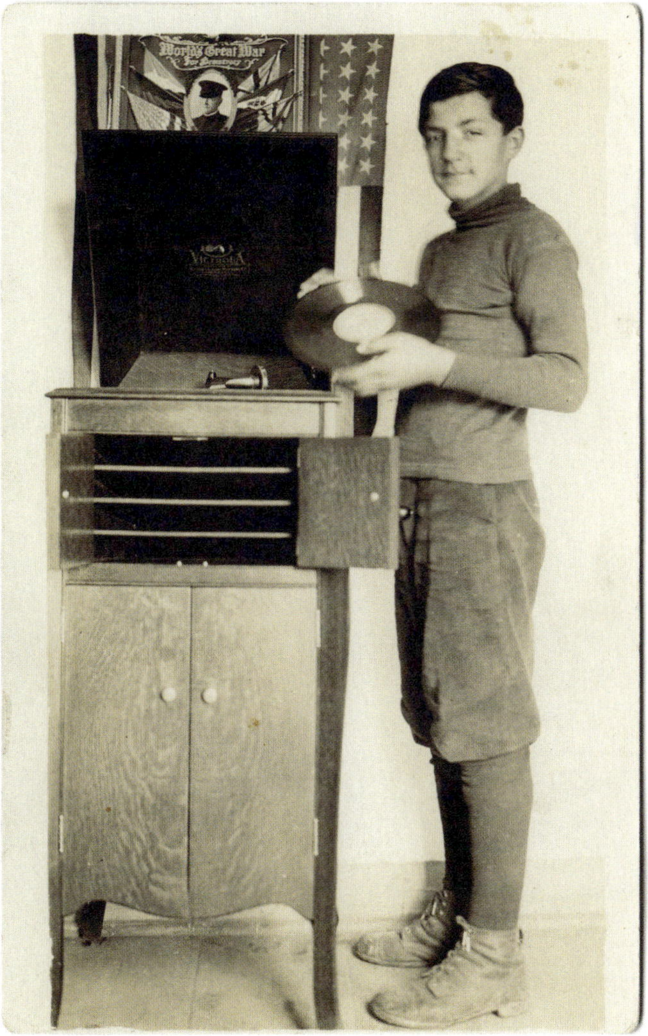
World's Great War
VICTROLA

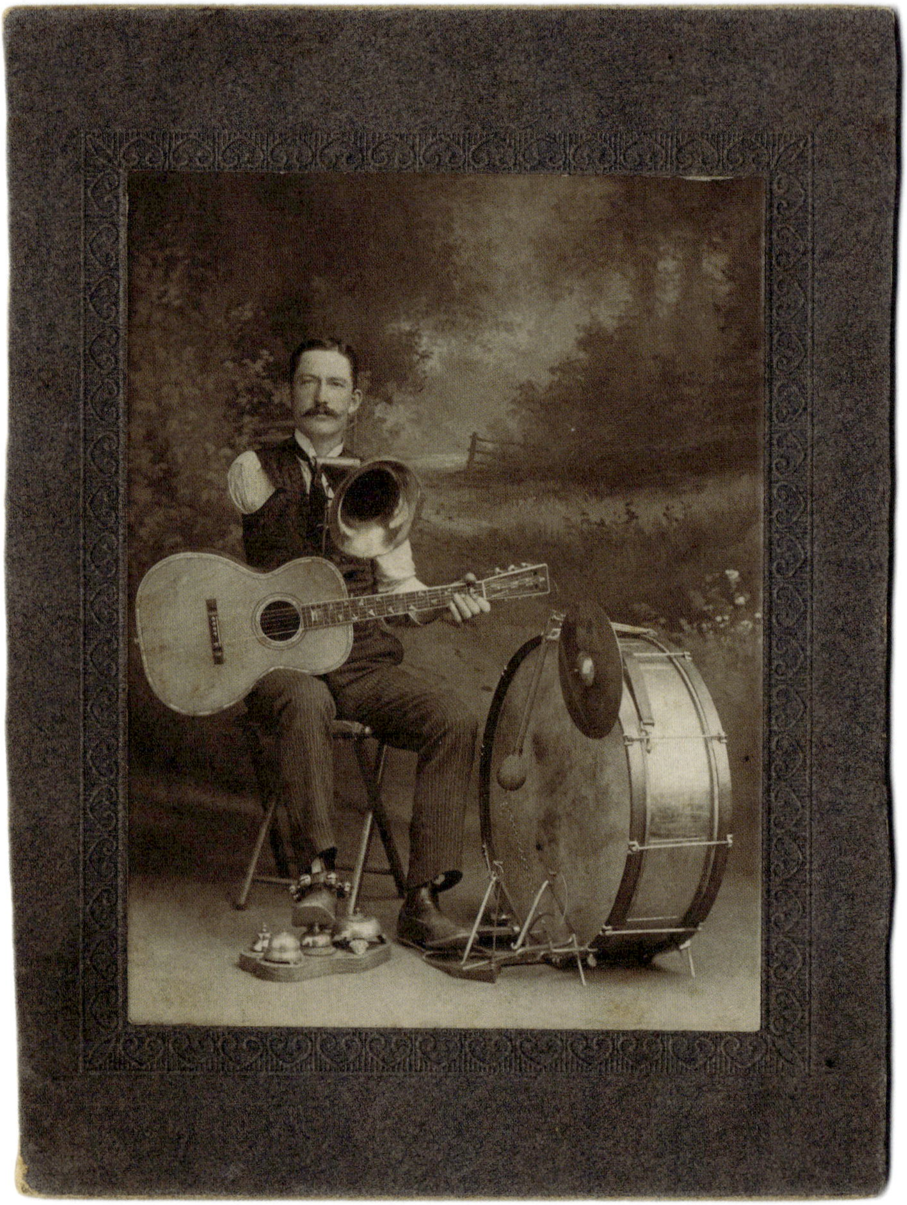

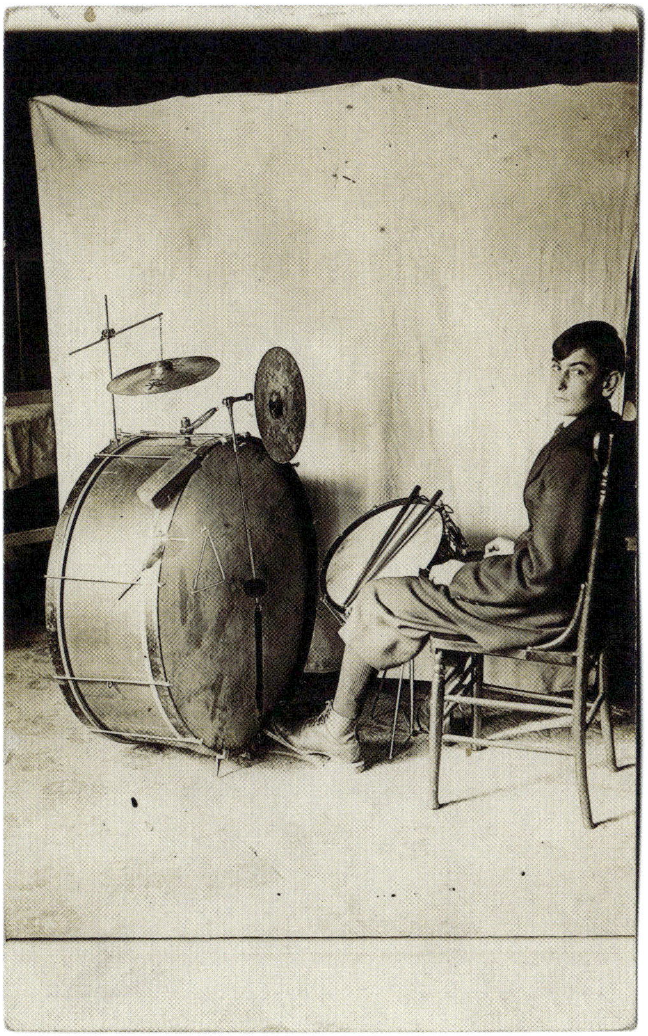

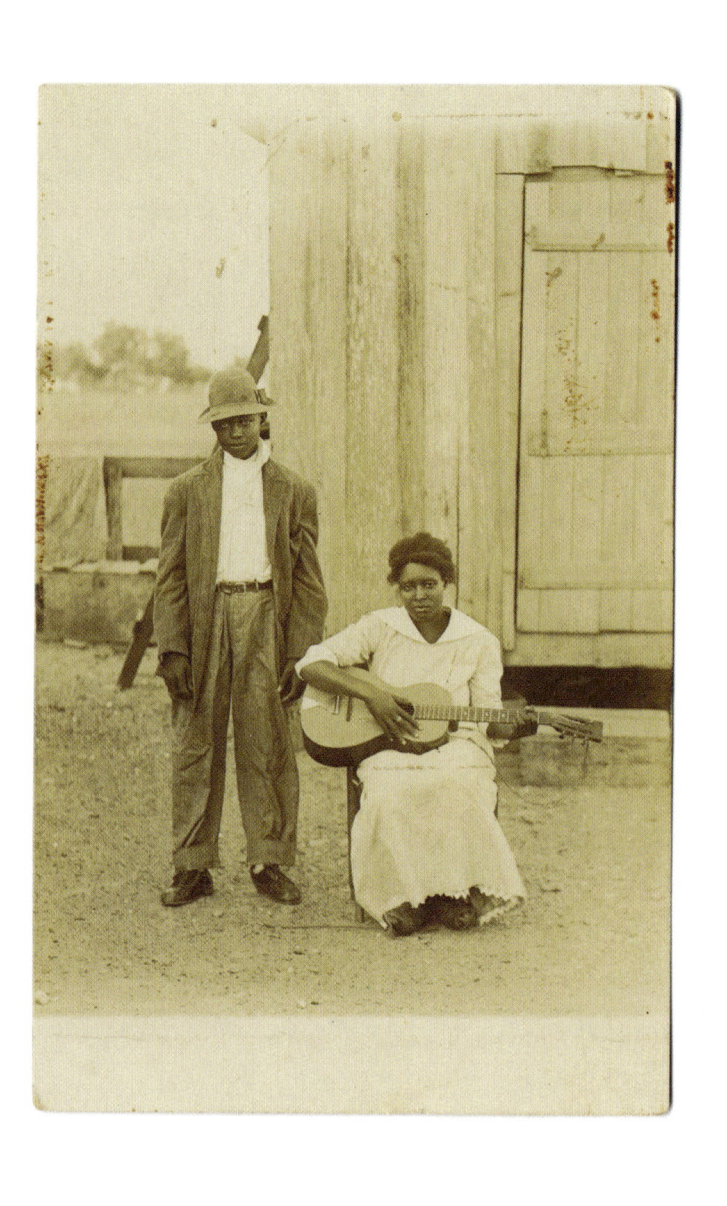

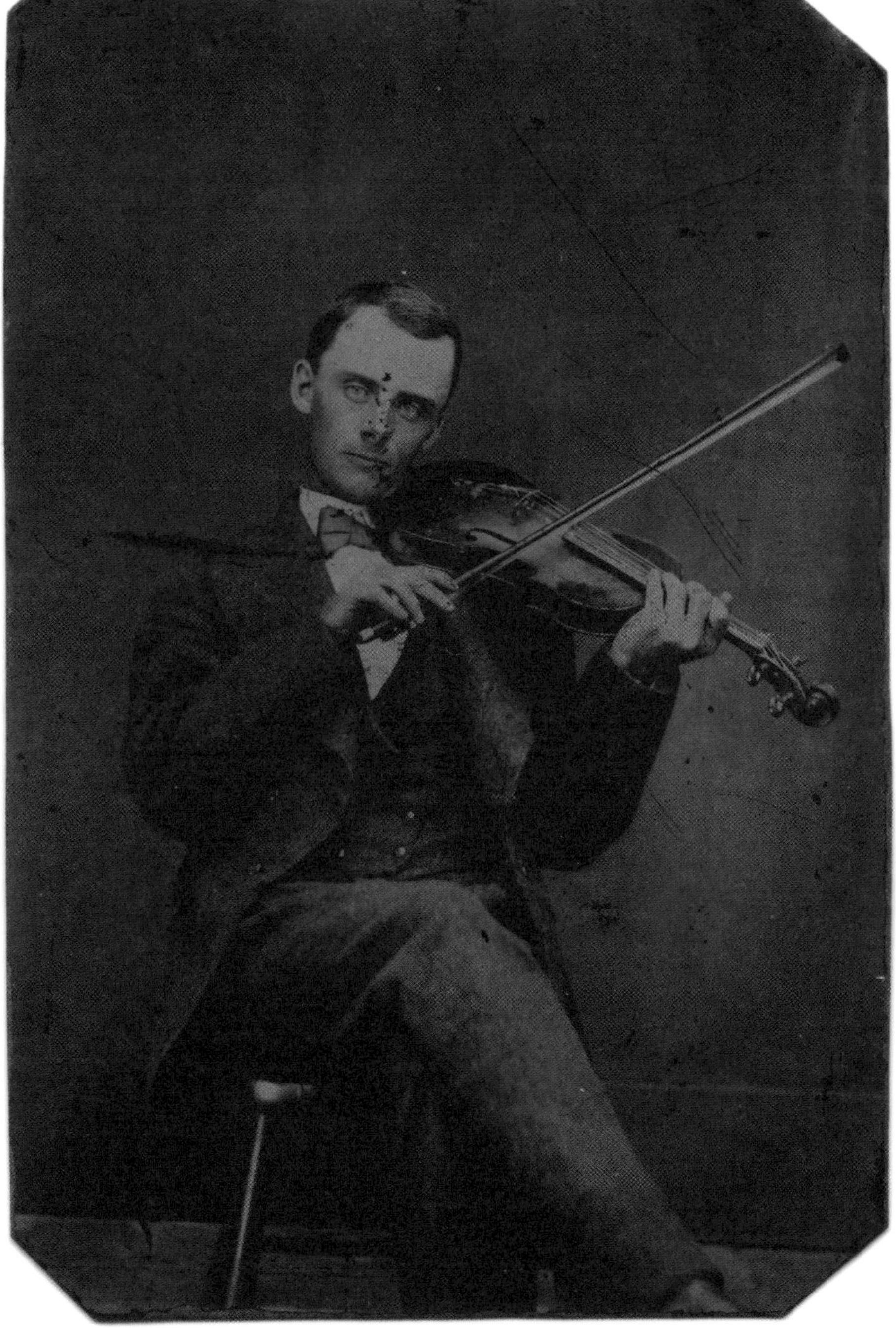

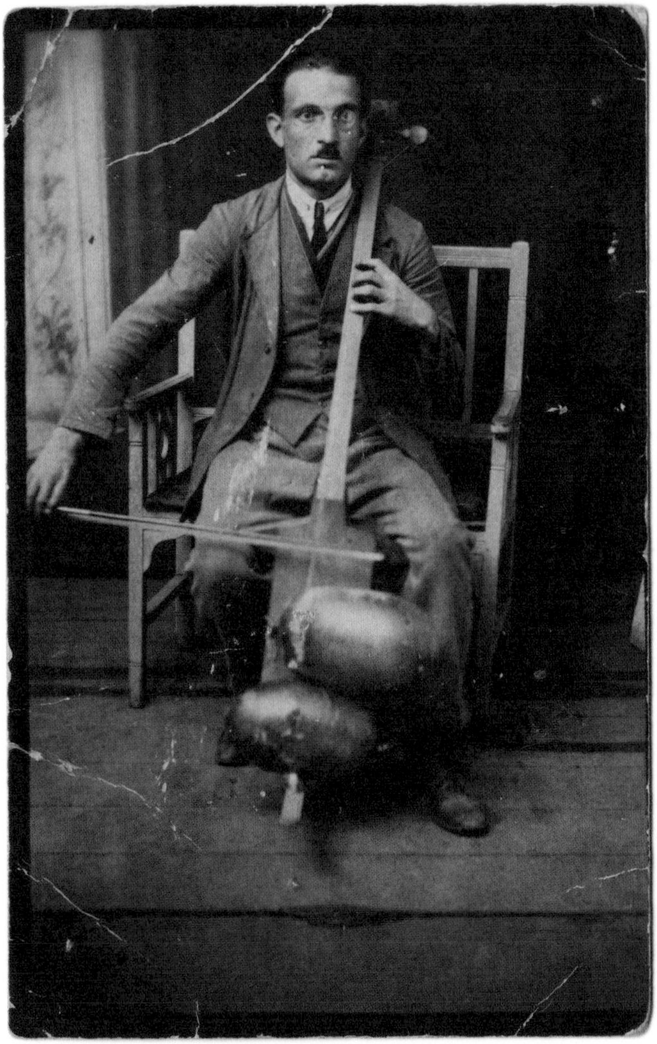

W. E. MERRILL, OVID, MICH.

Bousquet — 110 Main Street, Woonsocket, R. I.

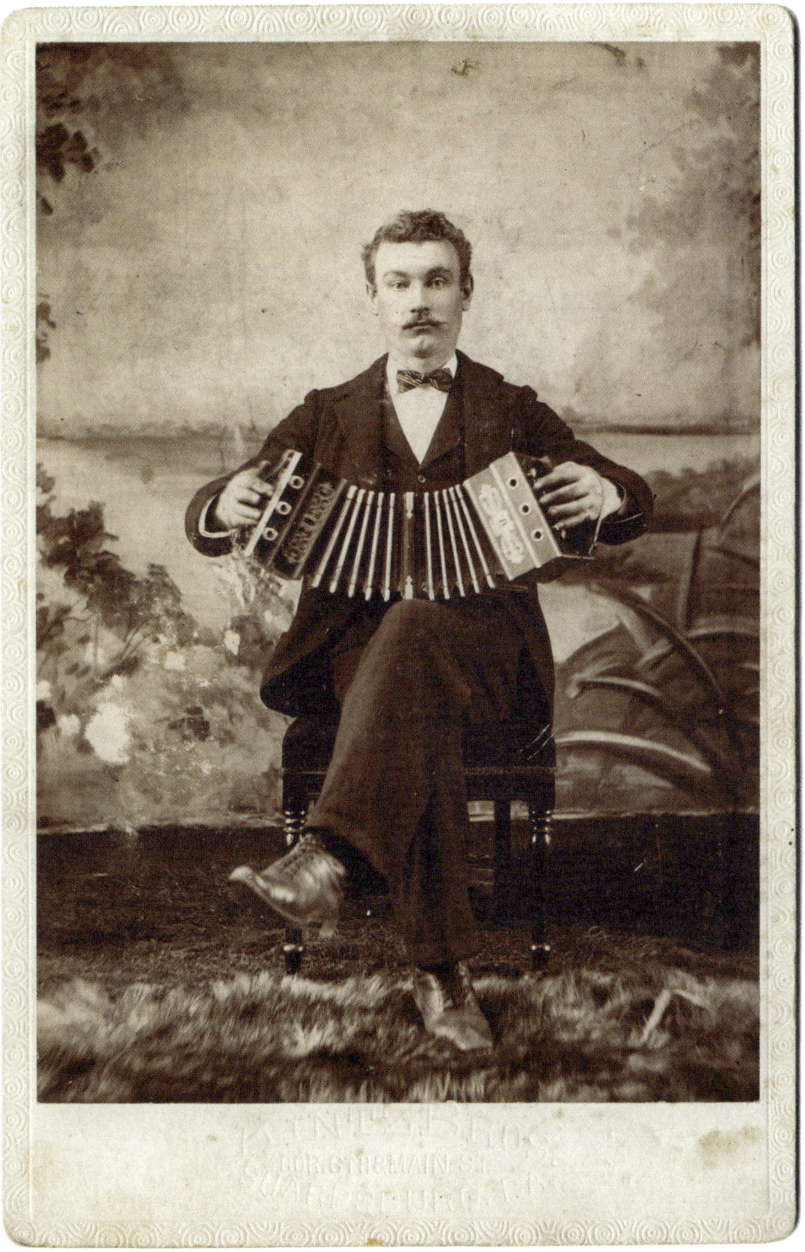
COR. 6TH & MAIN ST.

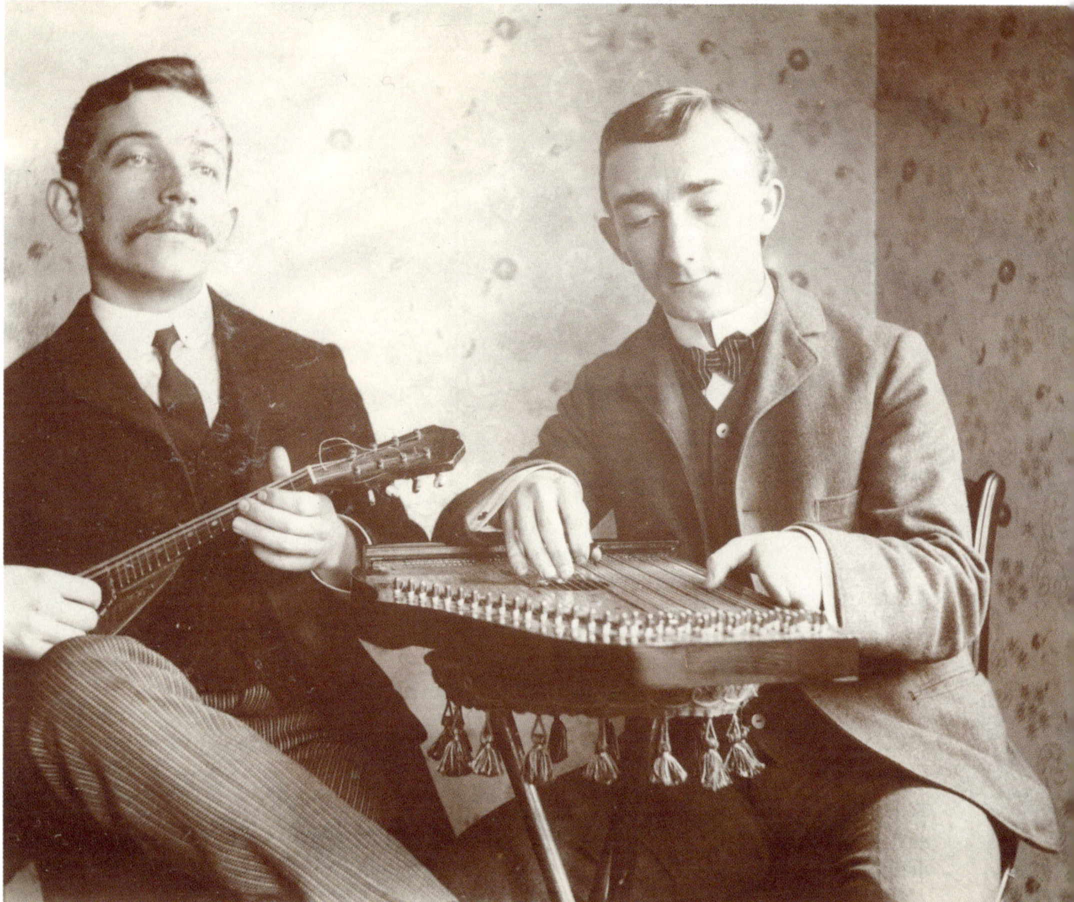

S. S. Vose & Son, PHOTOGRAPHERS.

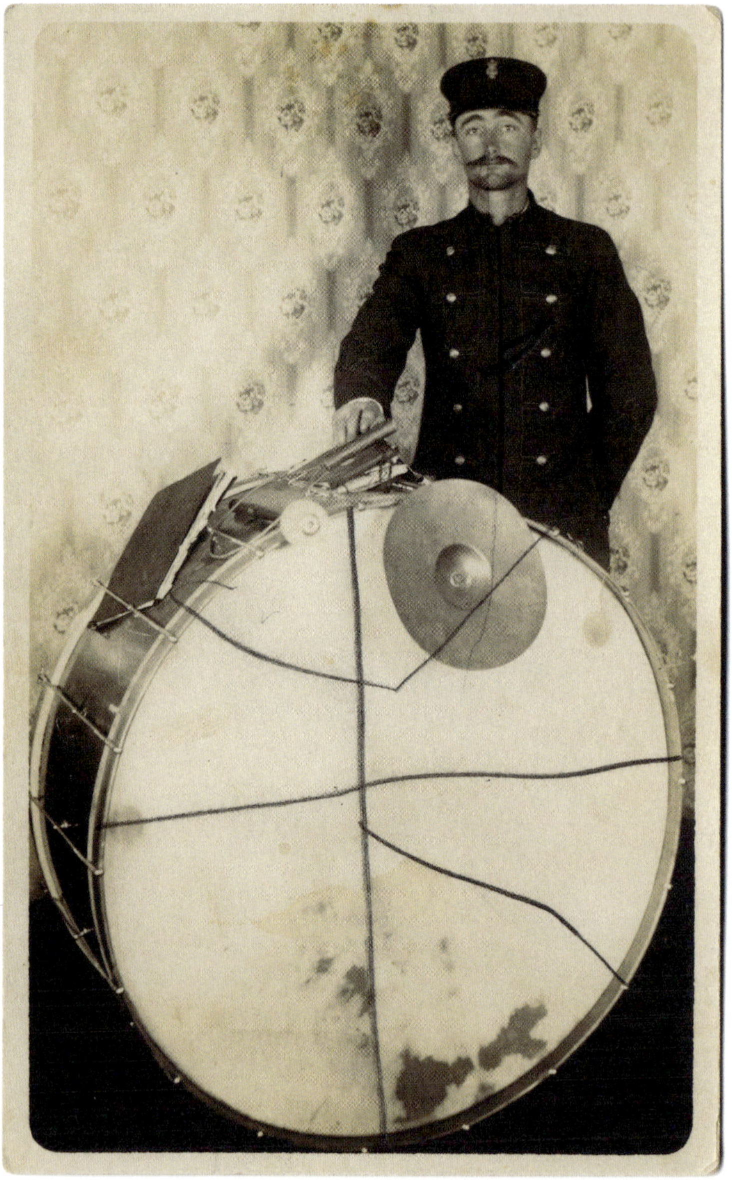

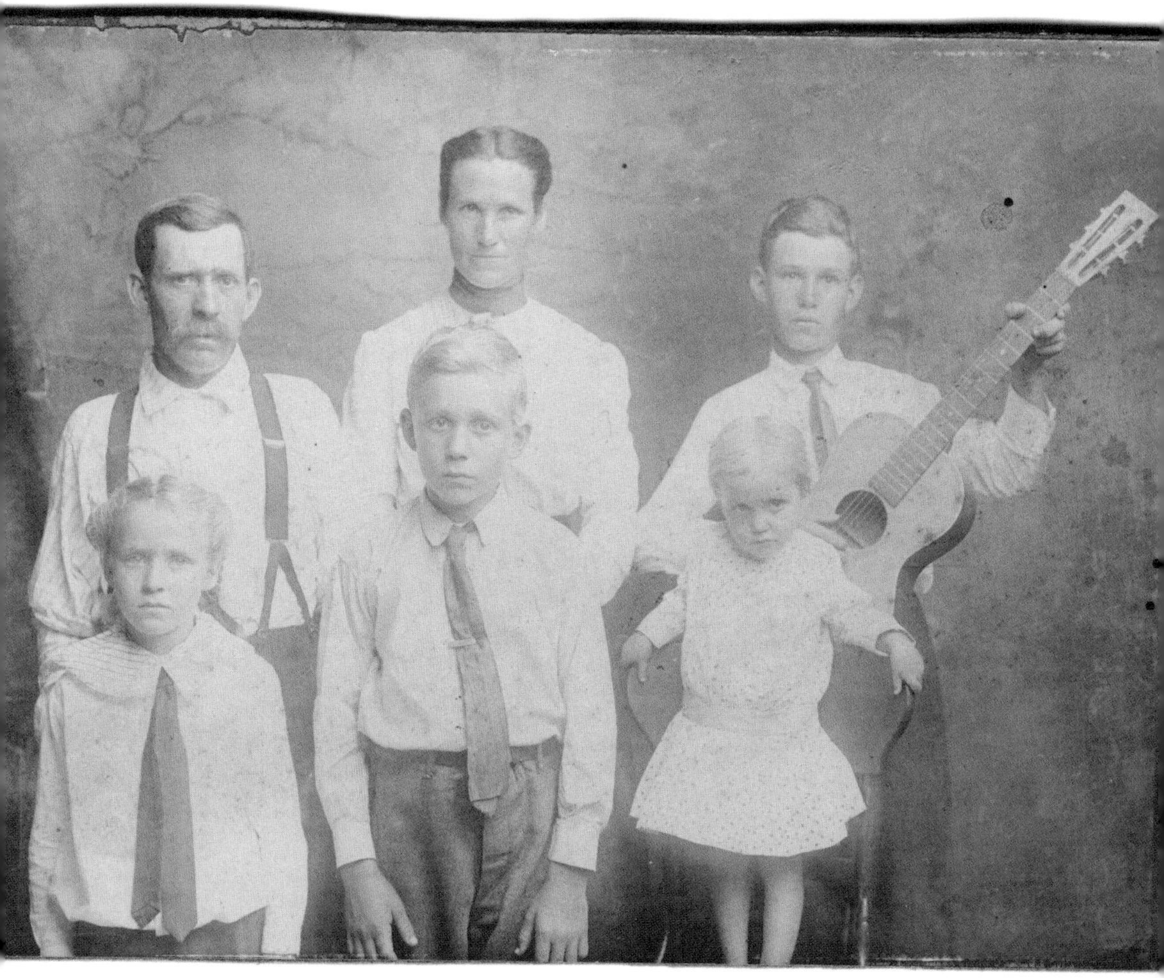

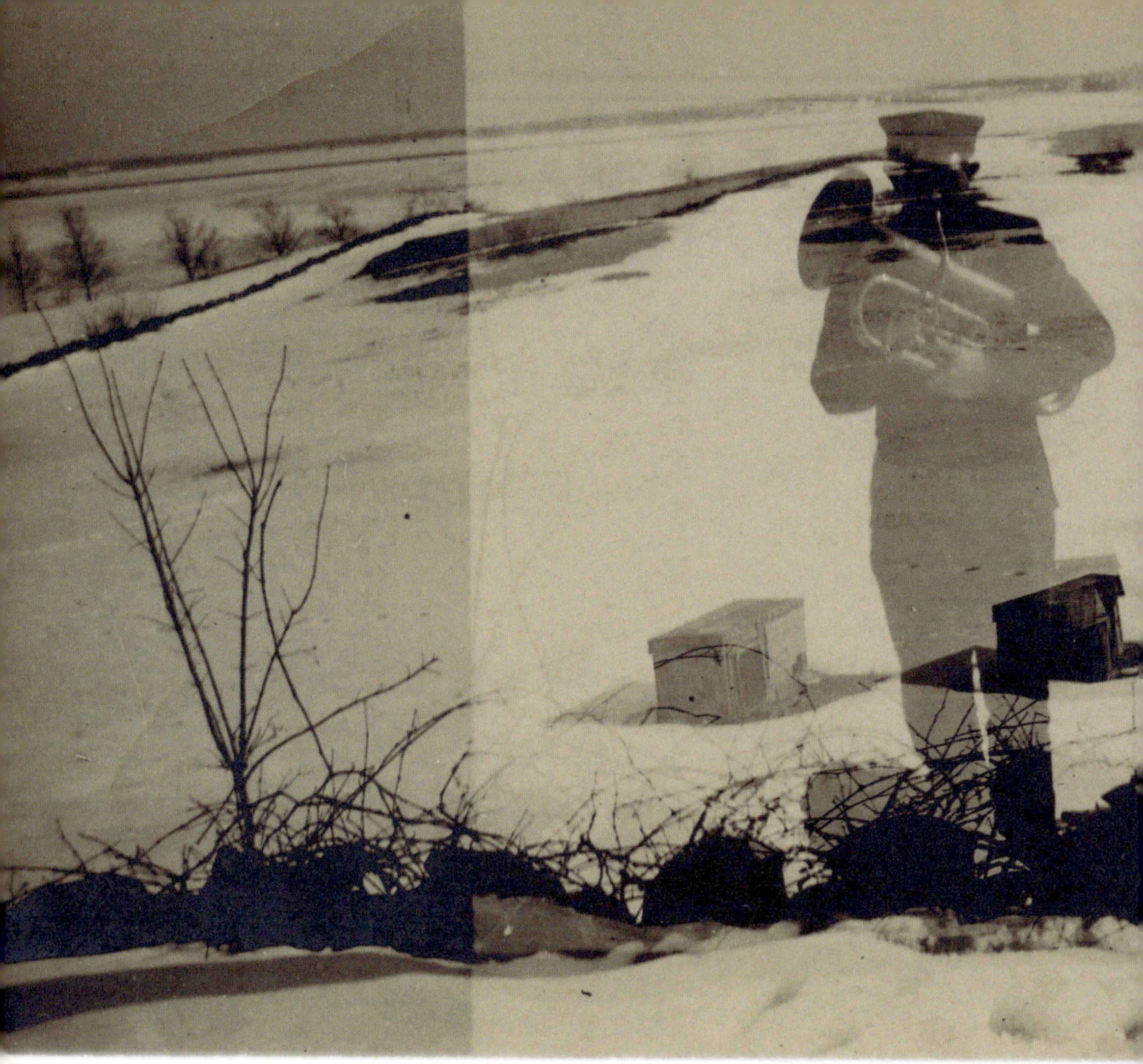

i stood for a long time upon the hillside, listening to the sough from heaven and earth; there was nothing else to be heard. then there might come a rustling sound, which would prove to be a shriveled, curled up leaf fluttering down through the frozen branches; it was like listening to a tiny fountain. then heaven and earth would sough again, a mildness enveloped me, as though all my strings were muted.

> knut hamsun
> *a wanderer plays on muted strings*

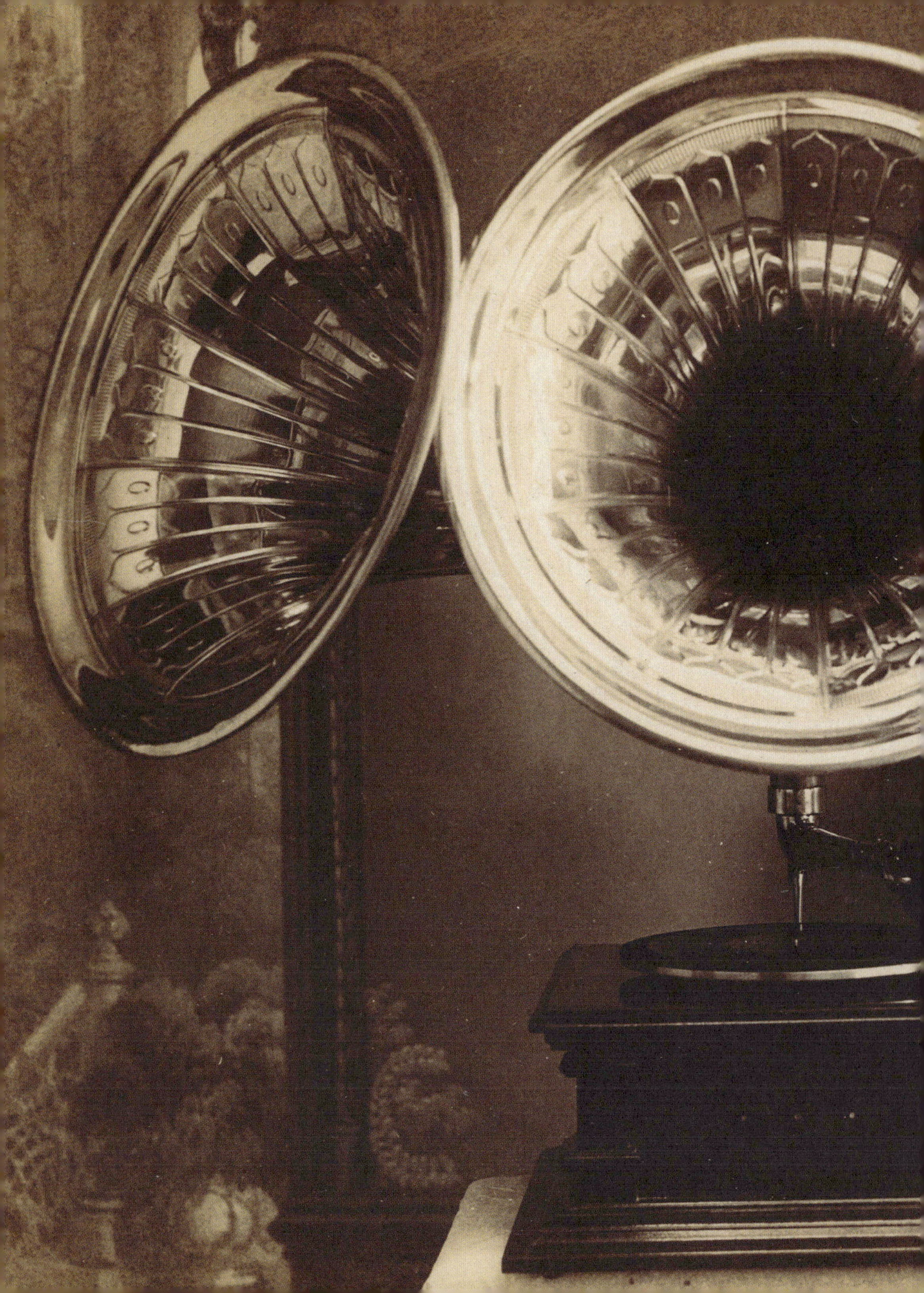

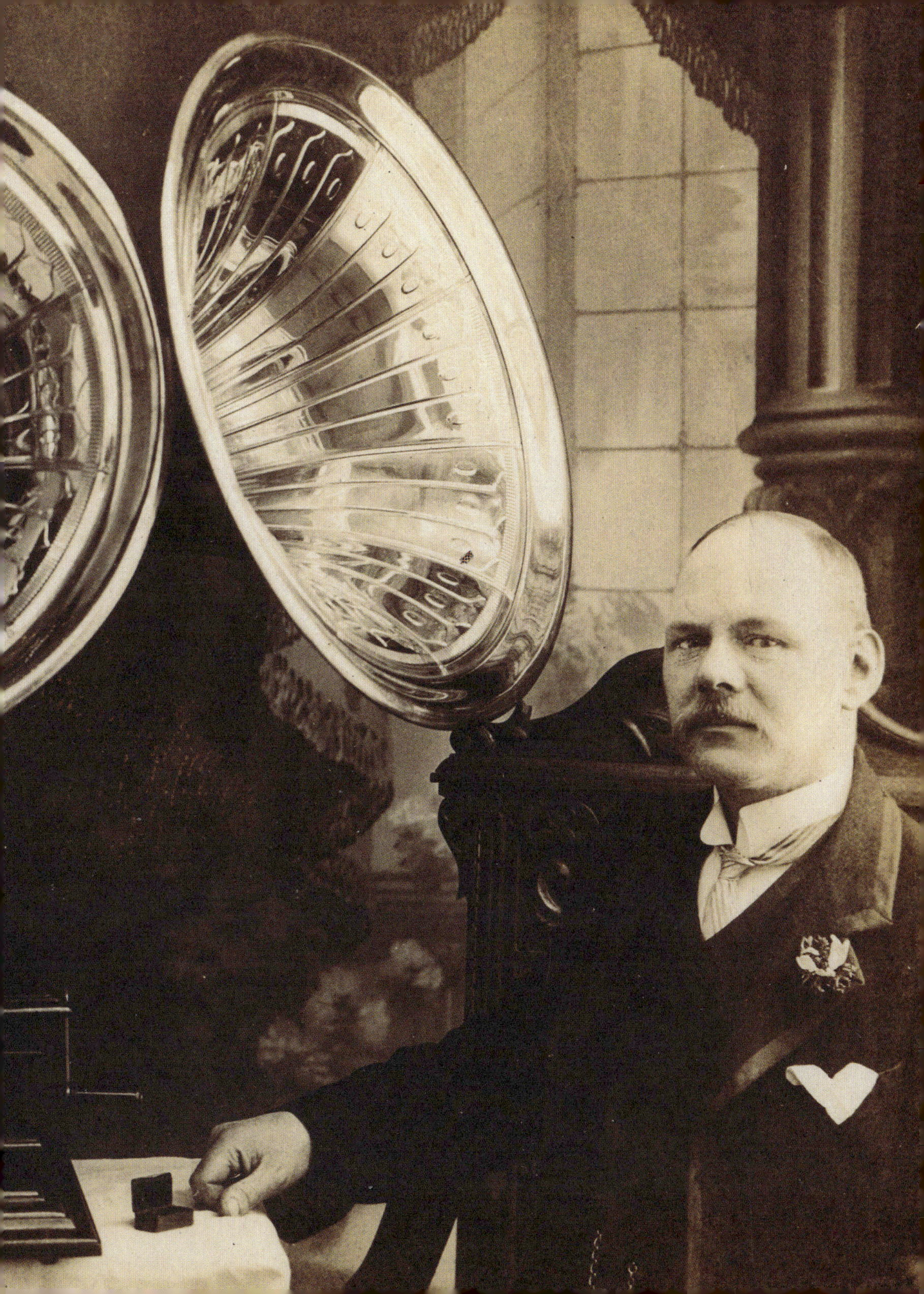

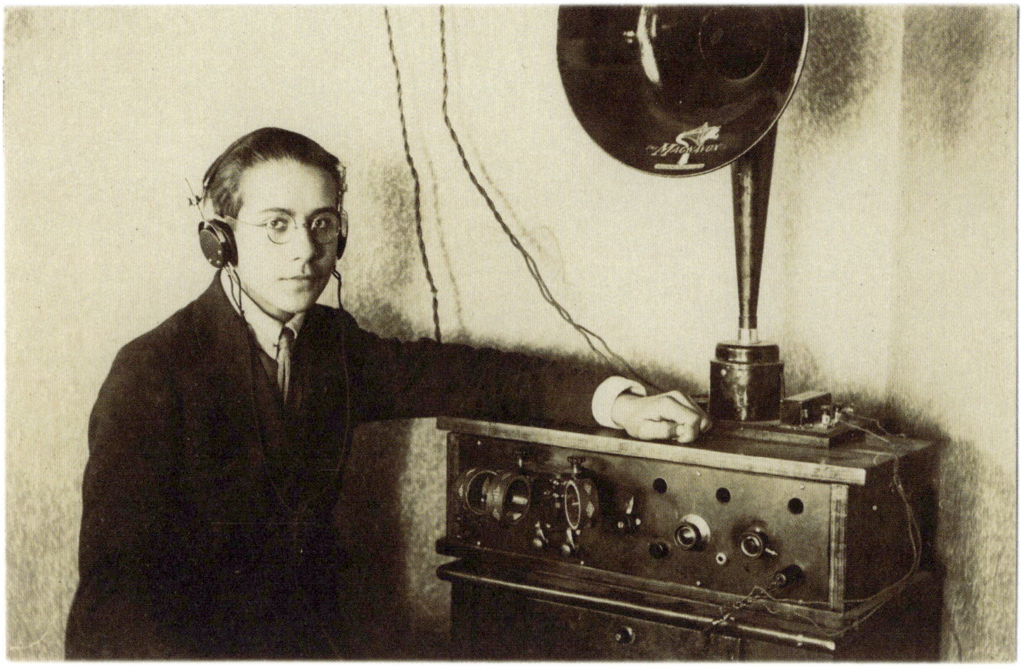

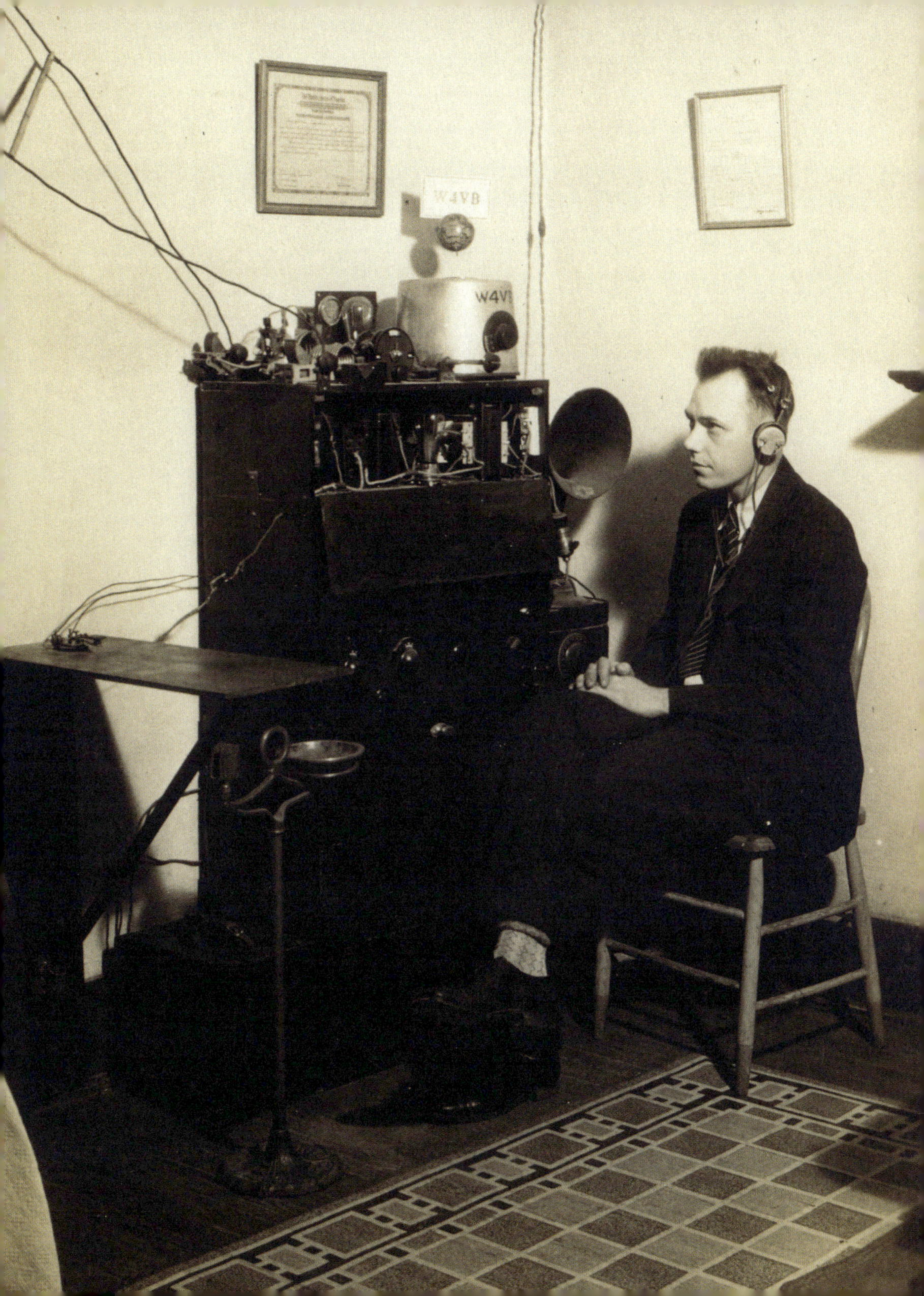
W4VB

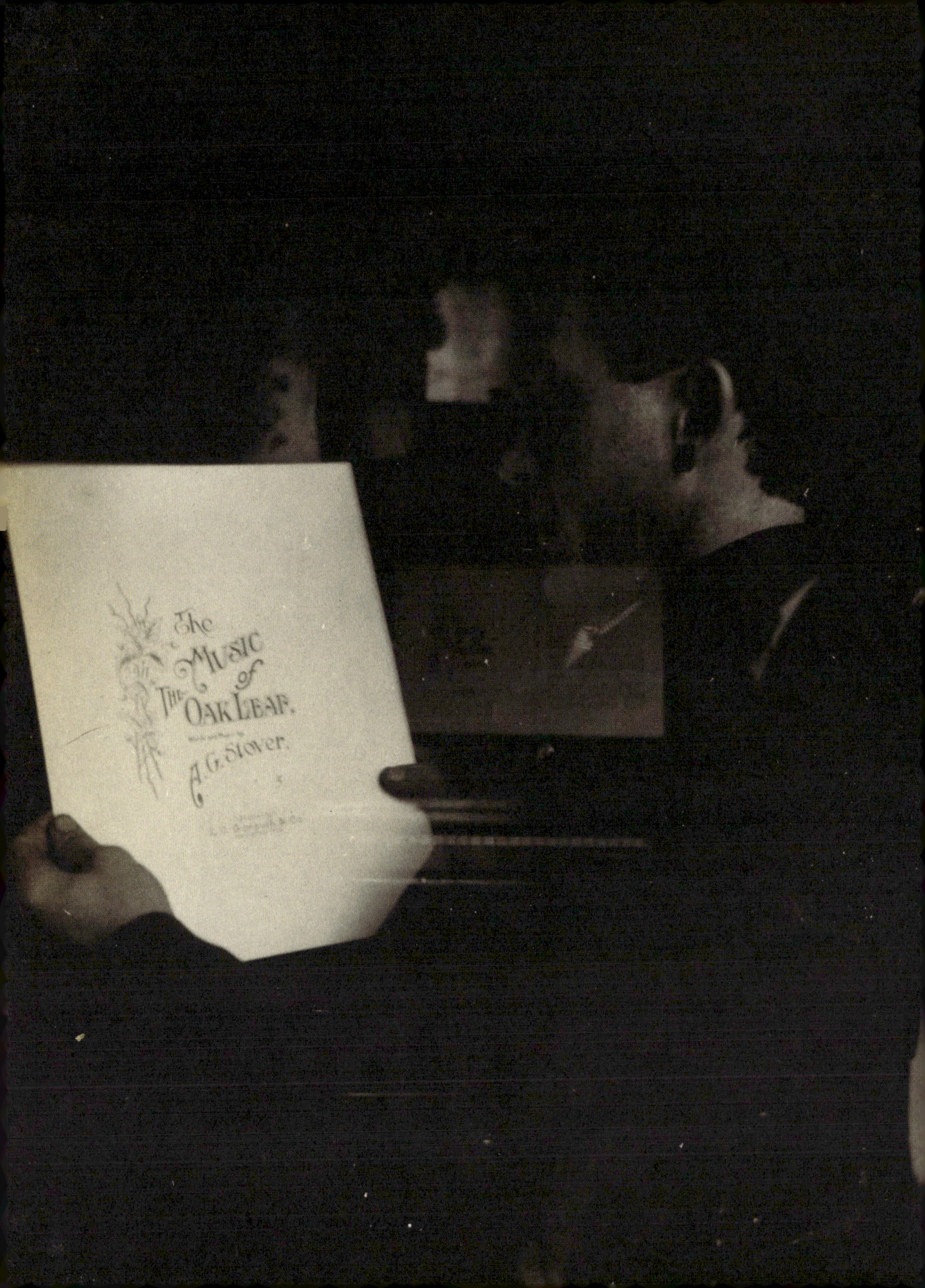
The Music of The Oak Leaf.
A. G. Stover.

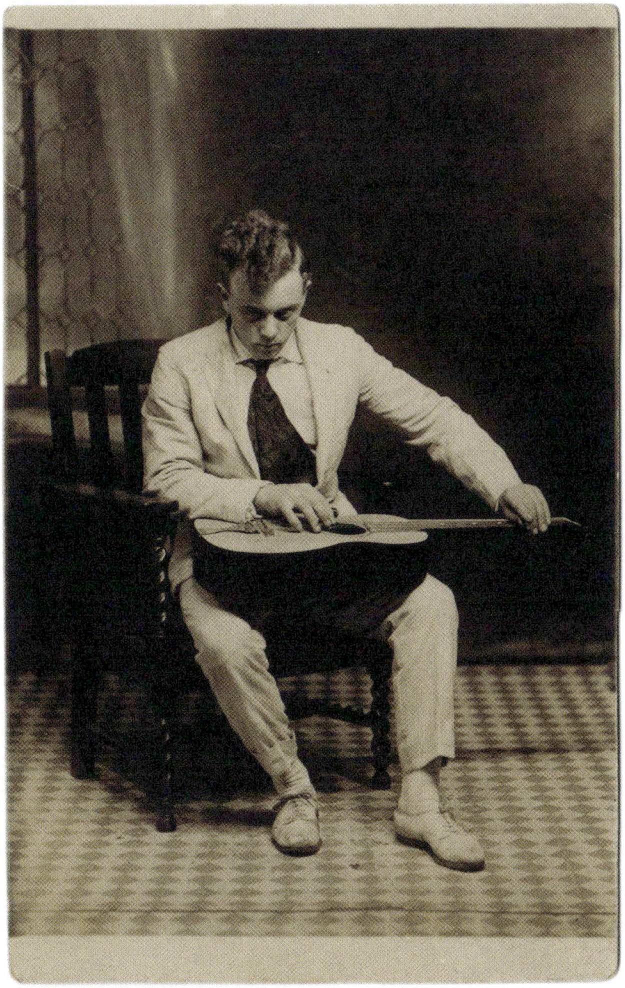

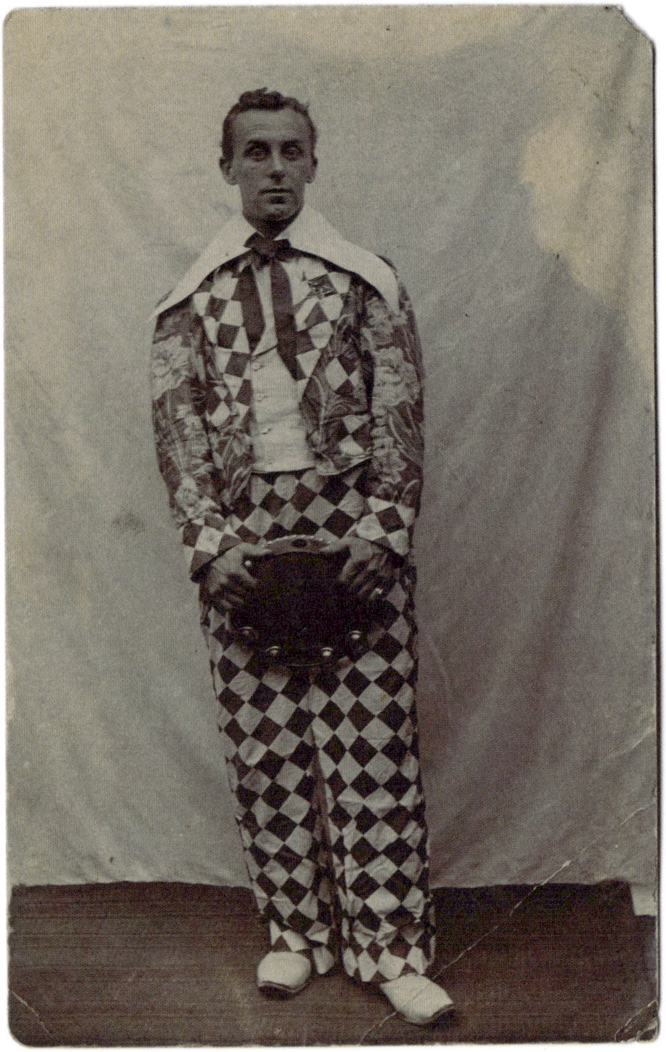

THE
SMITH
AMERICAN ORGAN
CHURCHES CHAPELS CONCERT HALLS
PRIVATE HOUSES

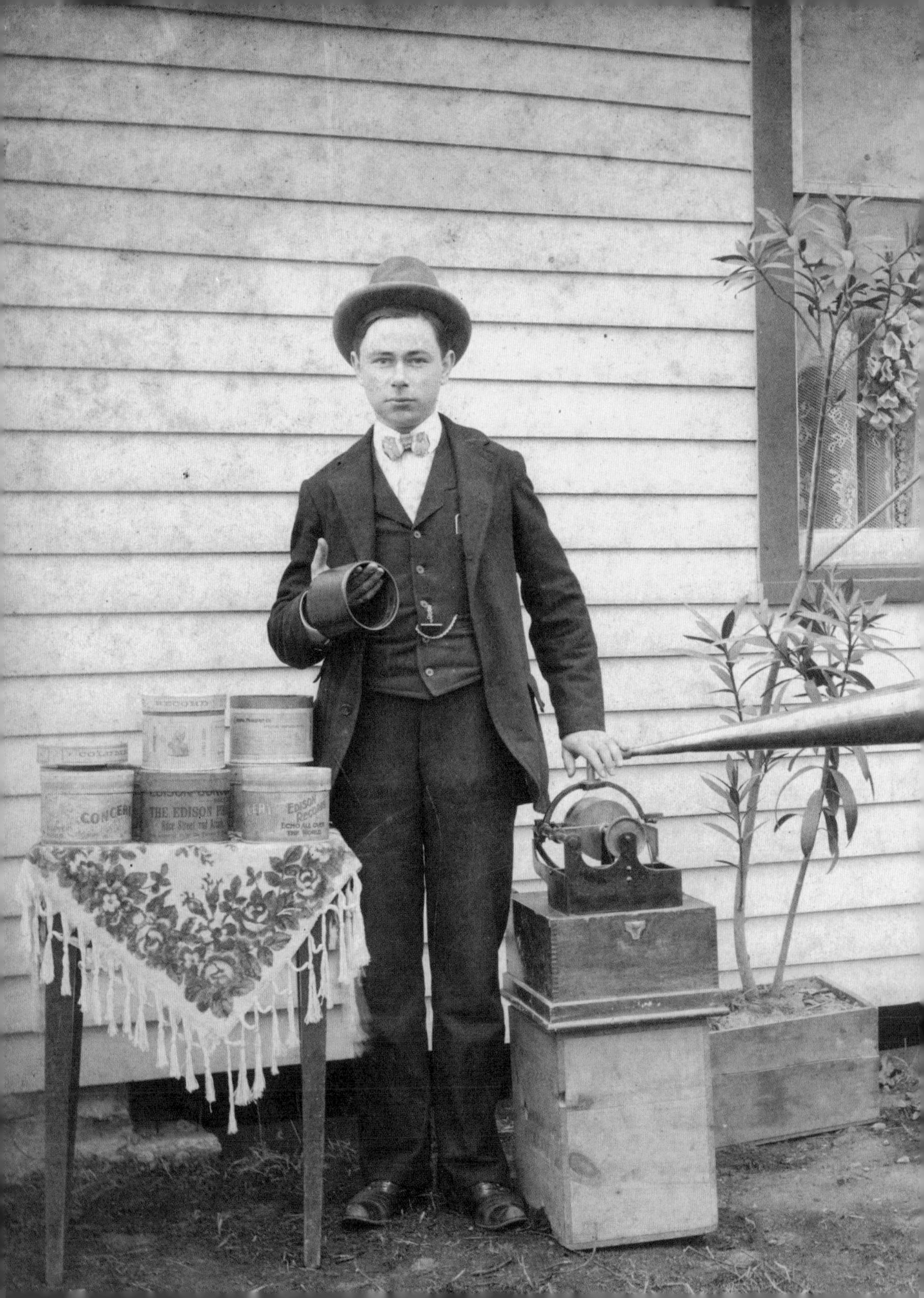
RECORD
THE EDISON
EDISON RECORDS
ECHO ALL OVER THE WORLD

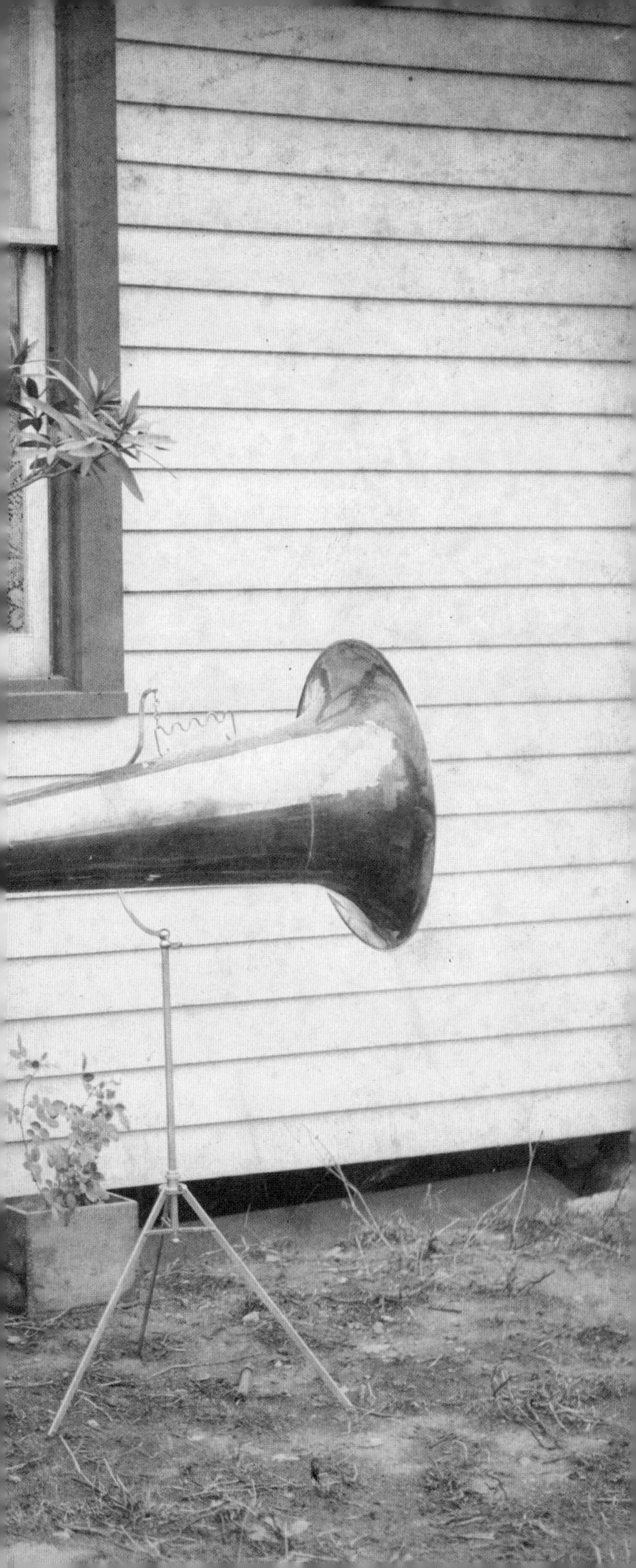

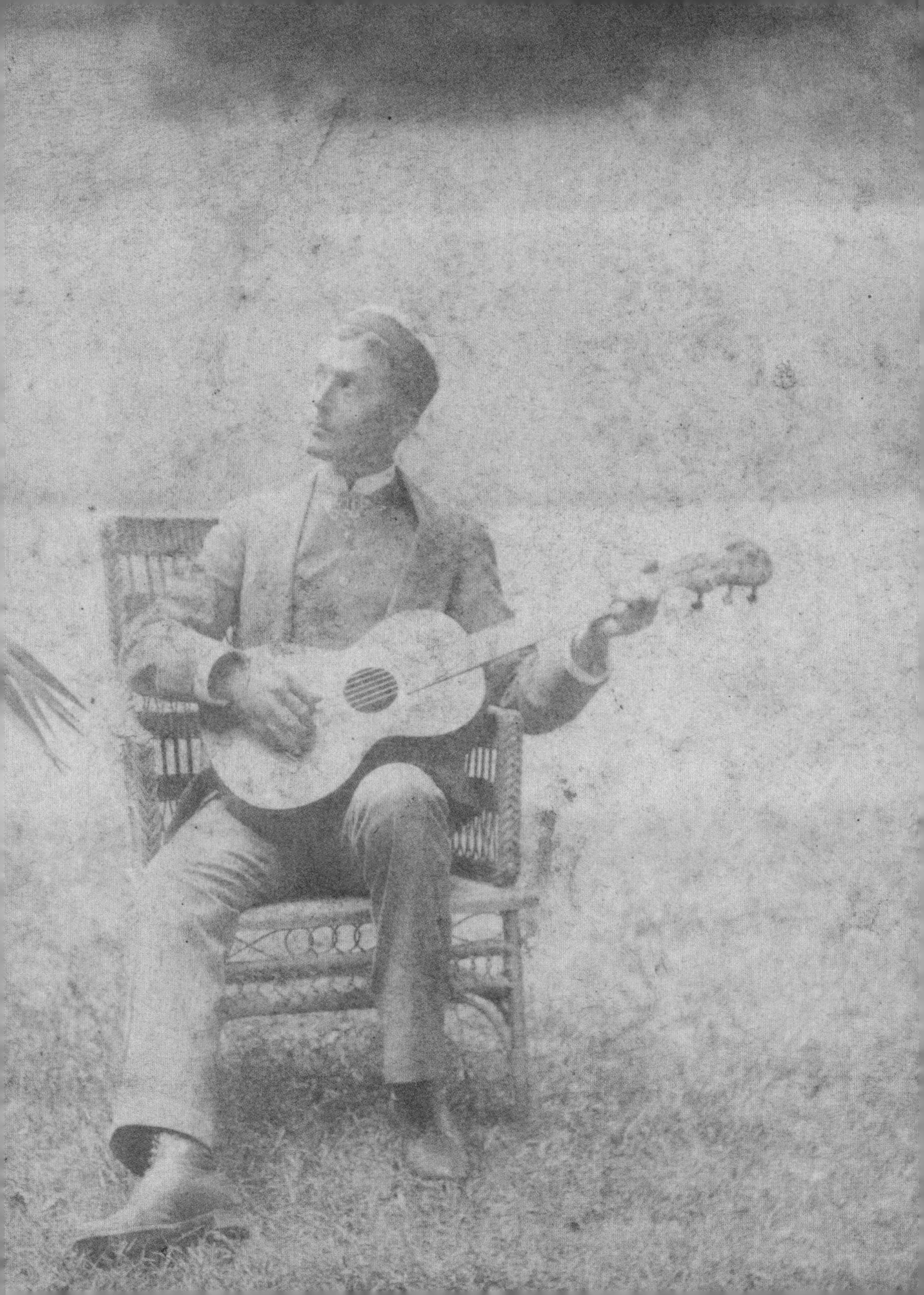

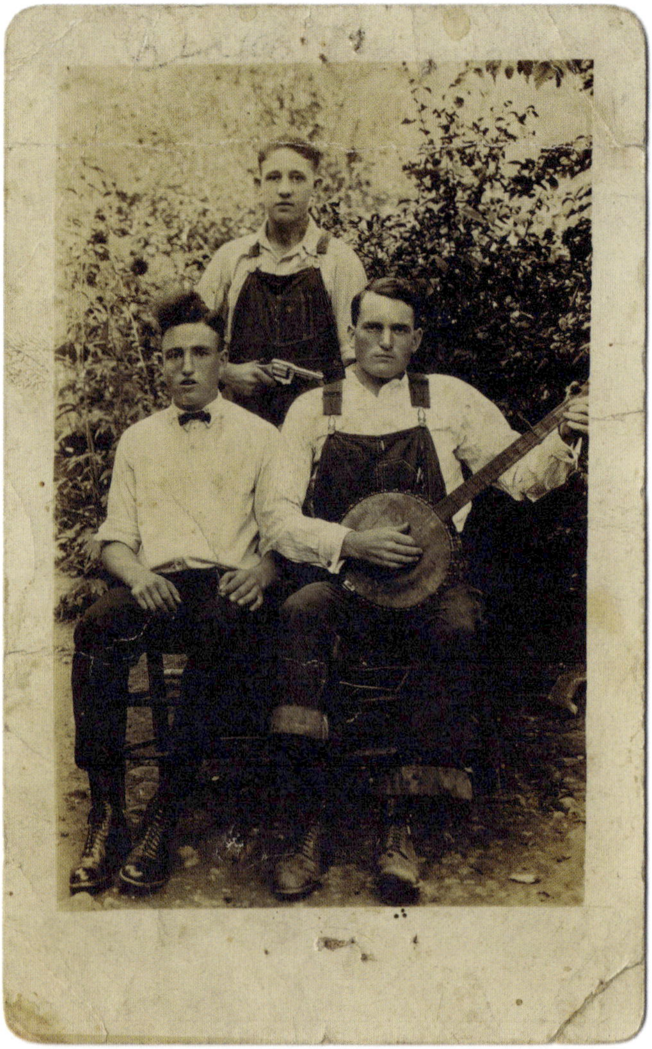

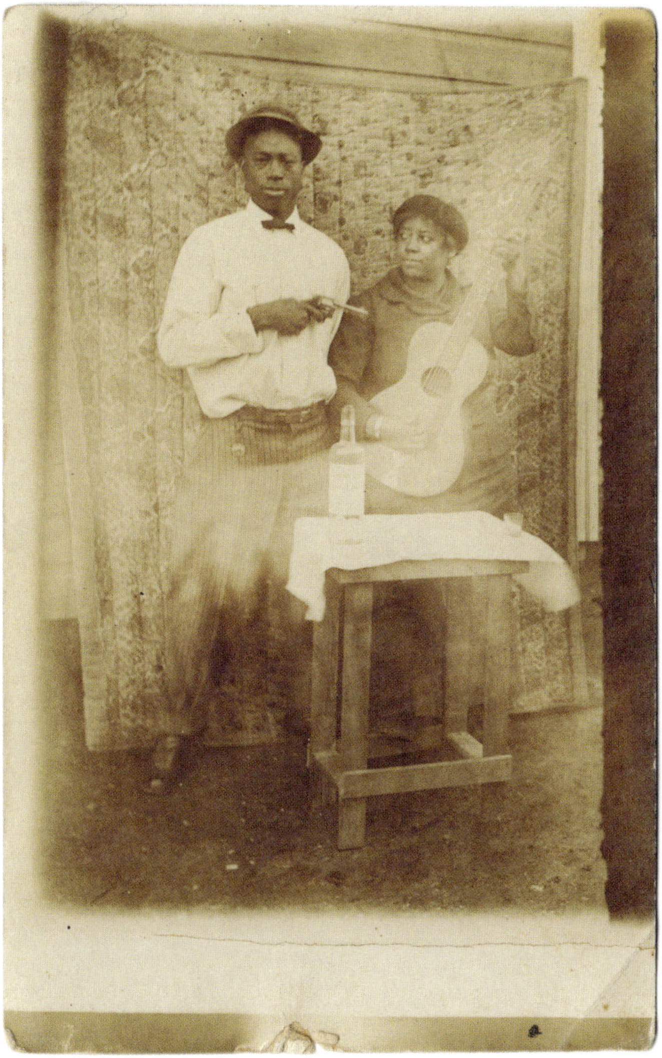

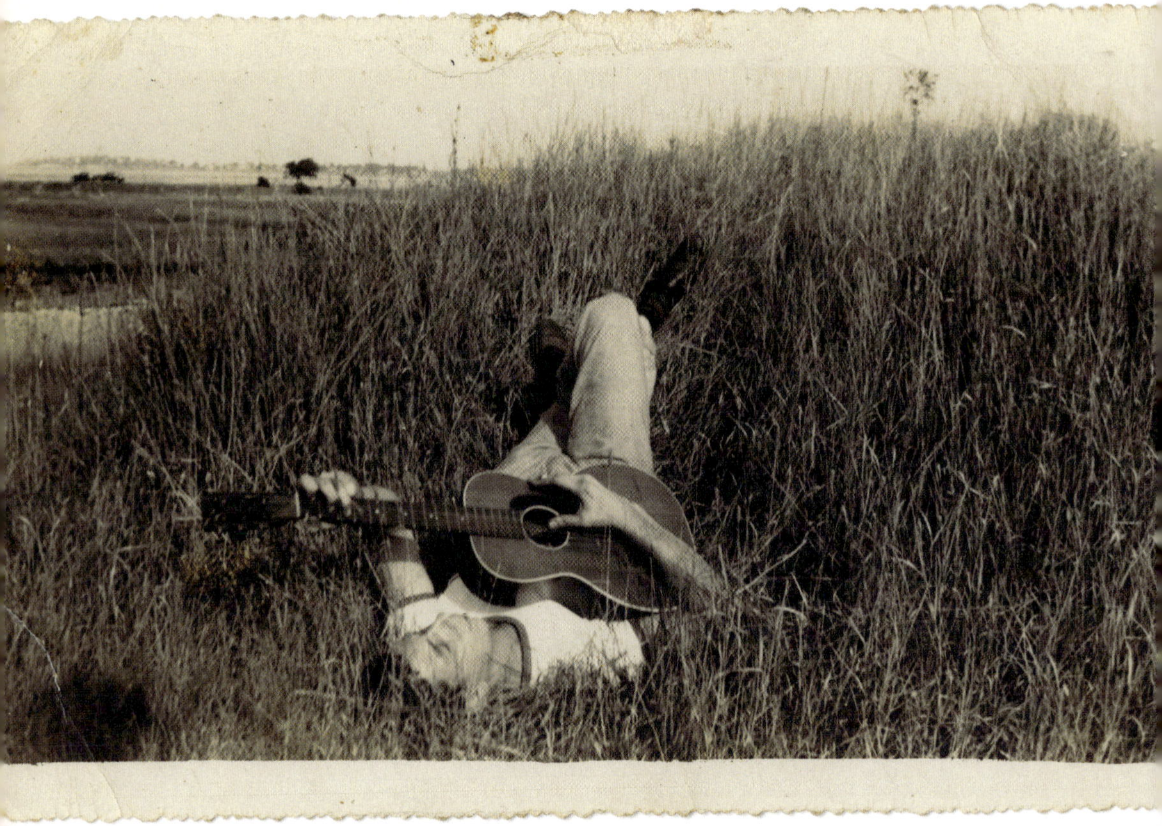

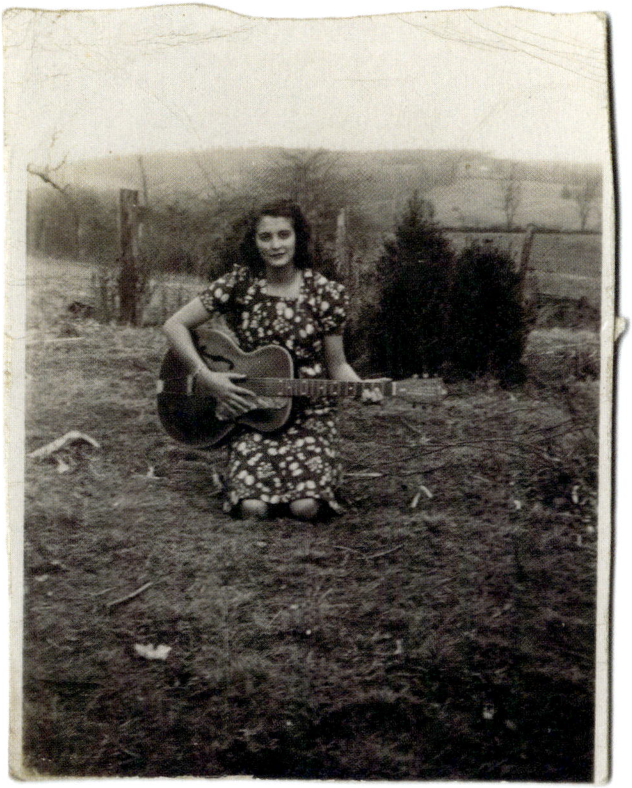

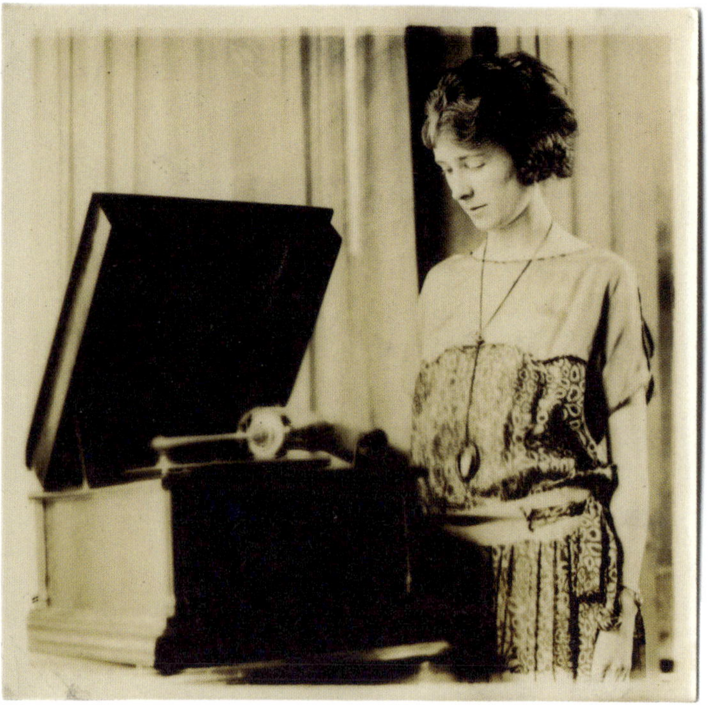

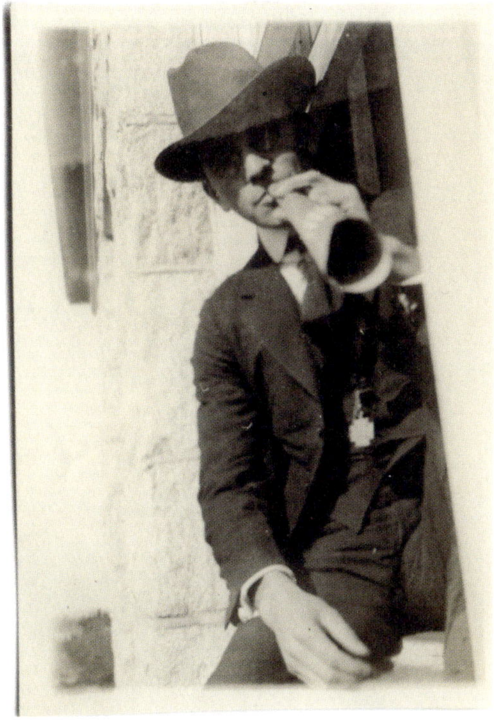

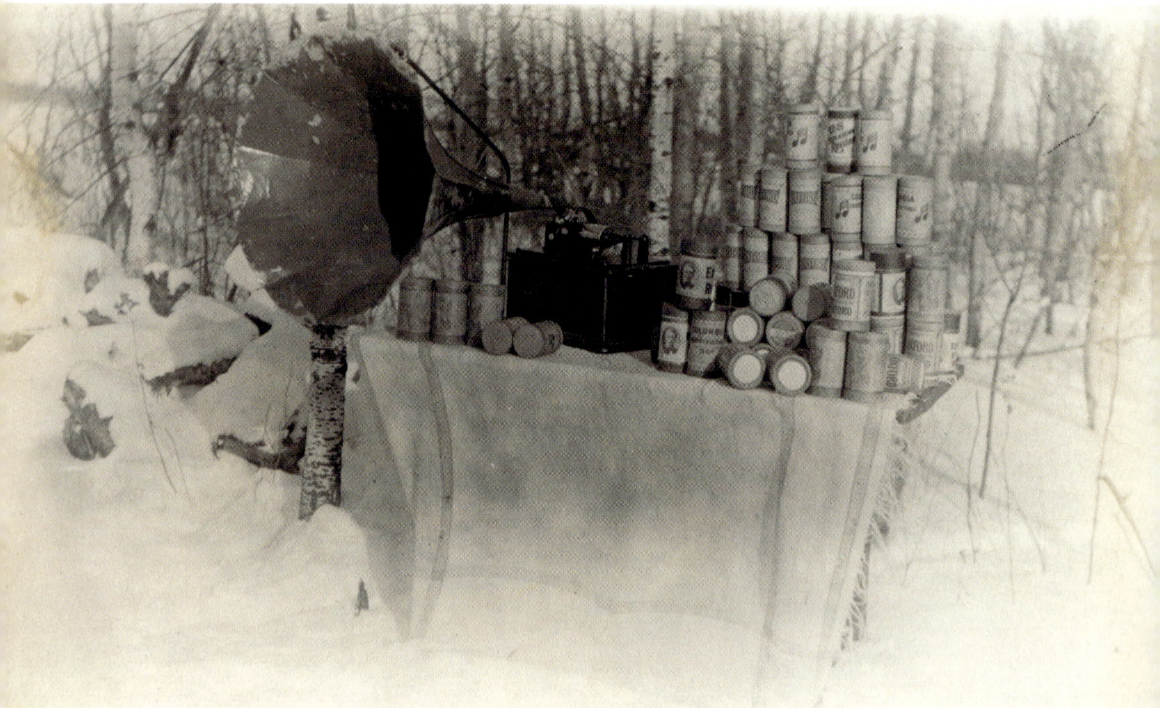

it seemed... that her voice sounded quite different in the silvery blue of the night... loud, clear and gentle, it had, as it were, arches and curves; he believed he could see the voice and almost catch hold of it. soon he had the sensation that it made an arch over his head and that he was standing directly beneath it.

joseph roth
weights and measures

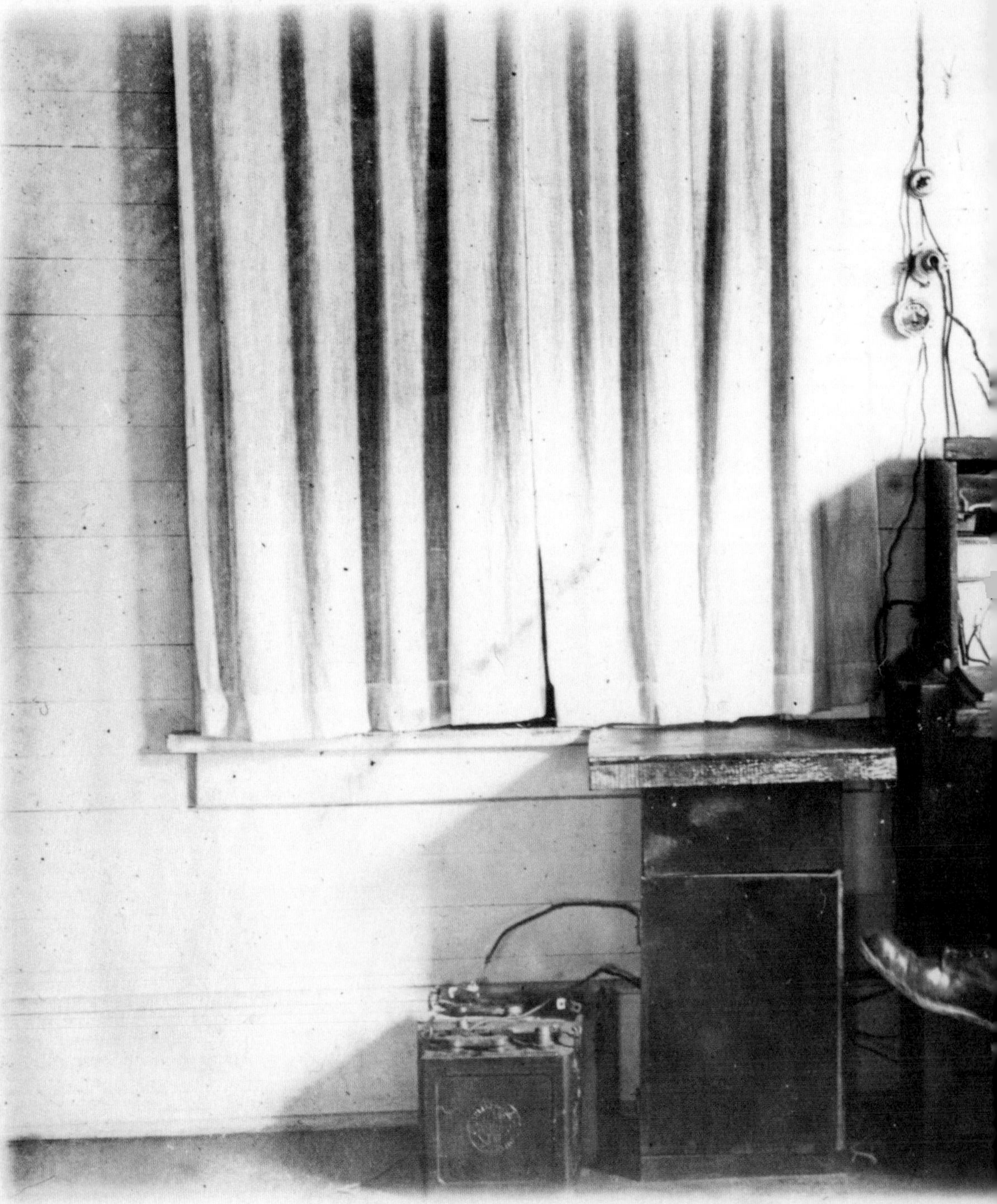

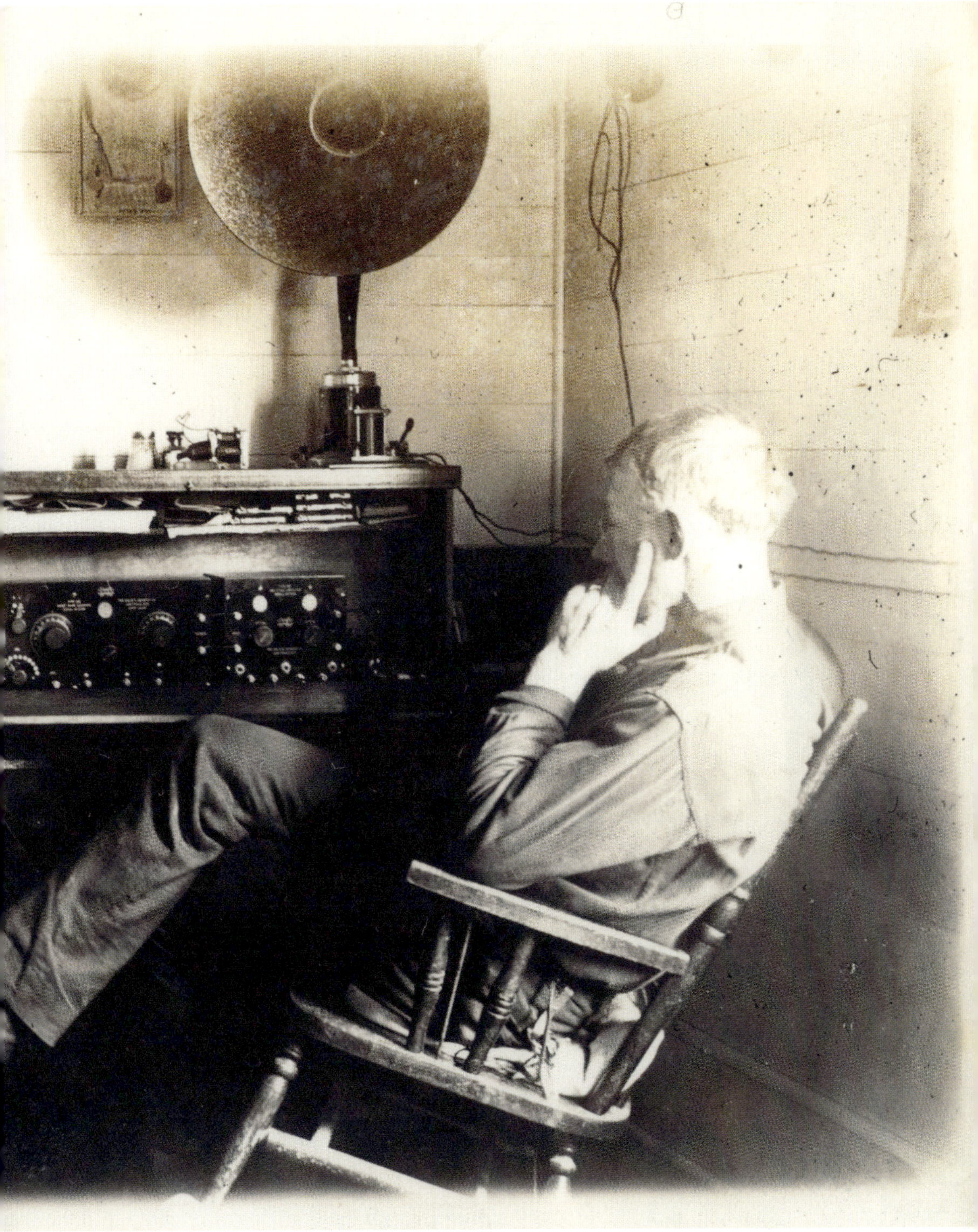

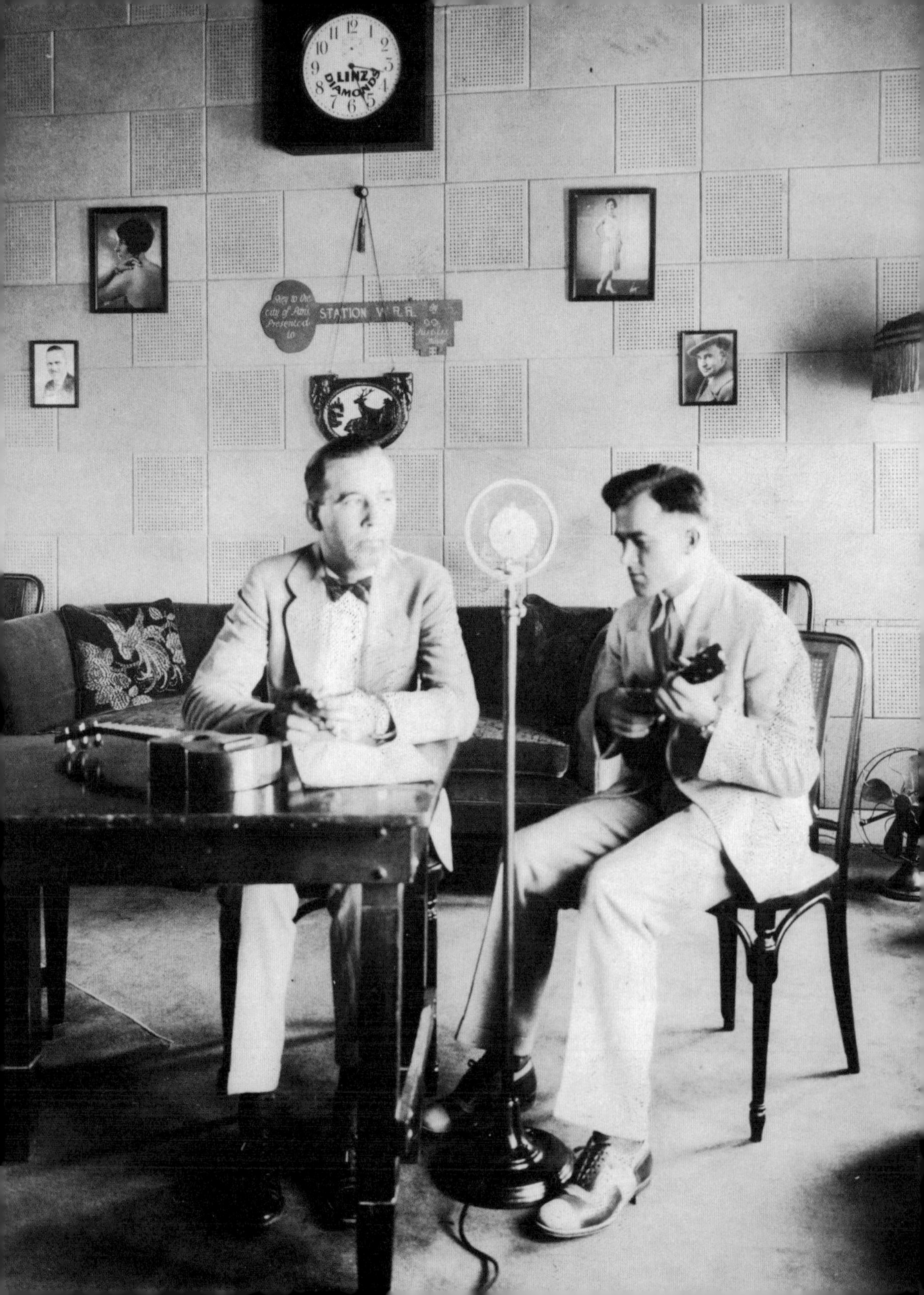
LINZ DIAMONDS
city of Paris
Presented
to
STATION

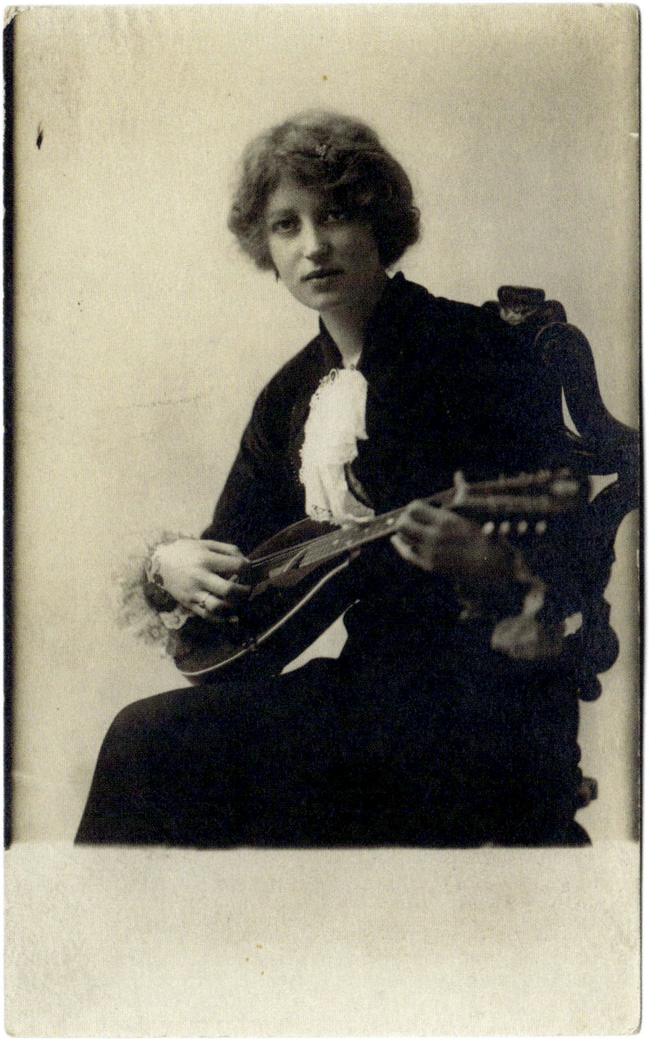

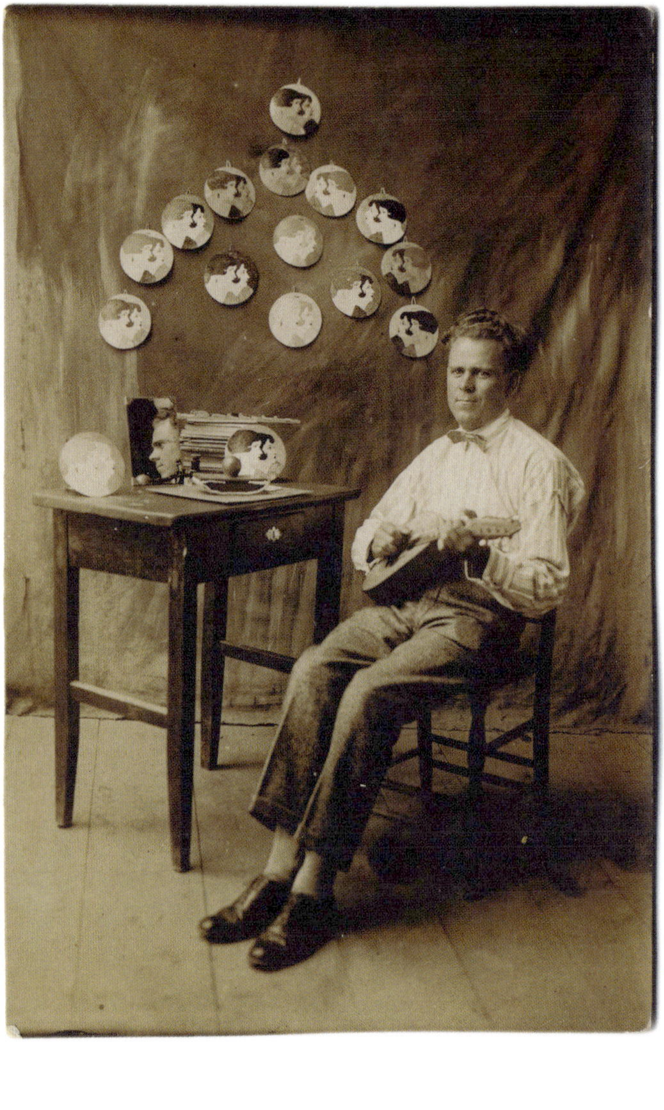

E. O. COFFIN.

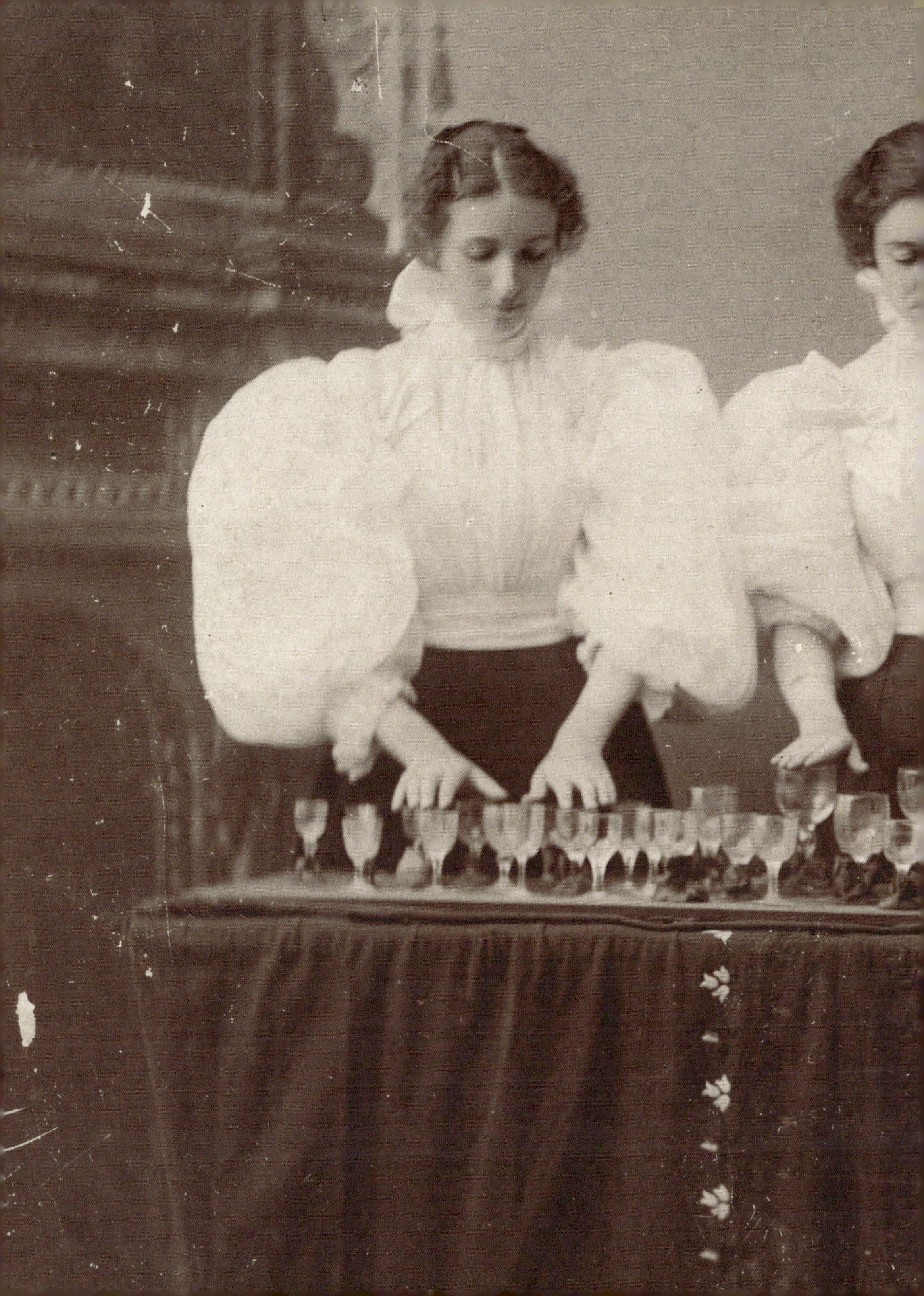

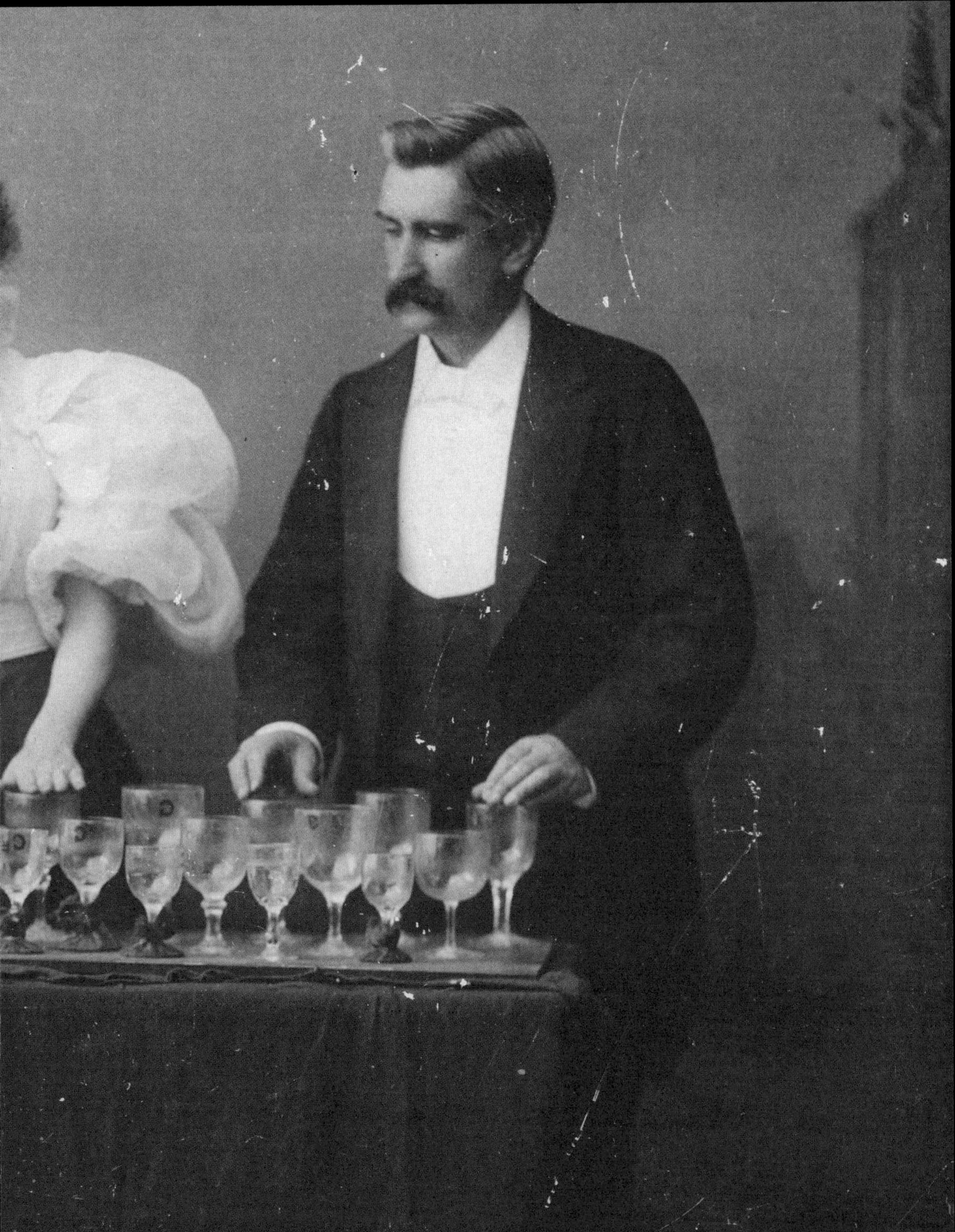

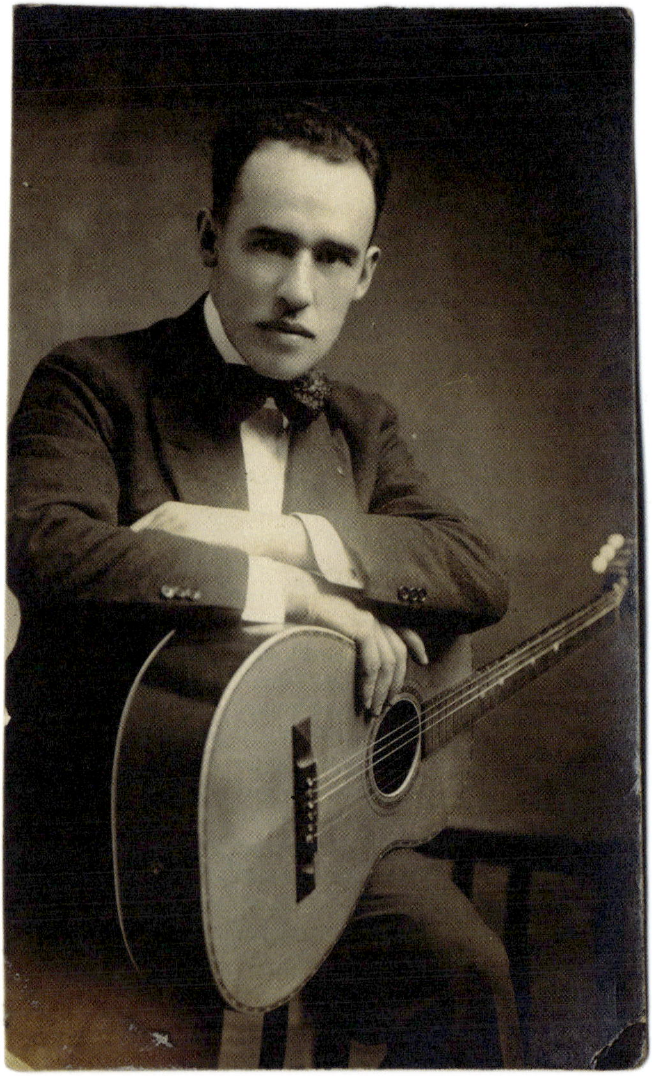

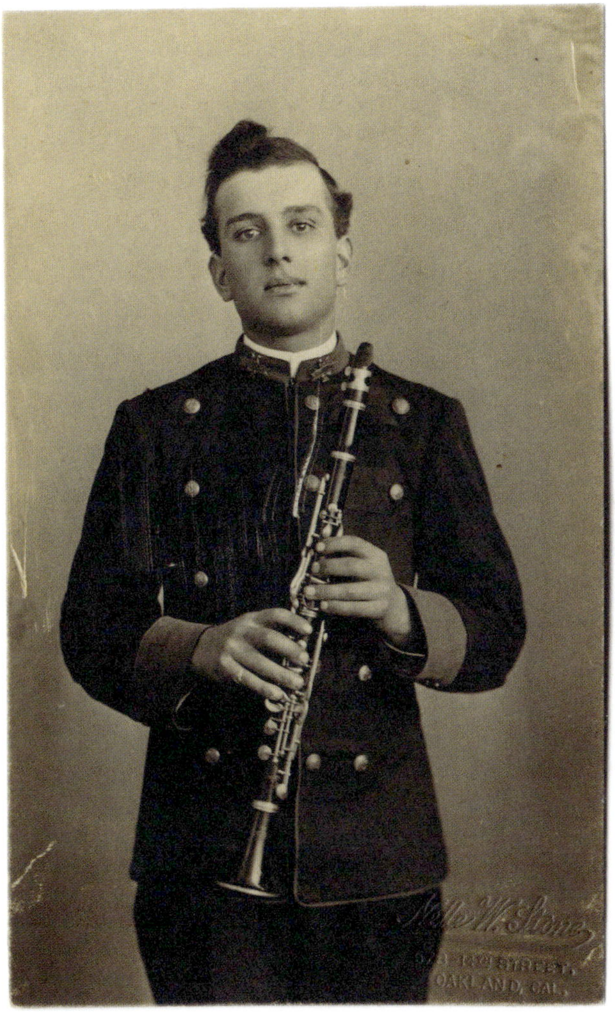
OAKLAND, CAL.

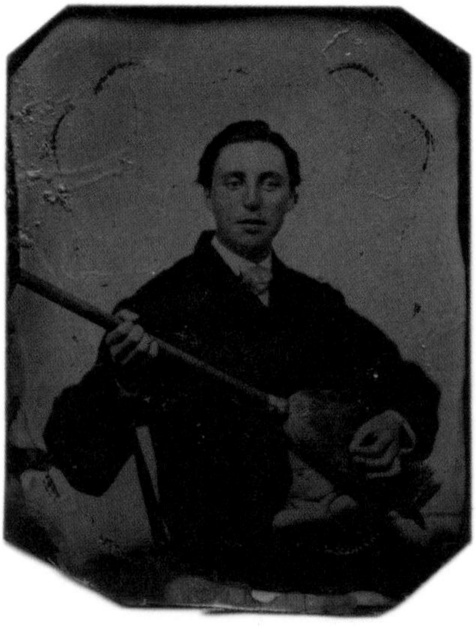

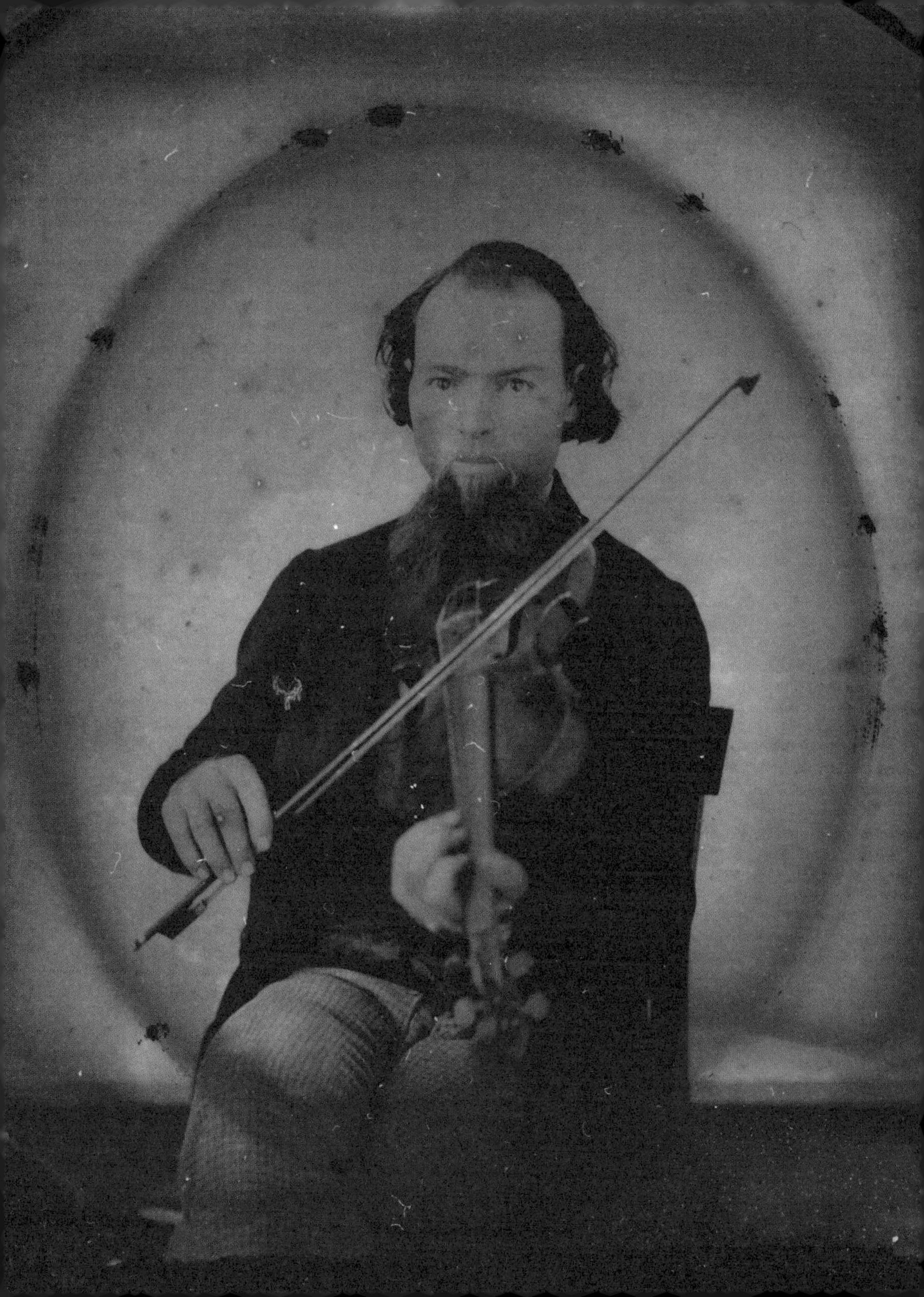

Apex Photo Gallery, 132 Water St., Fitchburg, Mass.

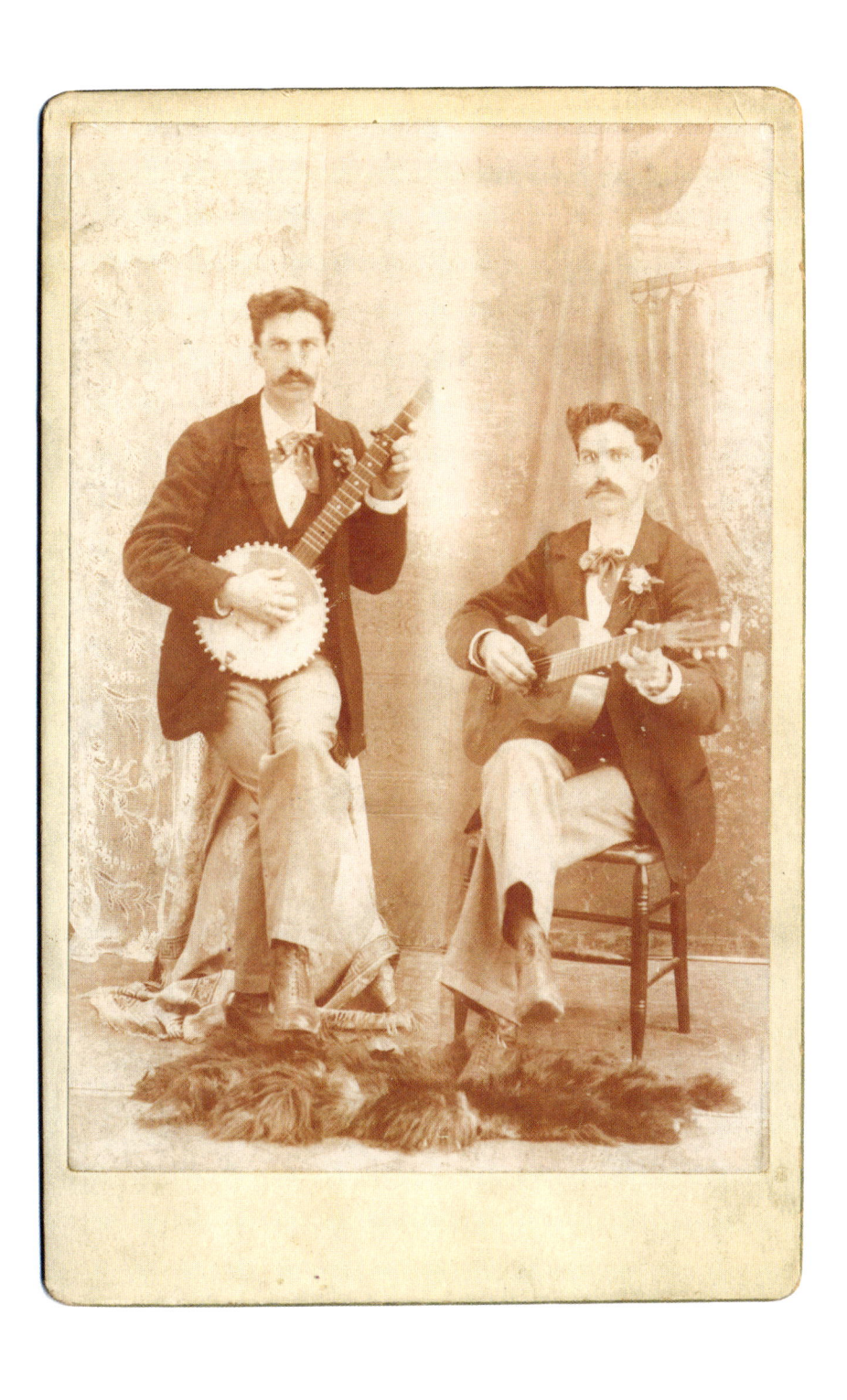

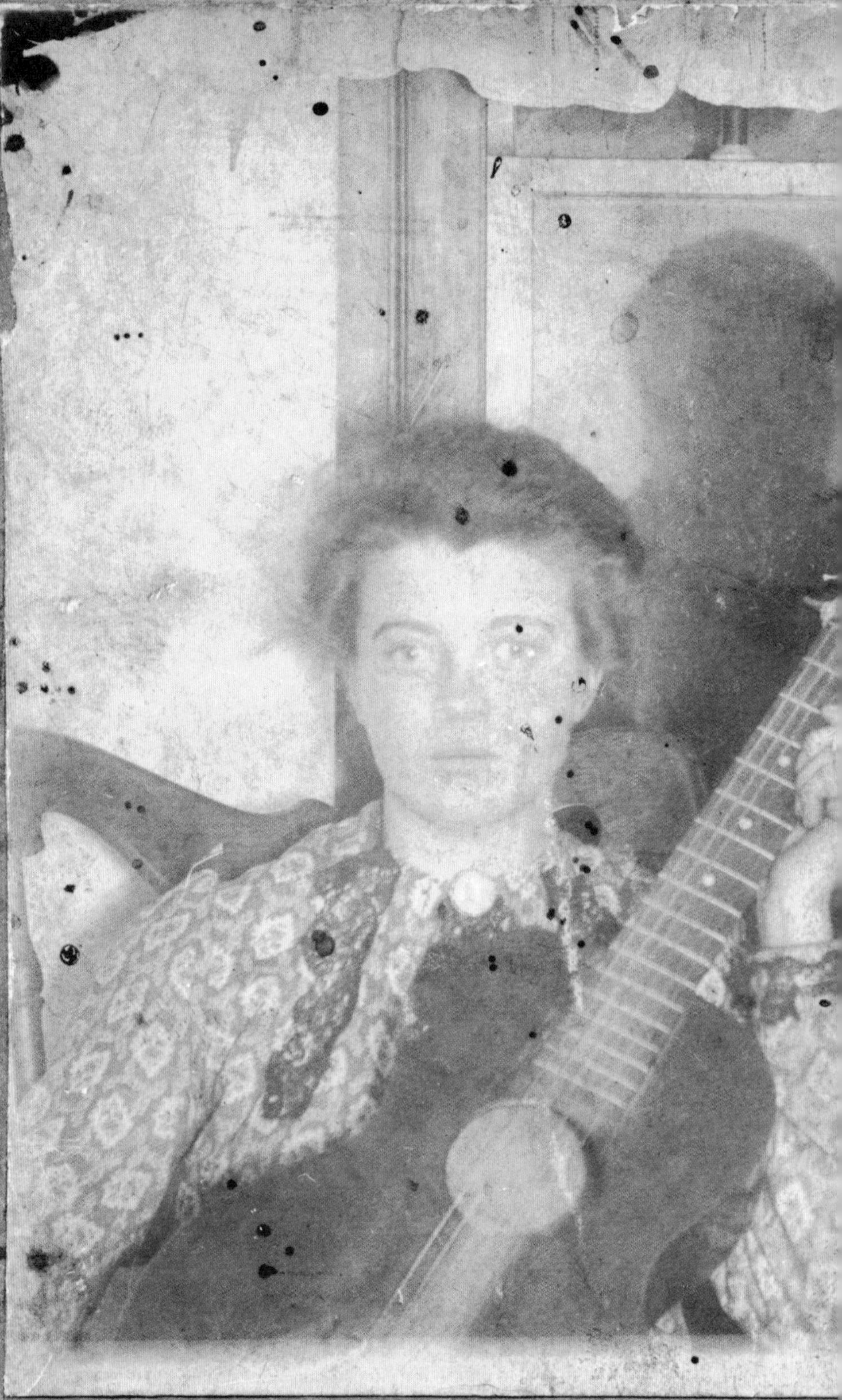

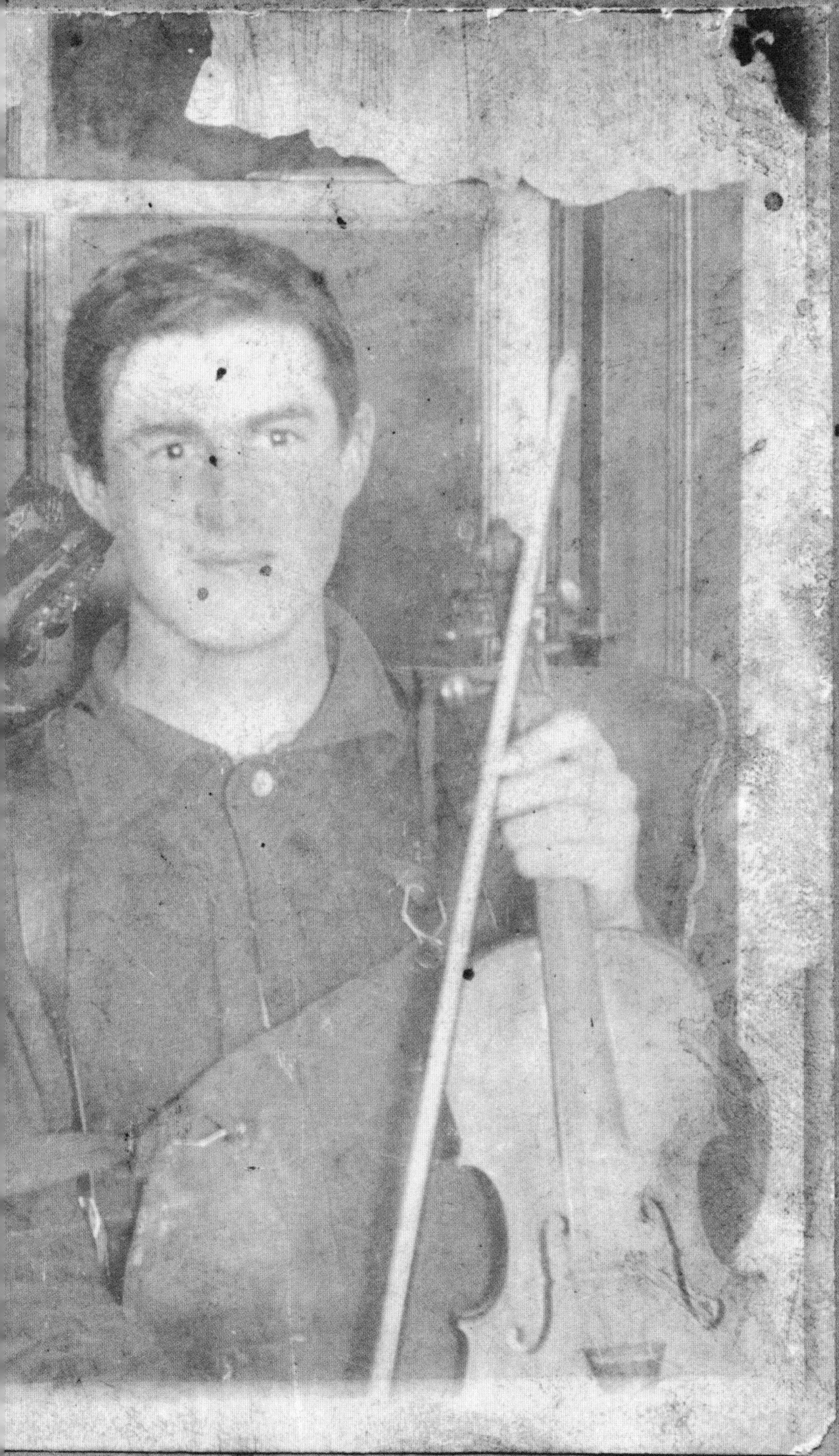

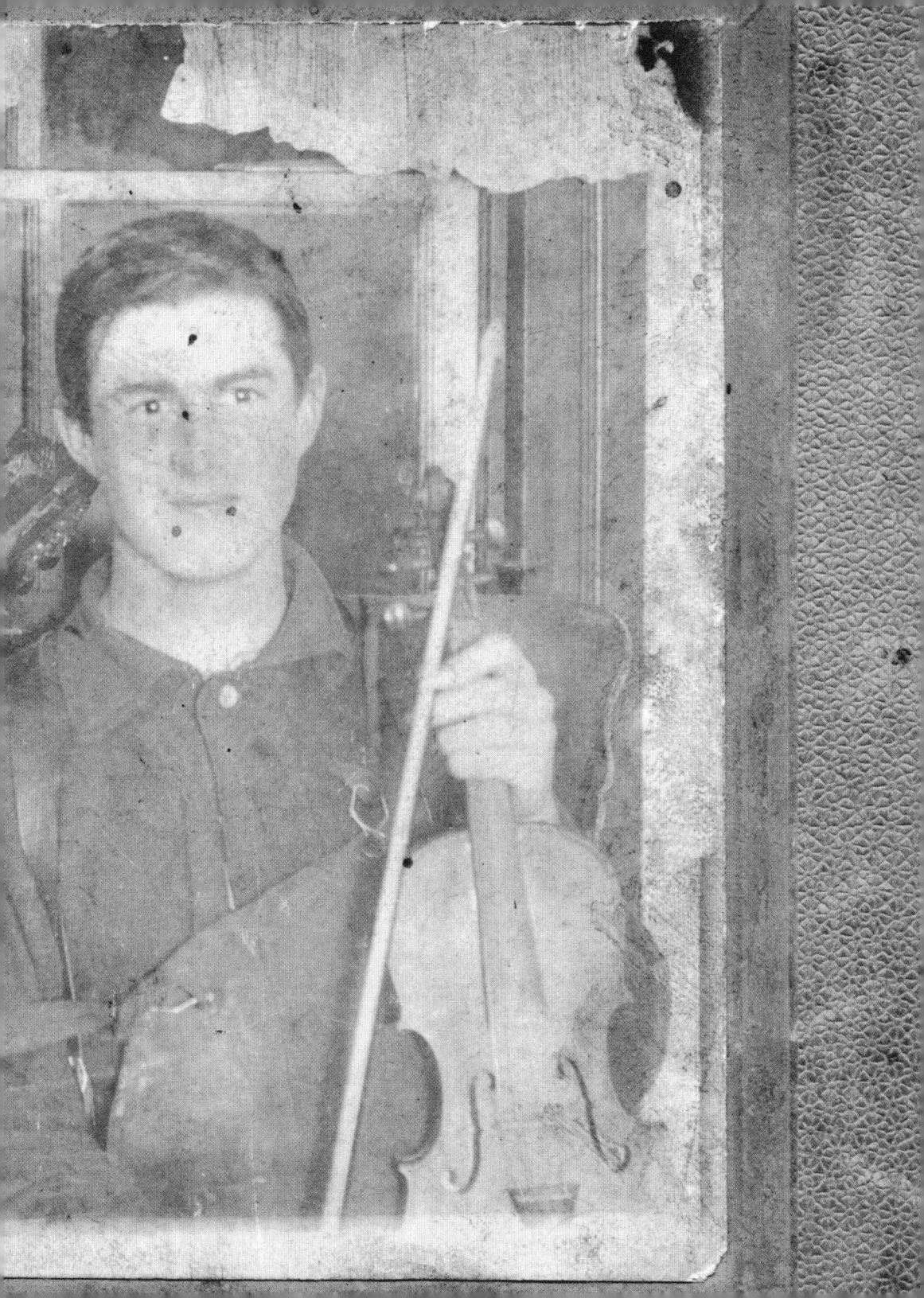

Johnson Studio — 3rd & Georgia St. — Louisiana, Mo.

Flaten — Moorhead, Minn.

i have seen a curious child, who dwelt upon a tract of inland ground, applying to his ear the convolutions of a smooth lipped shell; to which, in silence hushed, his very soul listened intensely; and his countenance soon brightened with joy; for from within were heard murmurings, where by the monitor expressed mysterious union with the sea.

william wordsworth
the prelude

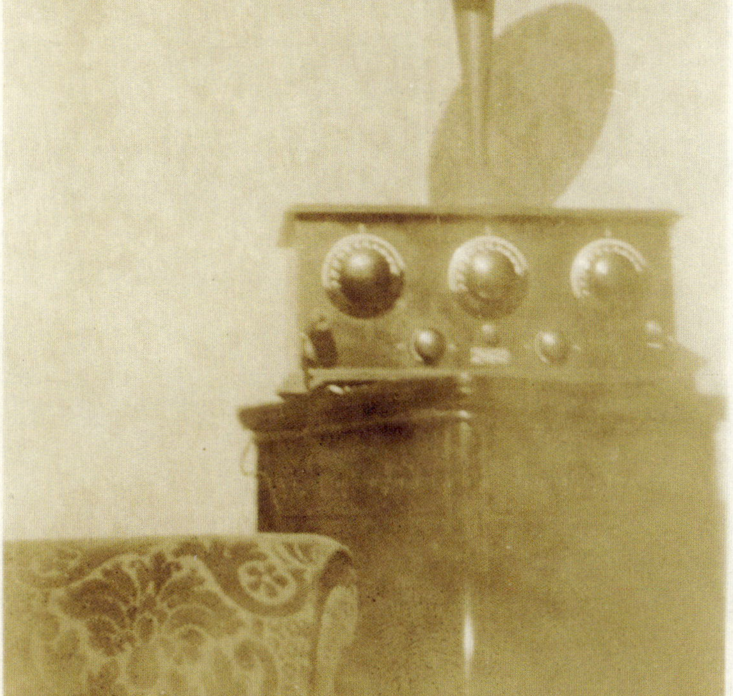

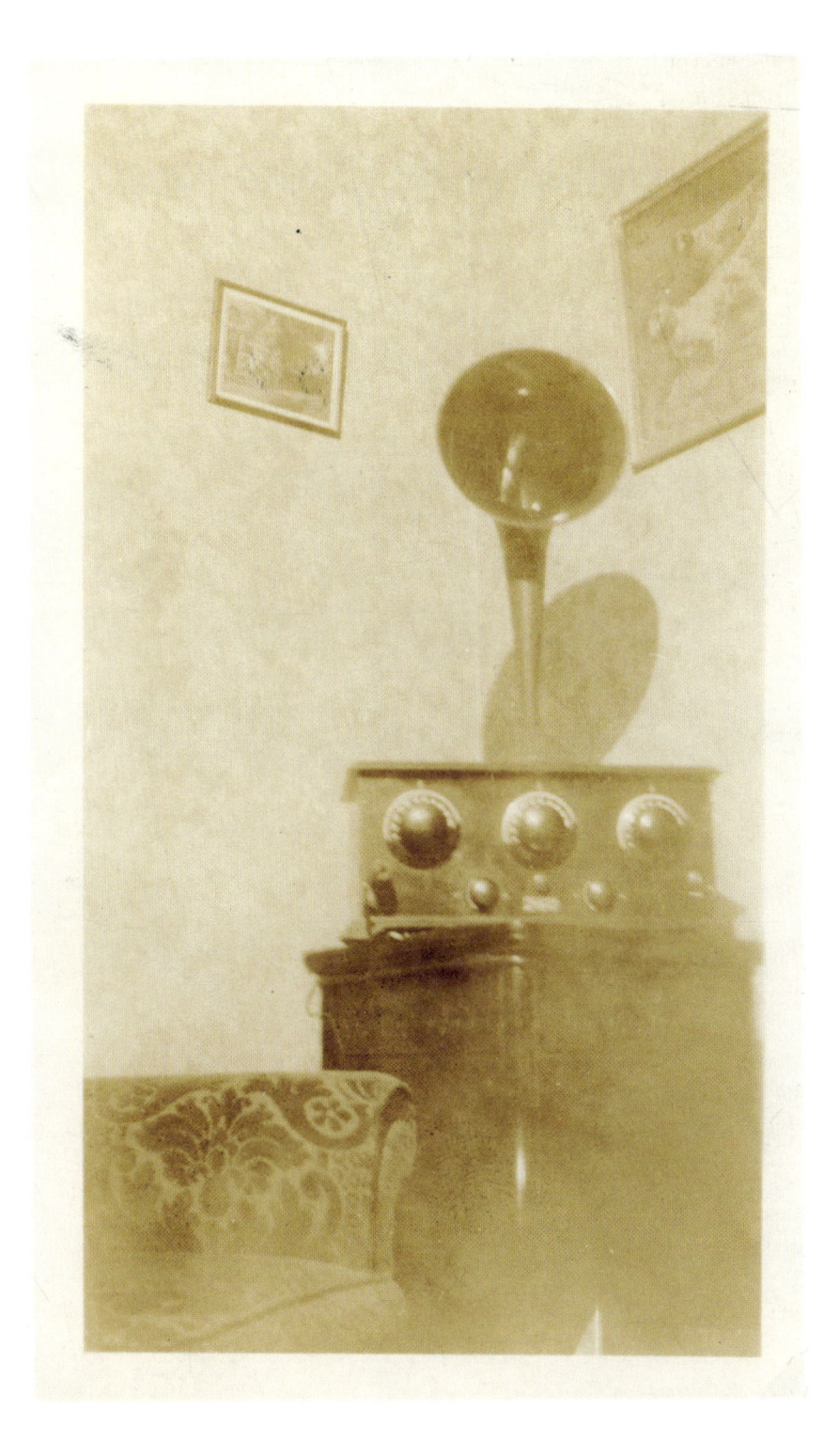

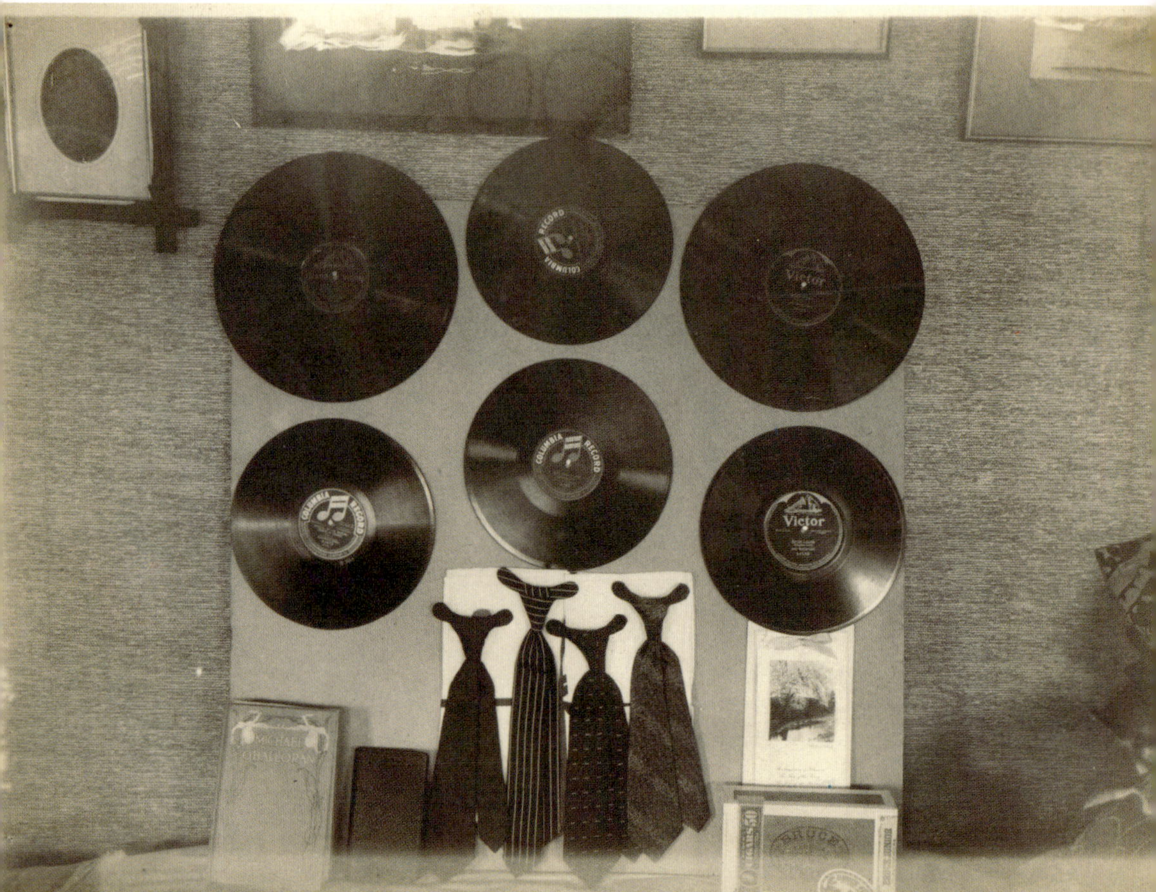
COLUMBIA RECORD
Victor

a strange wonderful sound filled the room, a sort of singing, though accompanied by words, was so supernaturally soft and touching that you could not believe it came from a human throat...

> gerhart hauptmann
> *the fool in christ*

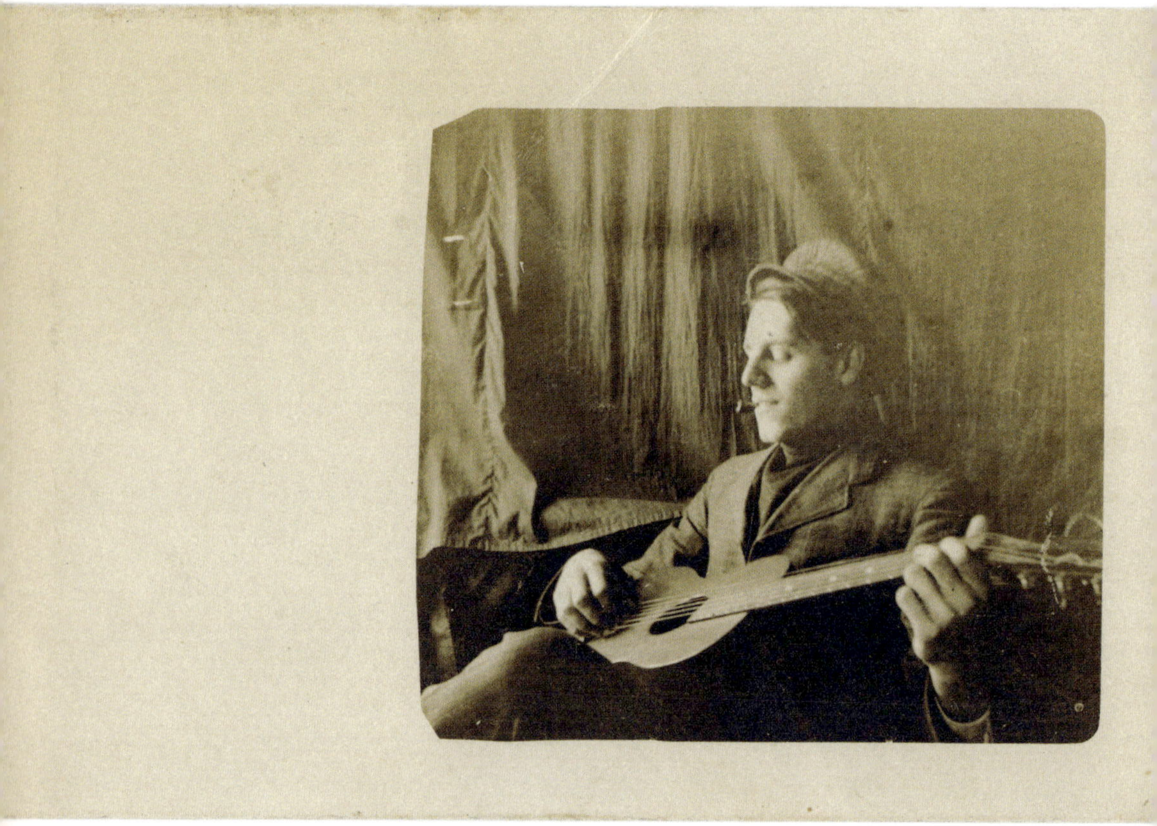

C. J. Jessup, one man
Drum + Bugle Corps.

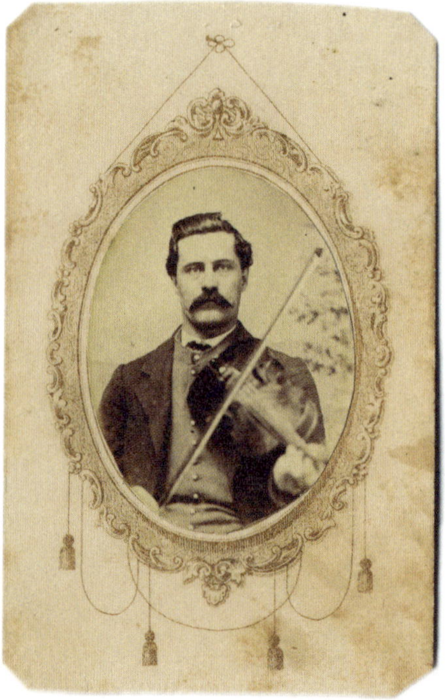

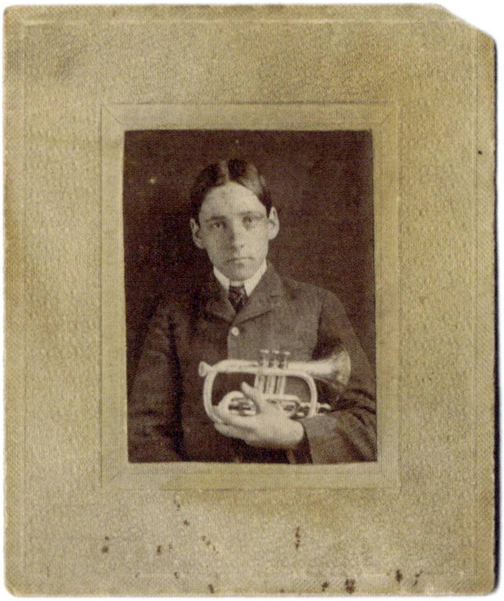

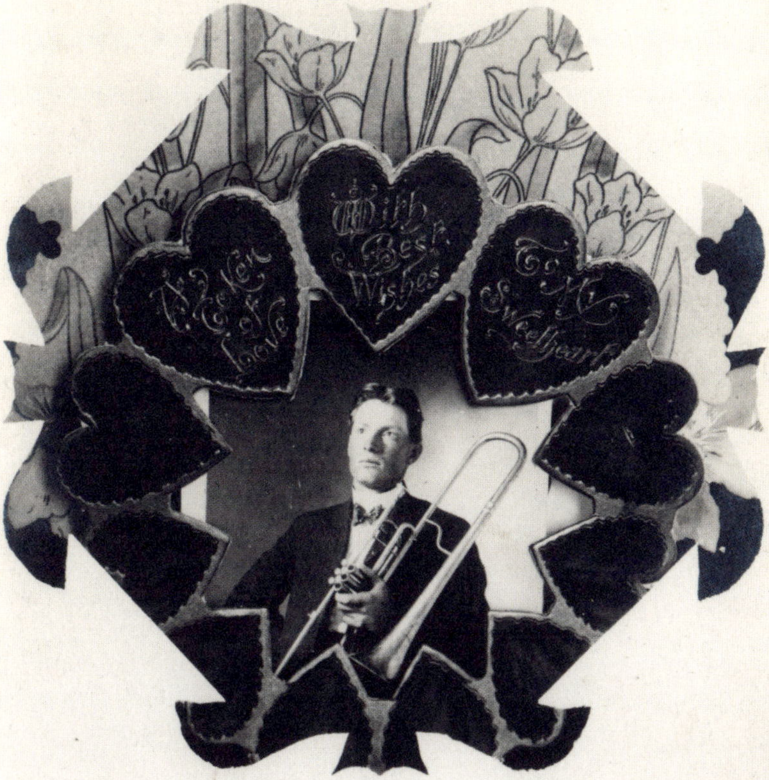
With Best Wishes
To My Sweetheart

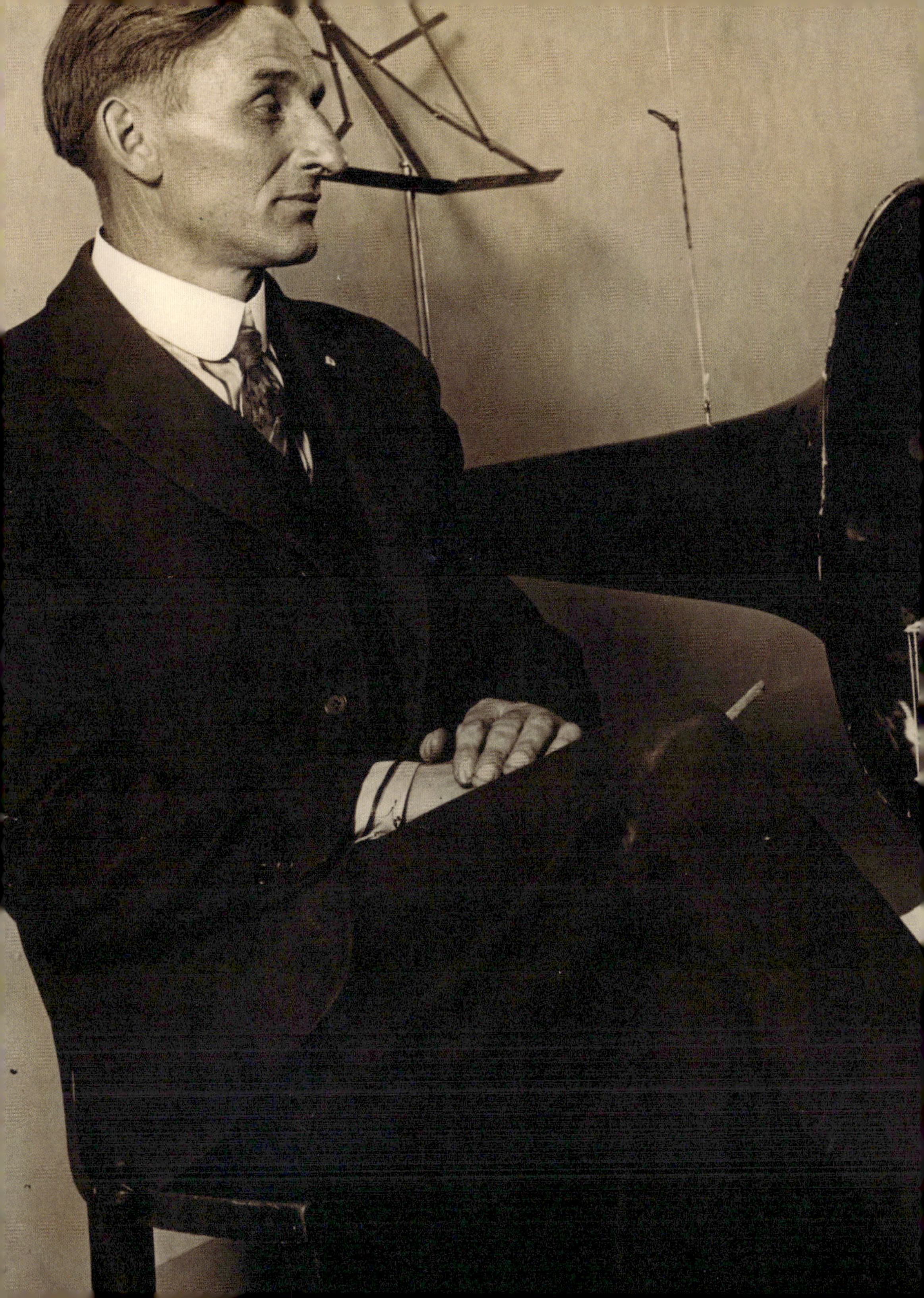

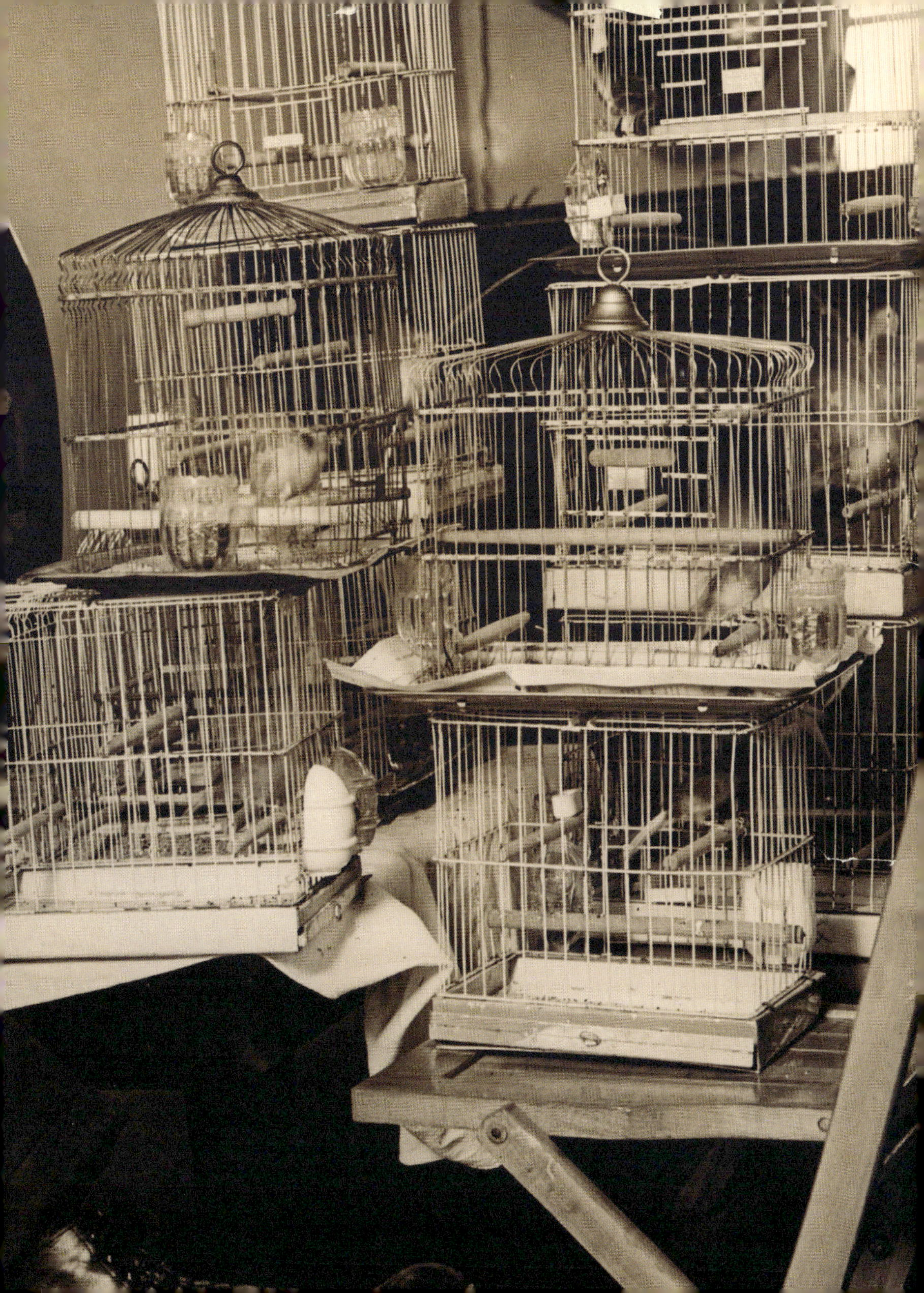

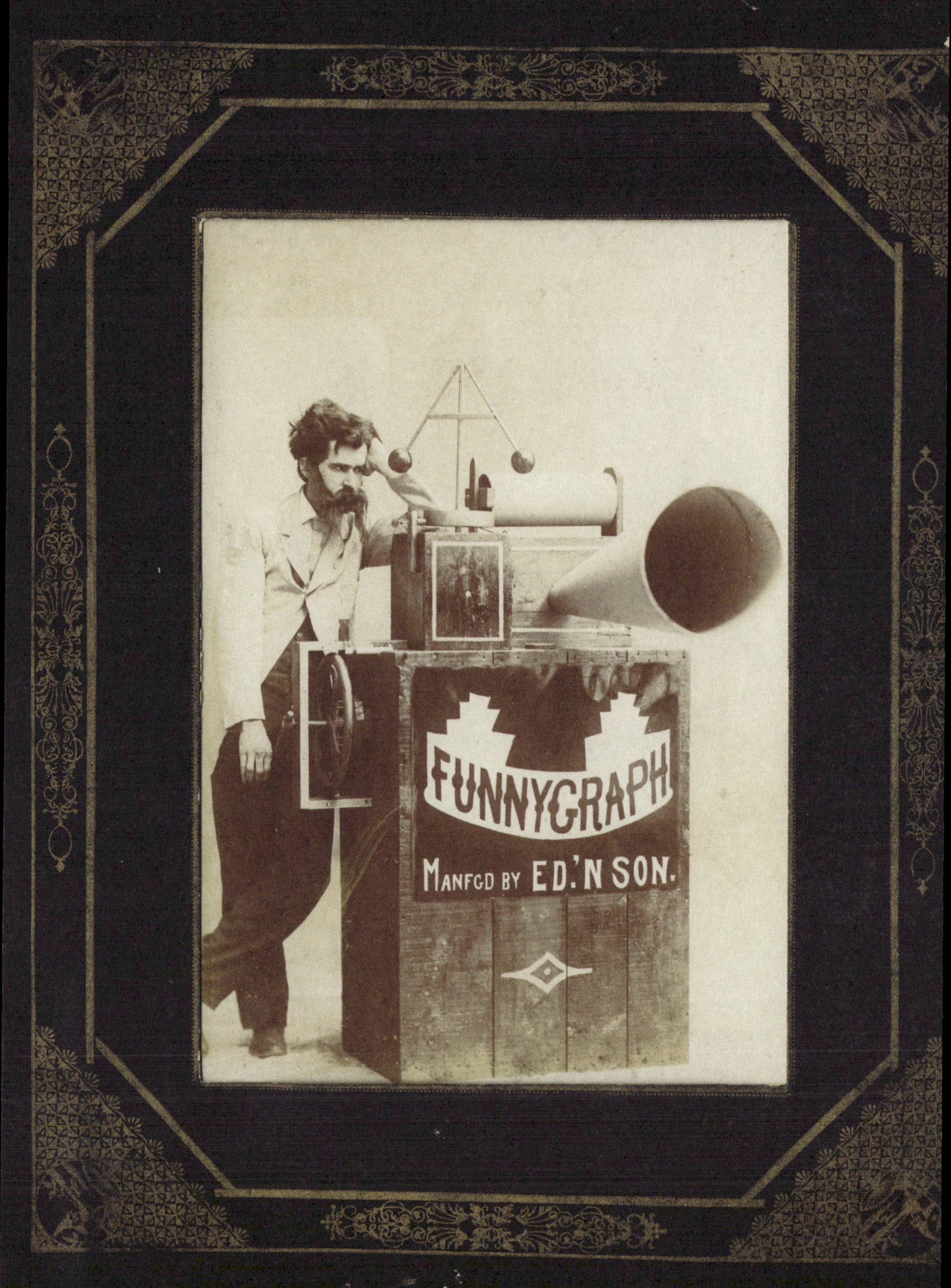
FUNNYGRAPH
MANFGD BY ED.'N SON.

Simon S. Kaufman

Taken Sept. 1885

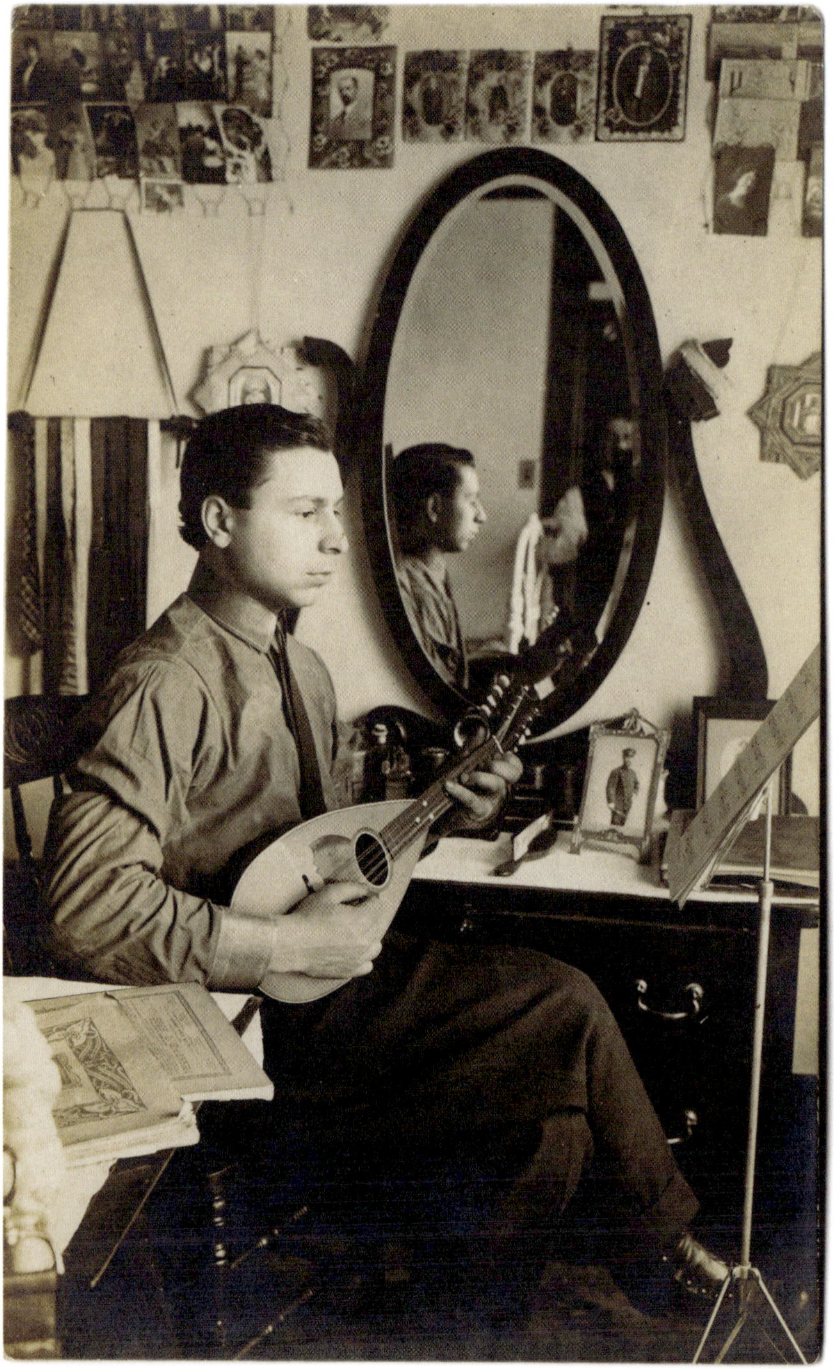

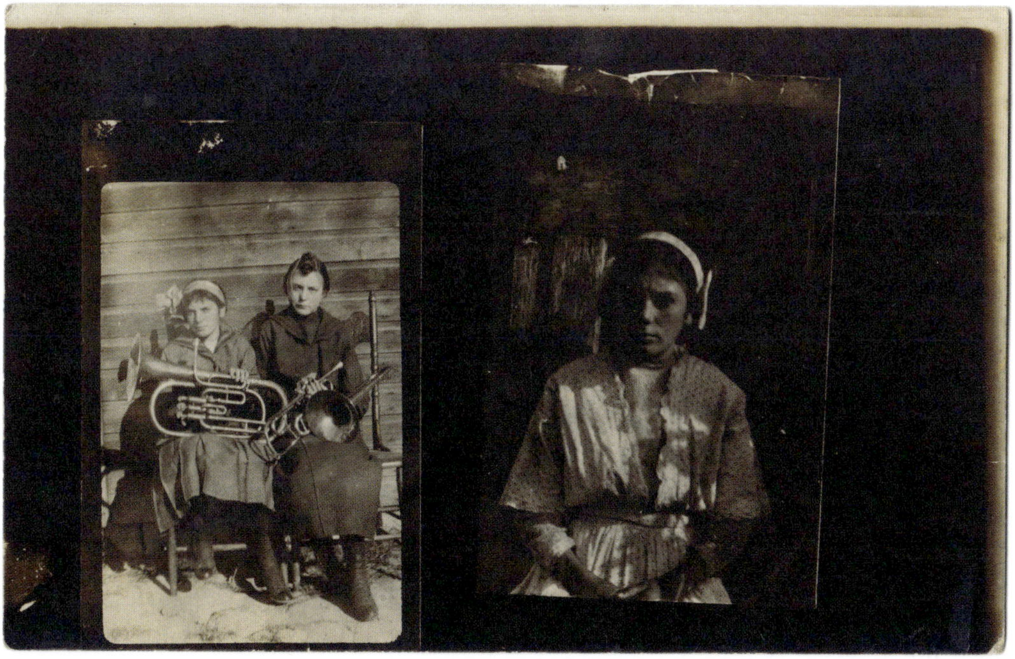

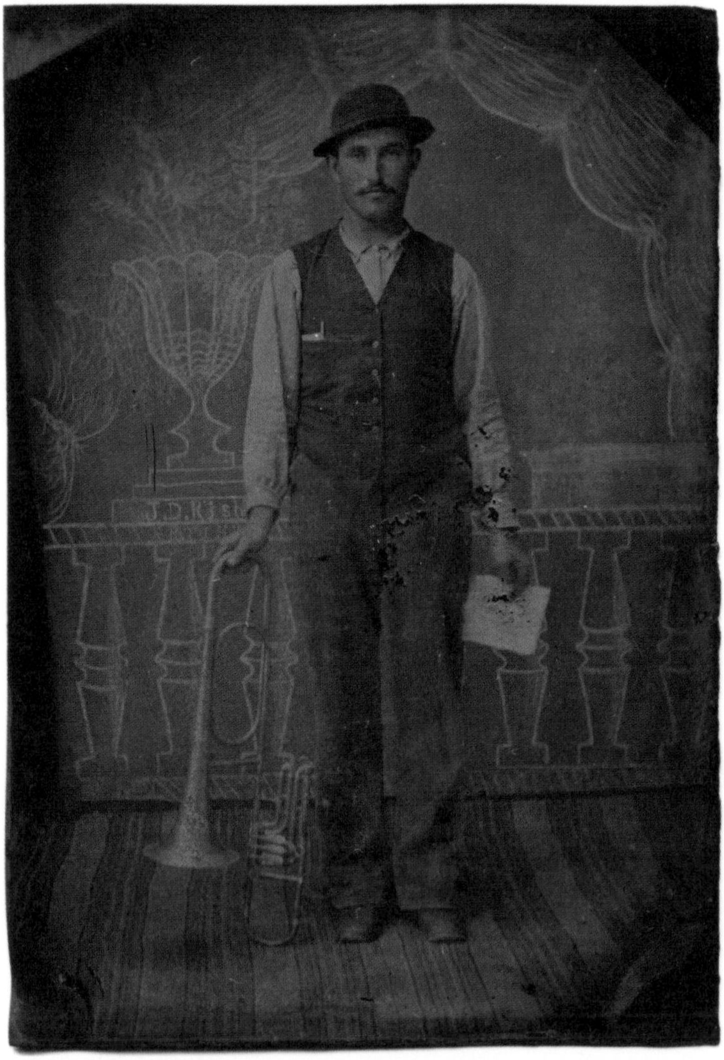

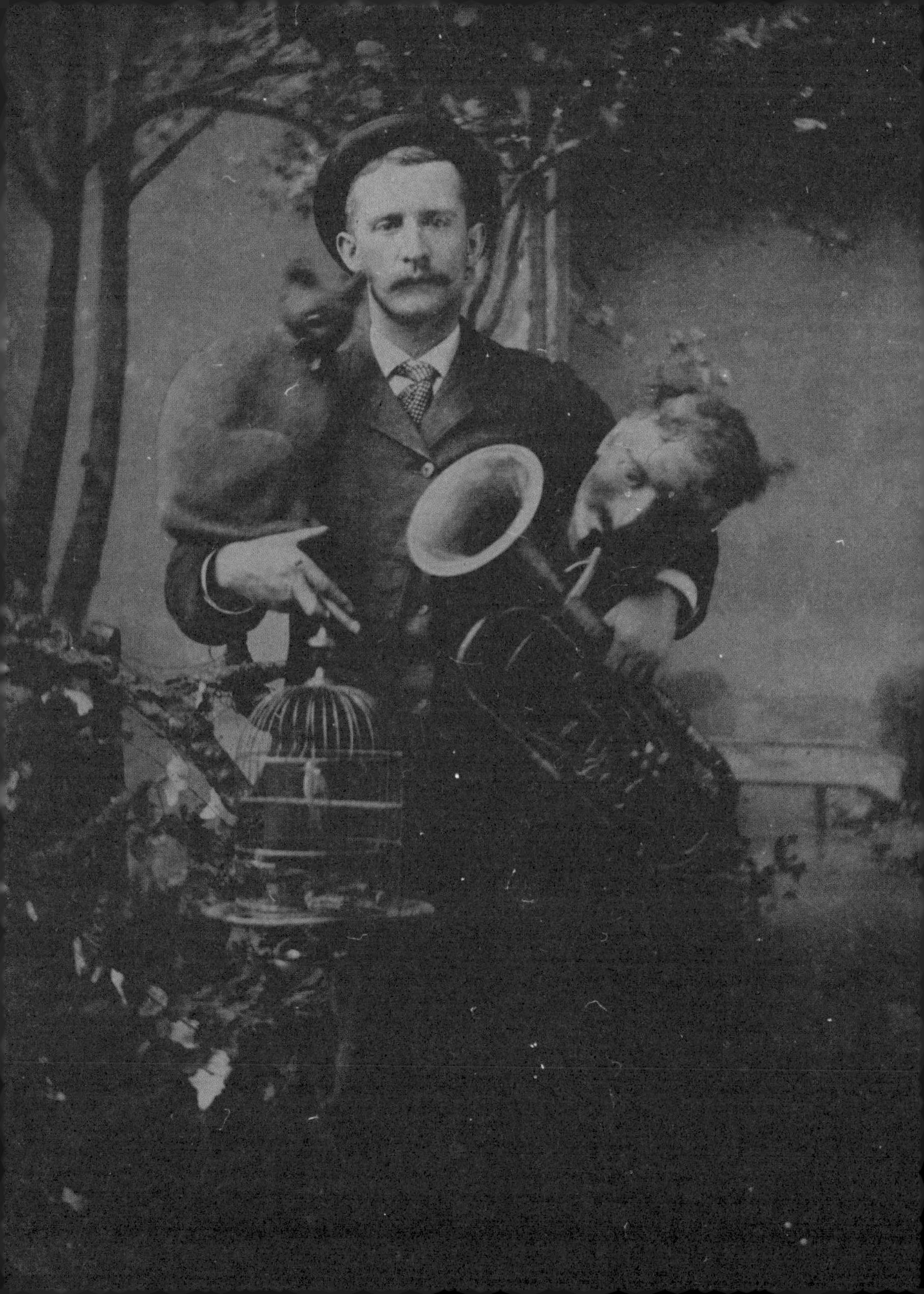

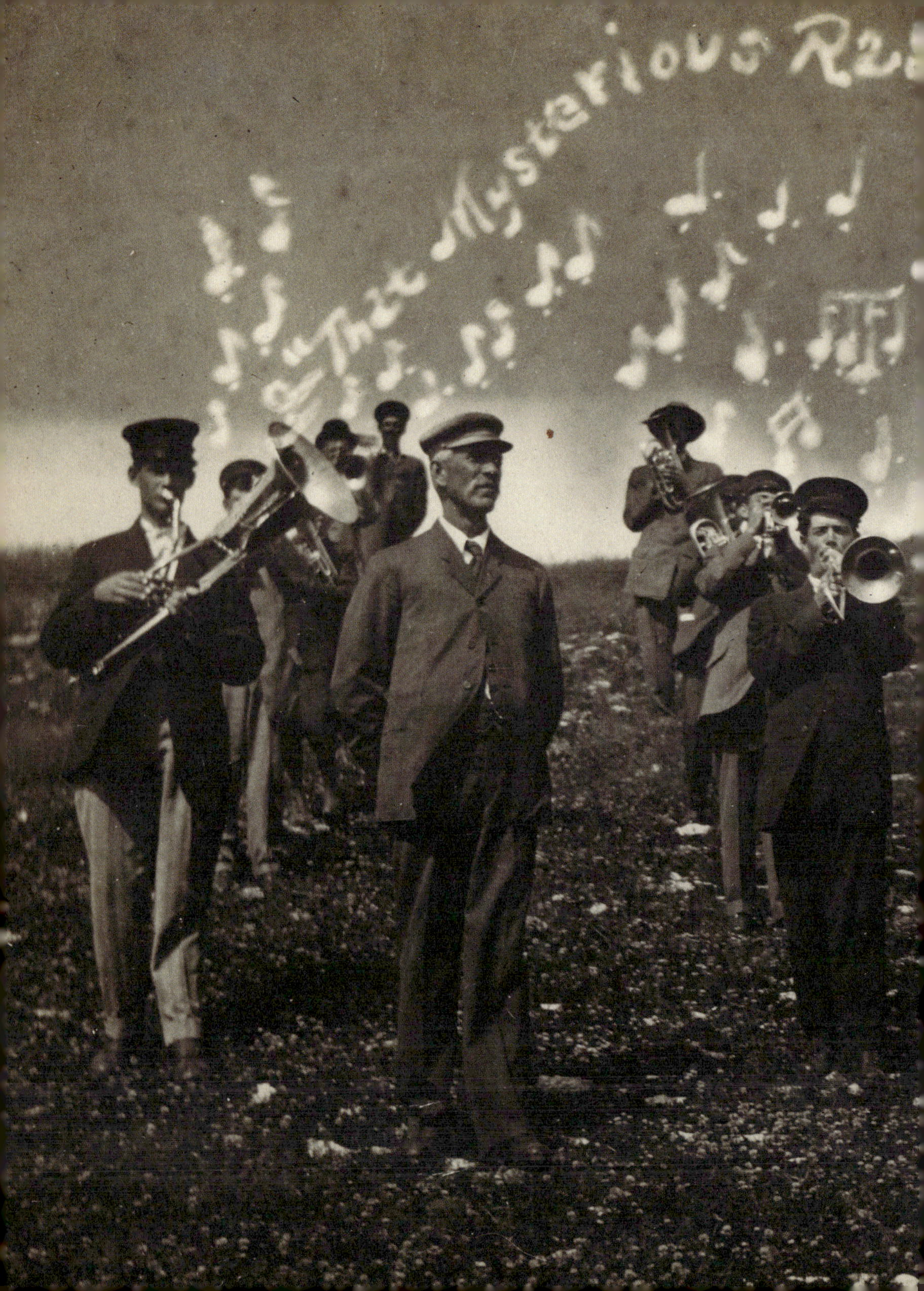
"That Mysterious Ra

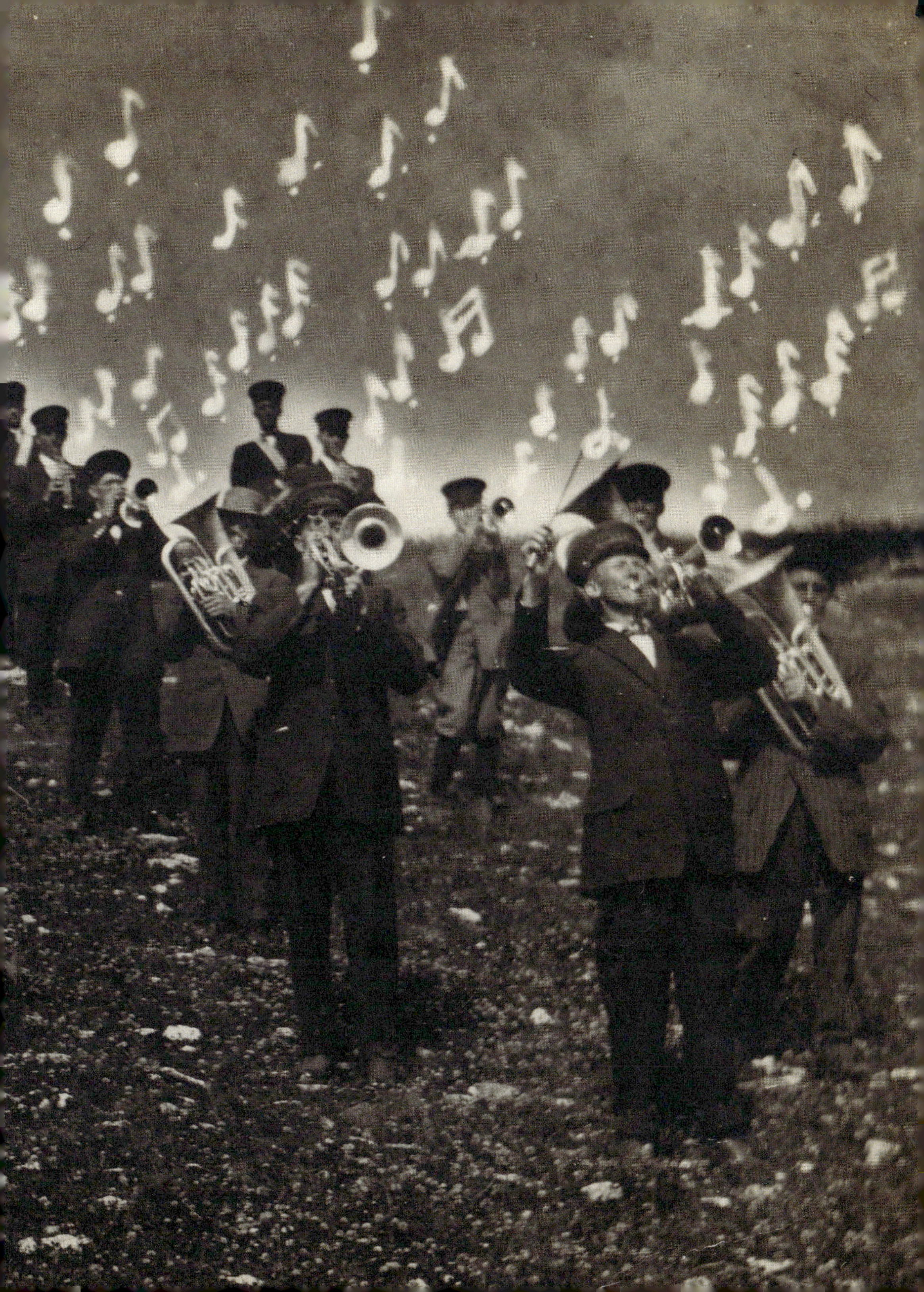

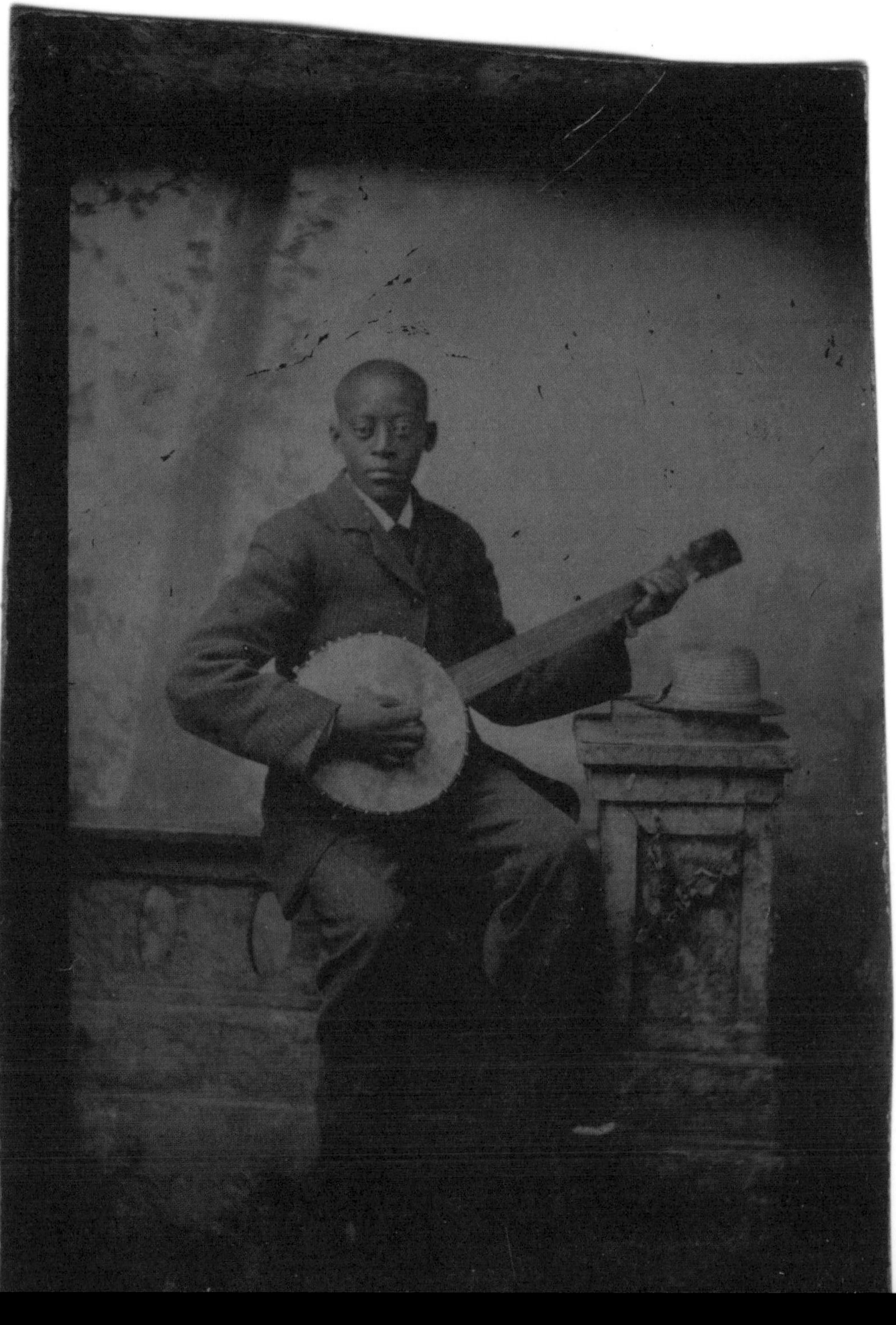

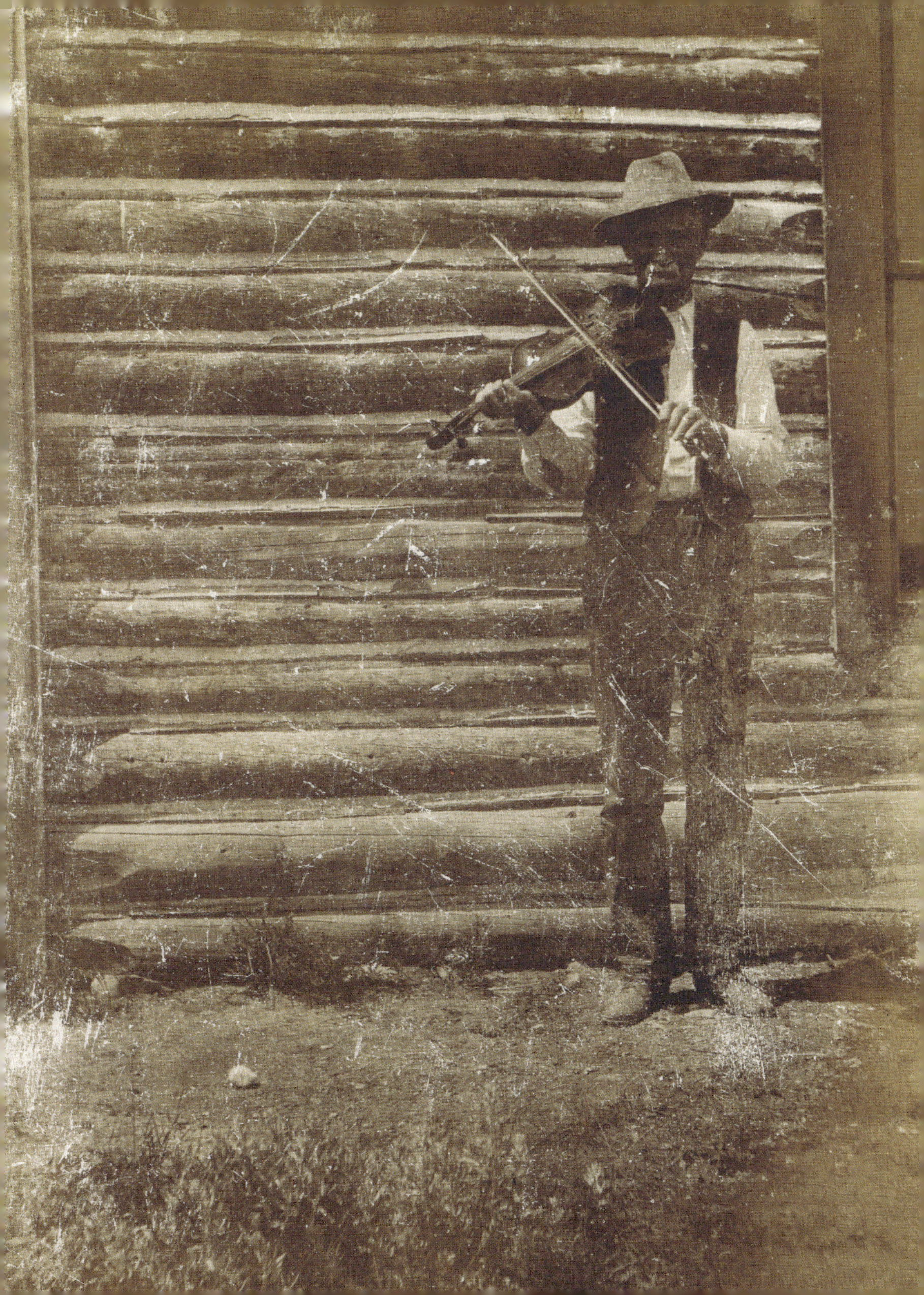

Ed. Gagné, Photo.   897 Rue Ste-Catherine
MONTREAL.

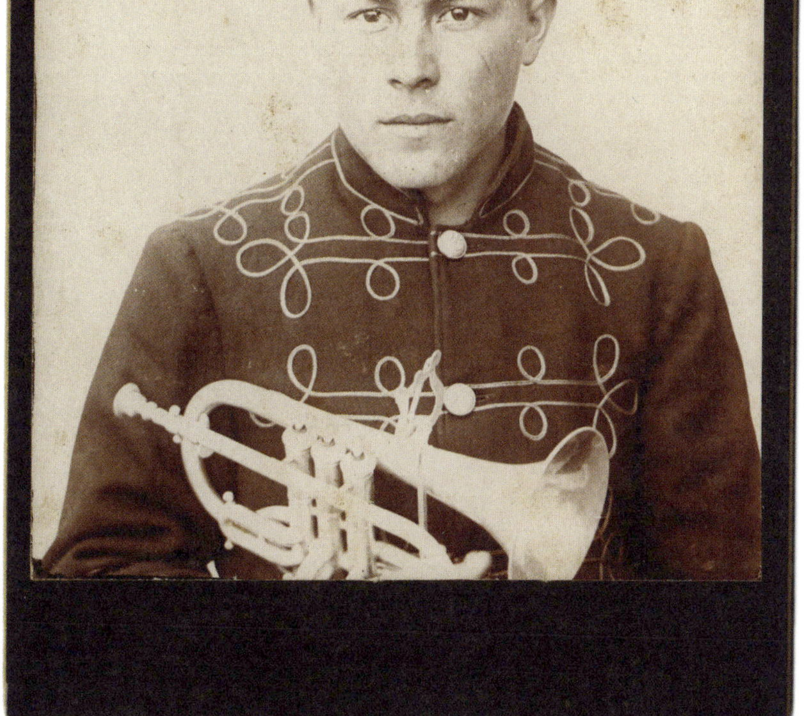
BCB

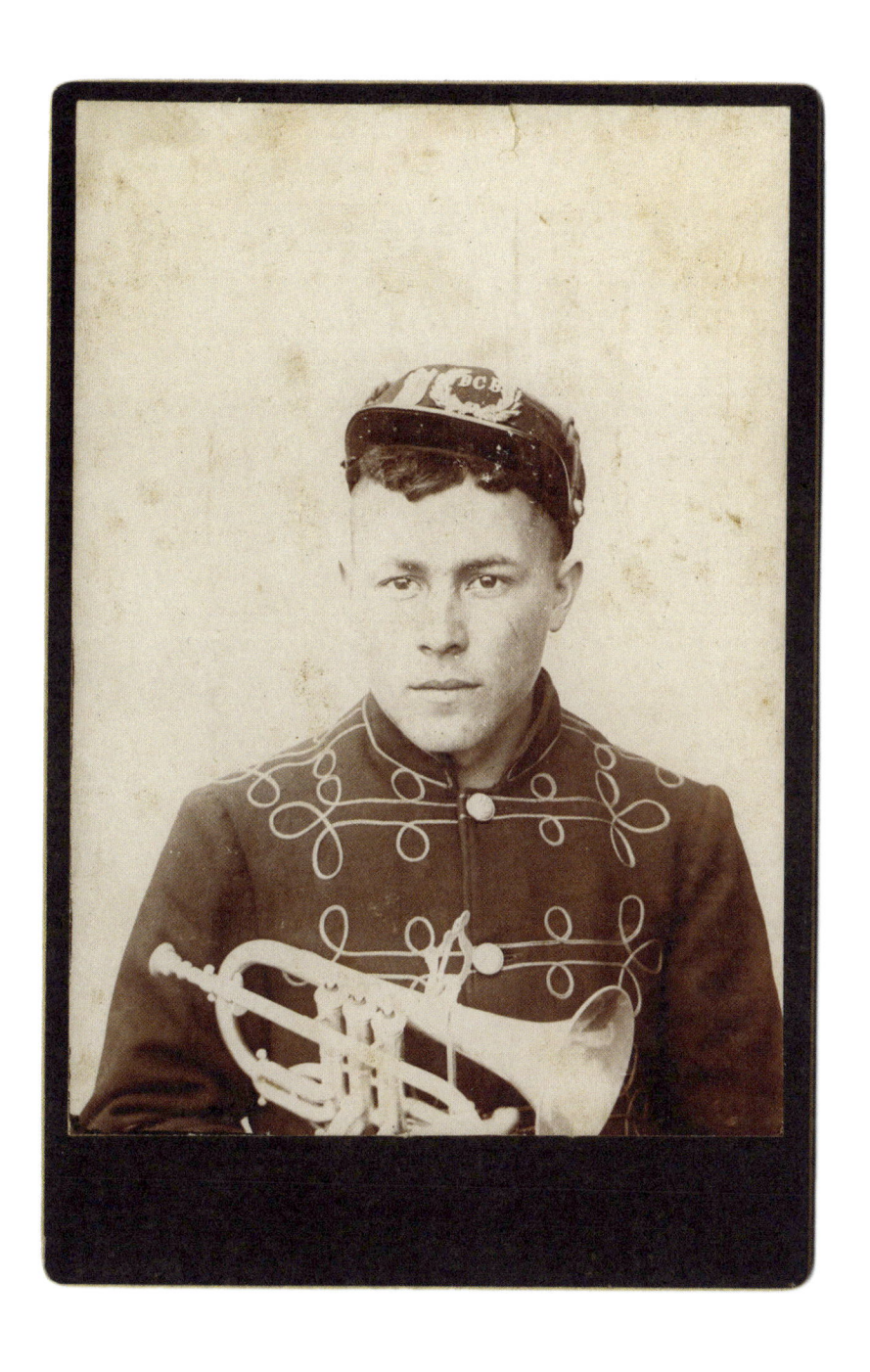

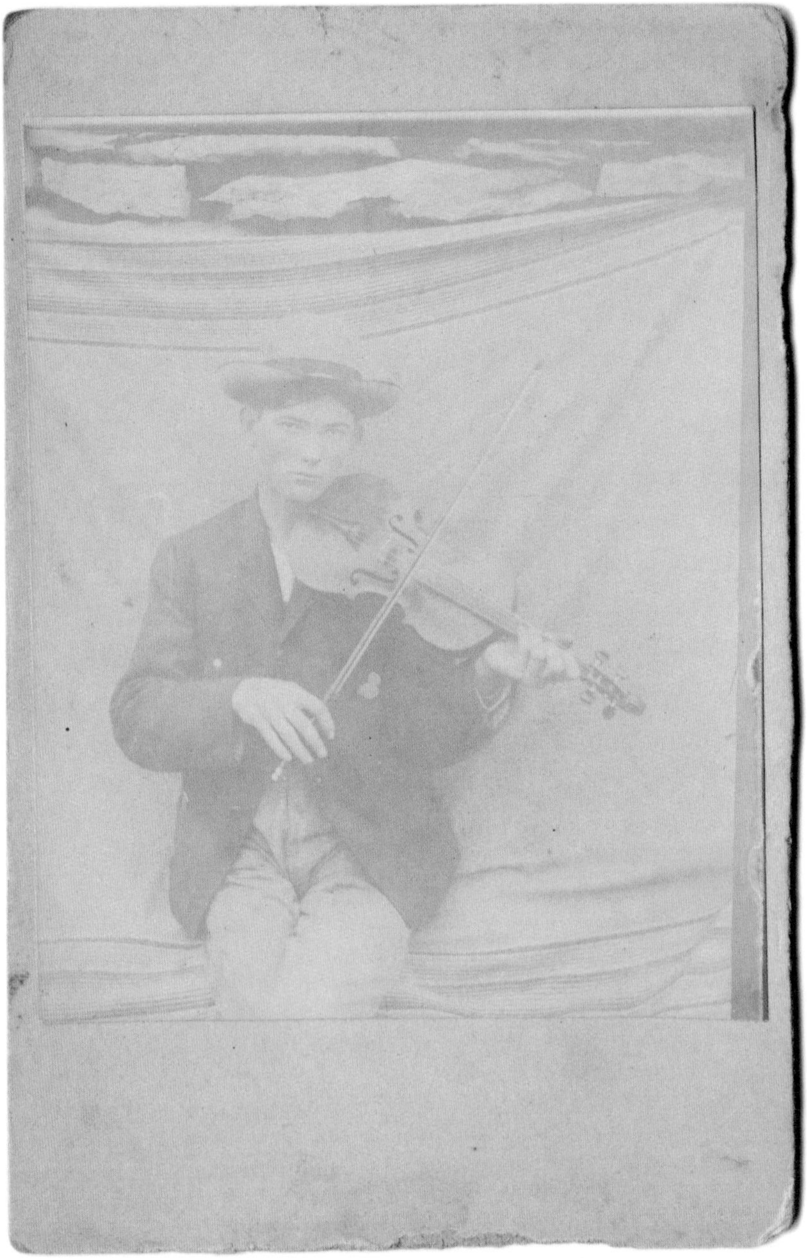

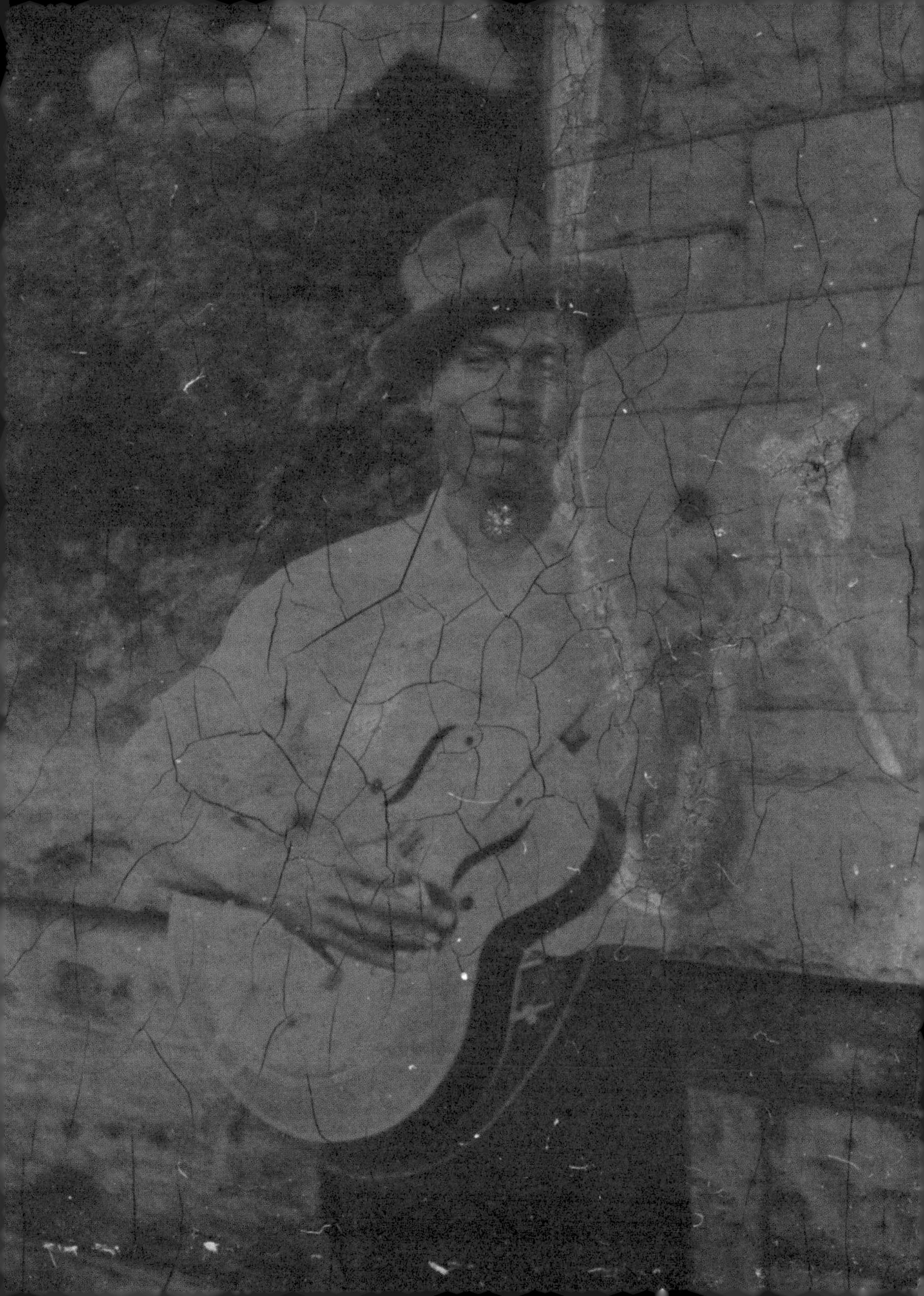

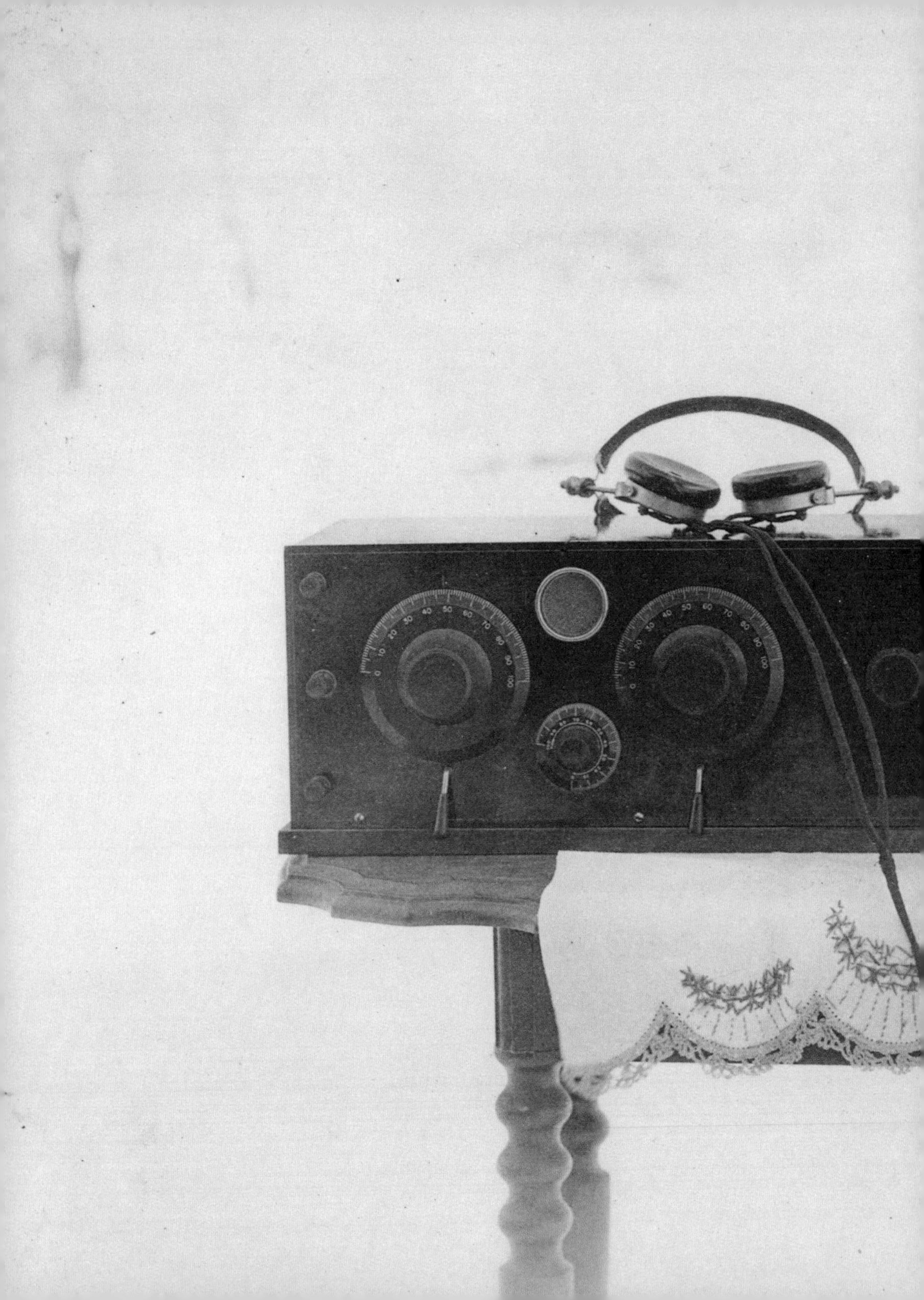

she was indeed like the fairy of silence, and only now, did i realize that even yesterday, in all that music and the milling crowd, she had walked in an island of silence, had floated in the purified atmosphere of silence, as if a few steps from her everything had gone quiet, and her big velvety eyes had muffled the noise of the soul as velvet cushions muffle sound.

mihaly babits
the nightmare

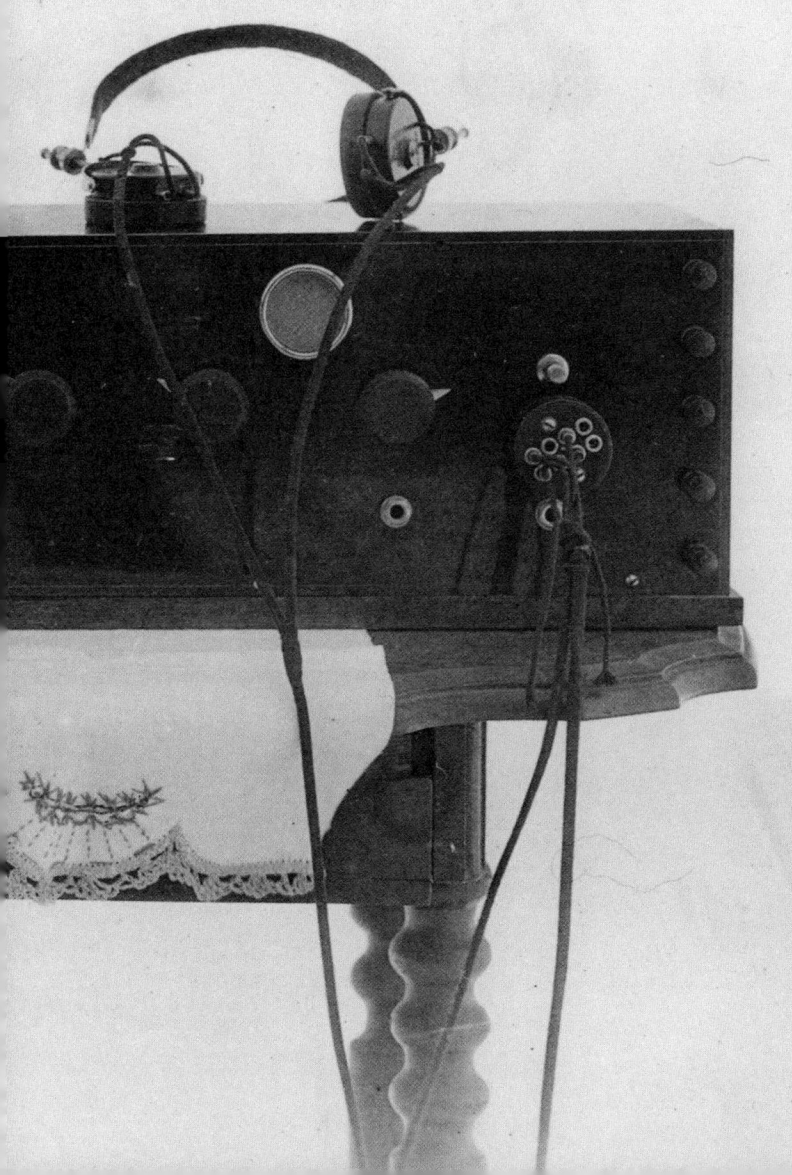

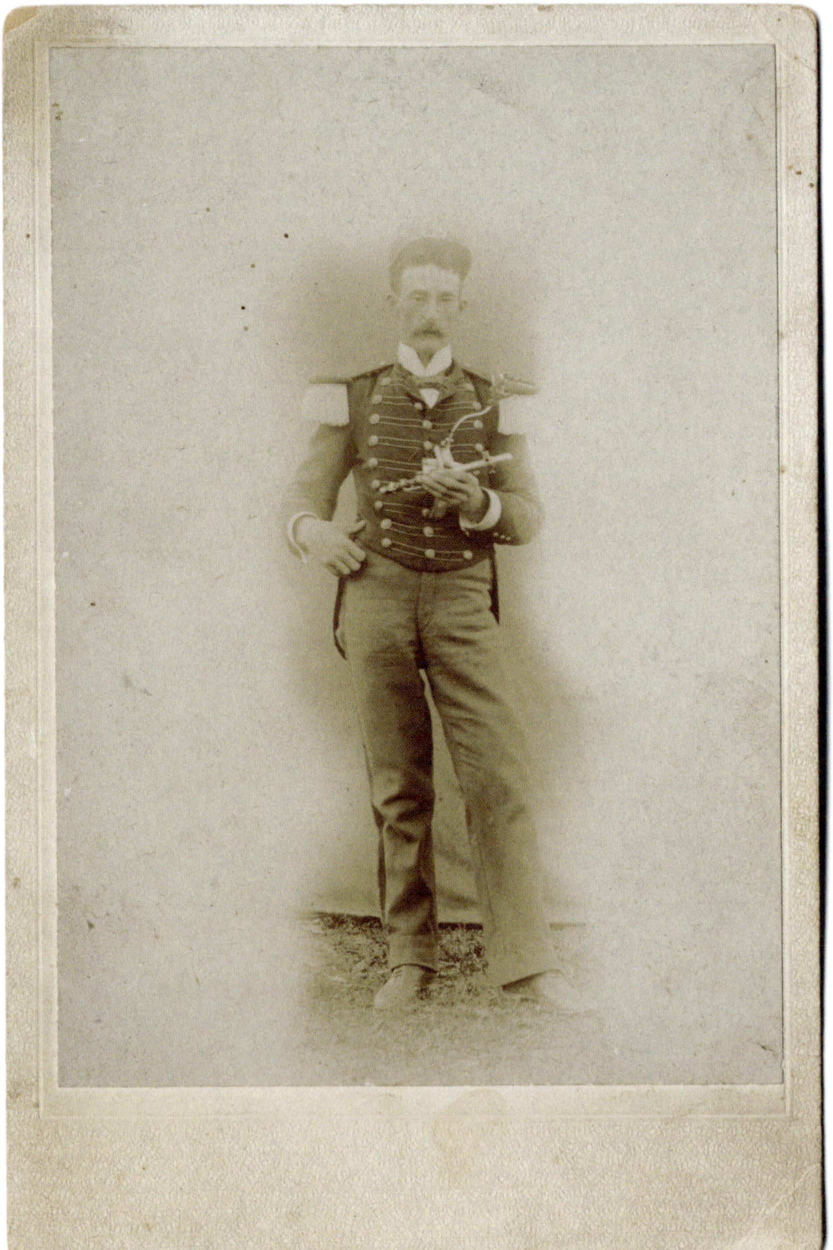

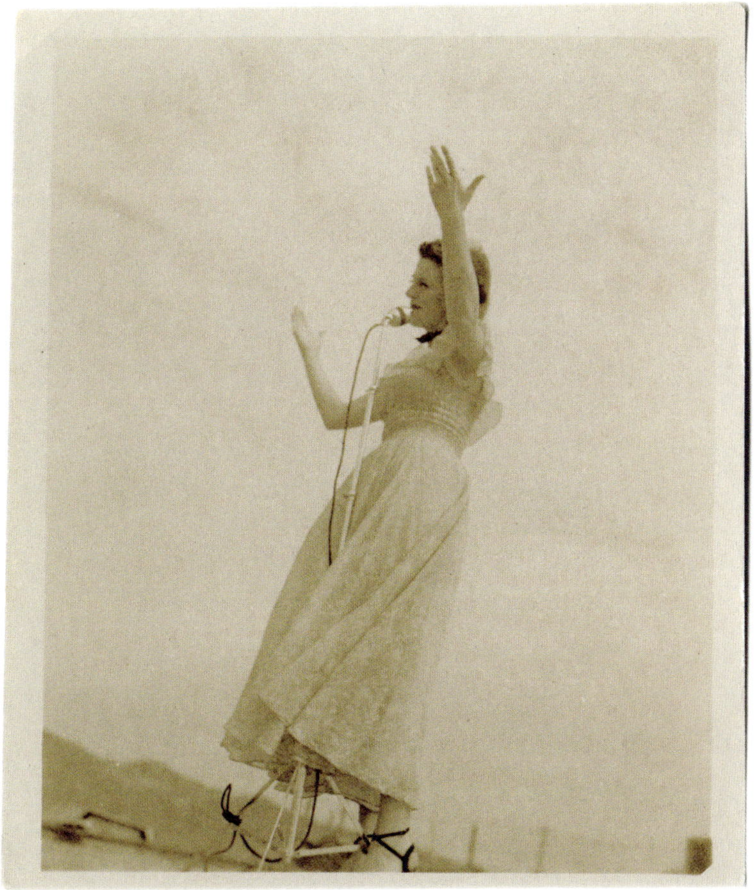

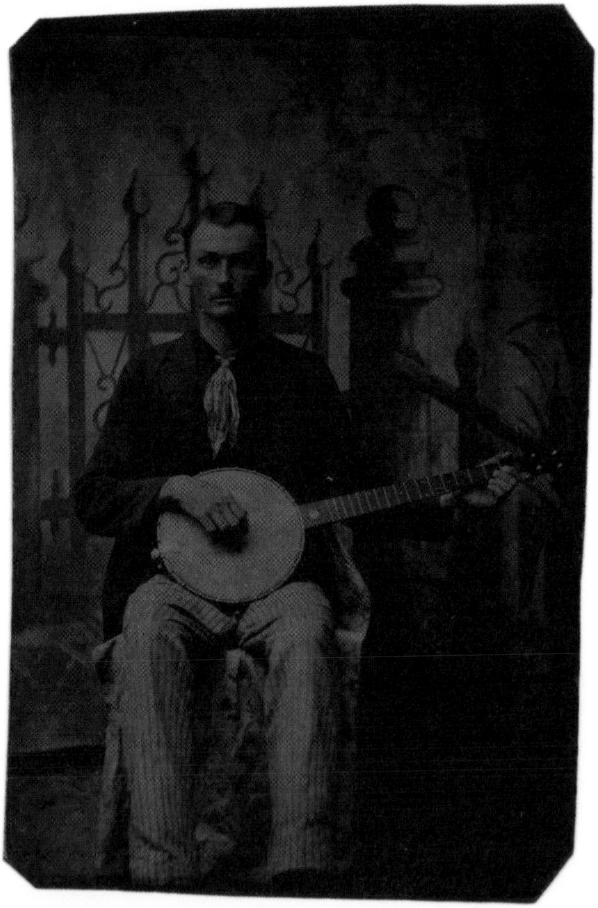

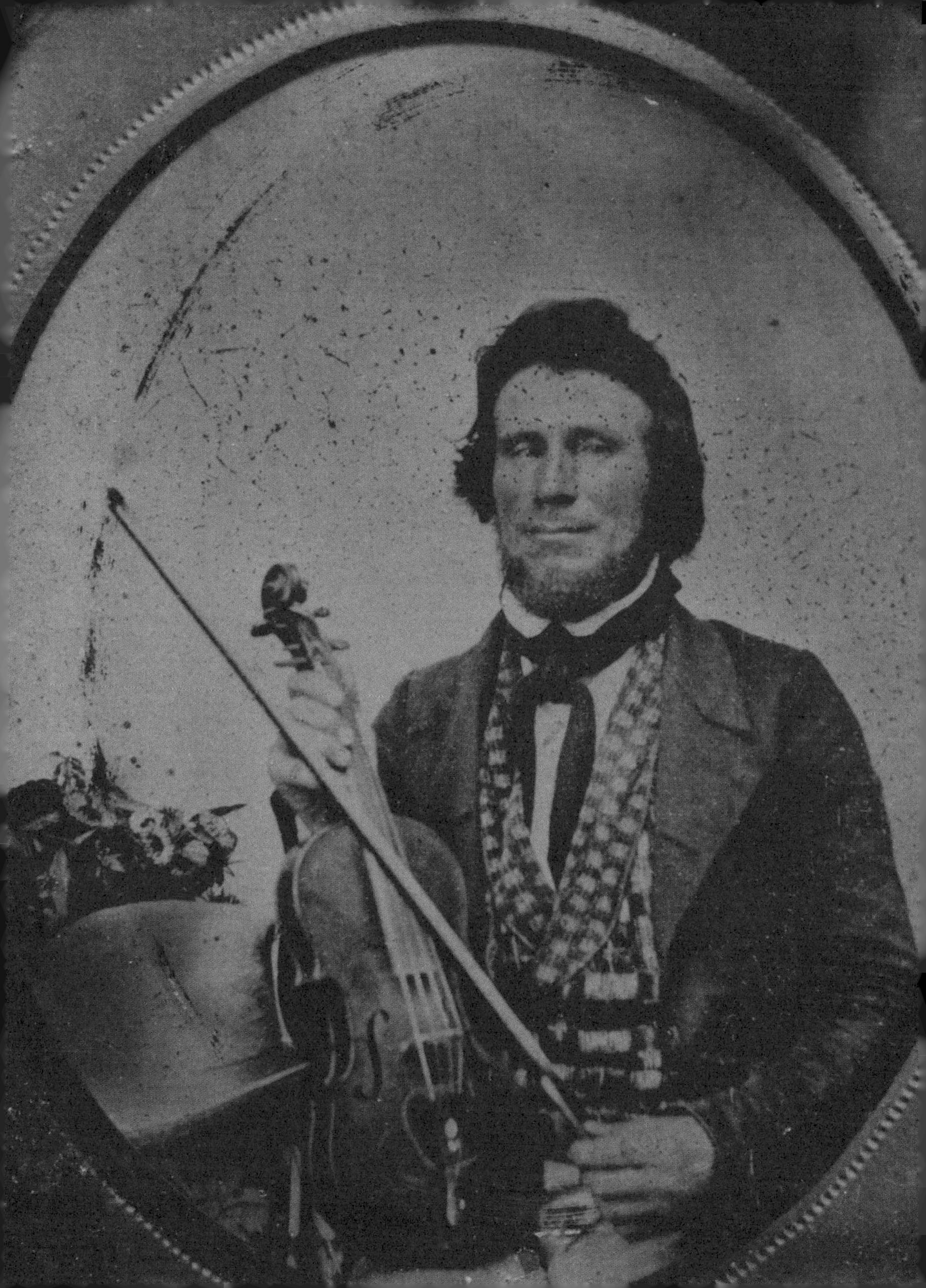

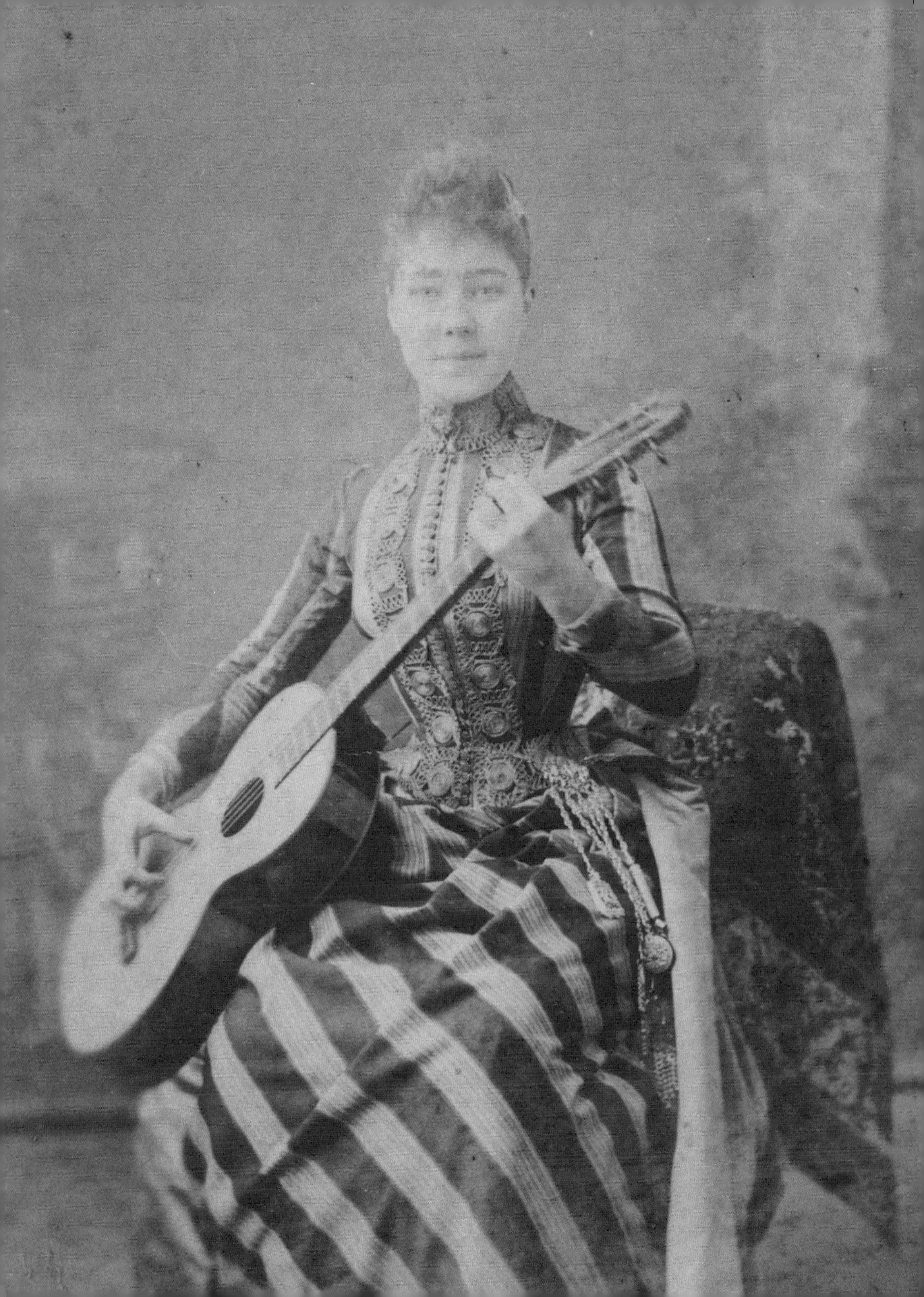

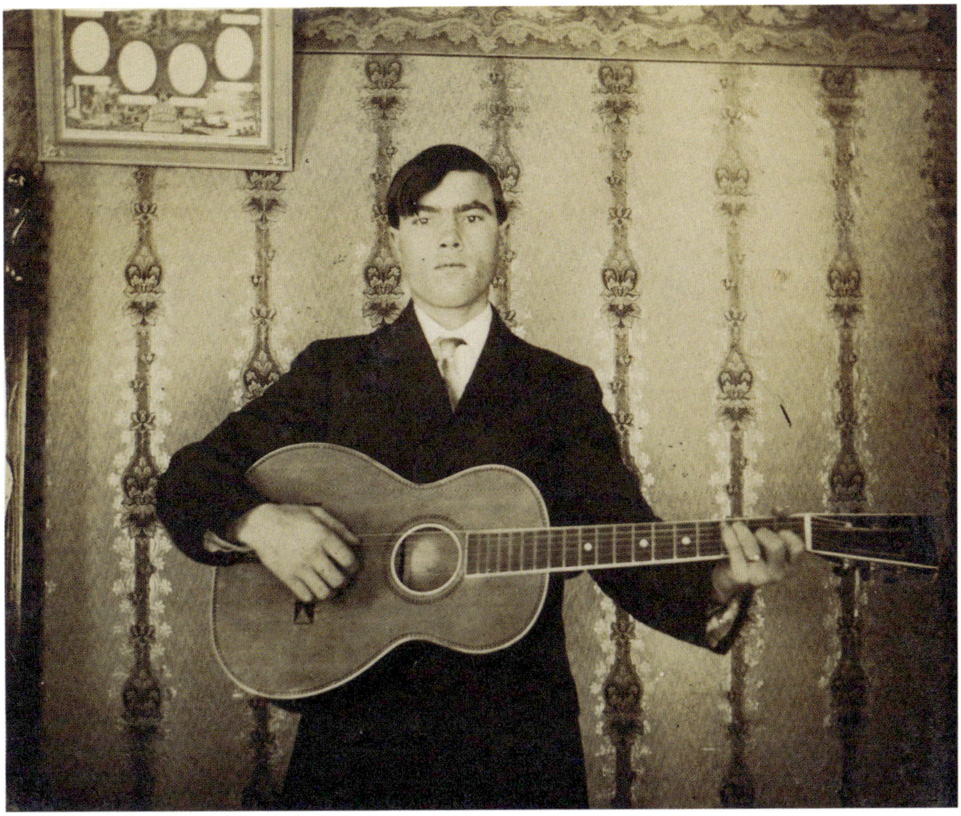

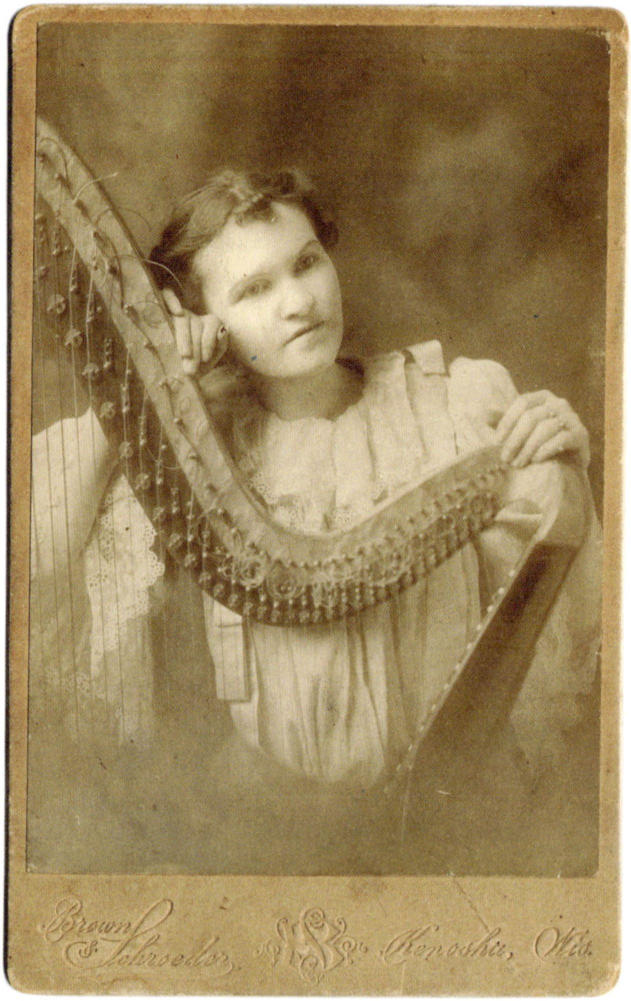
Brown & Schroeder
Kenosha, Wis.

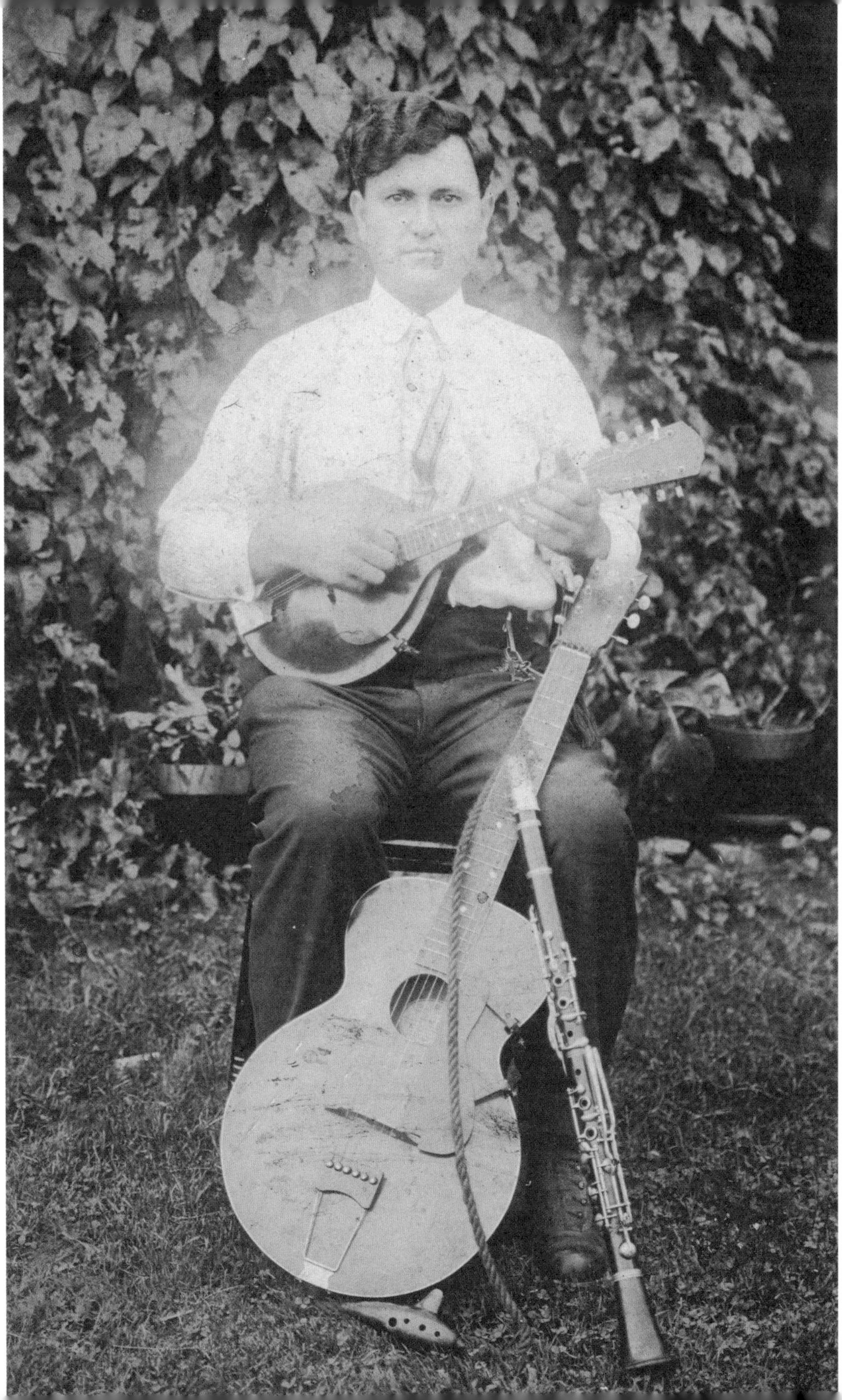

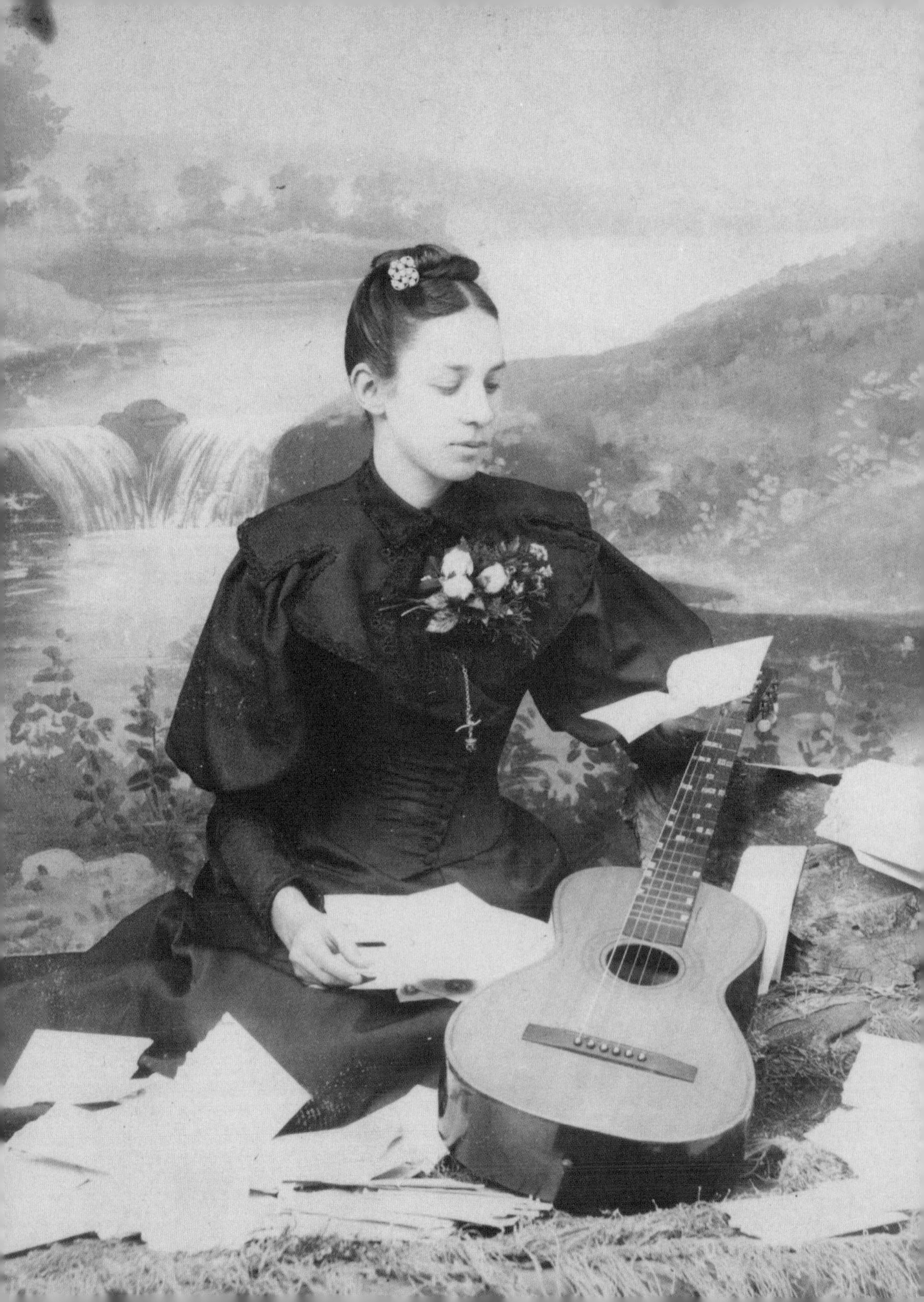

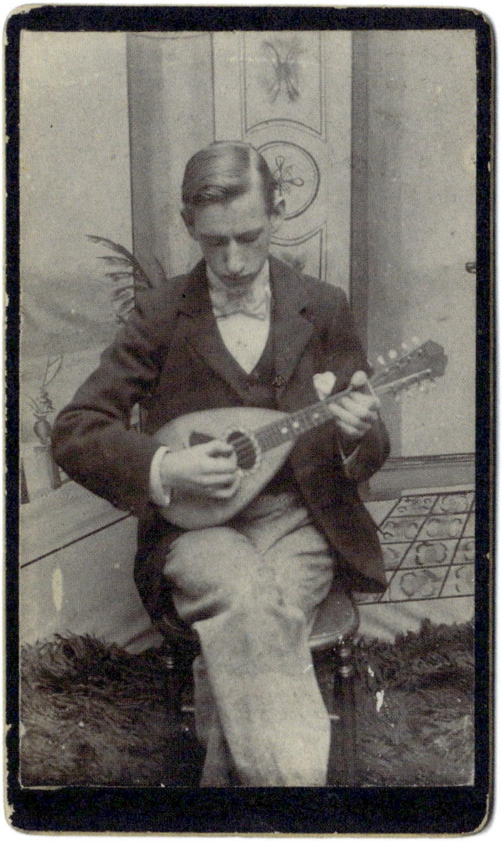

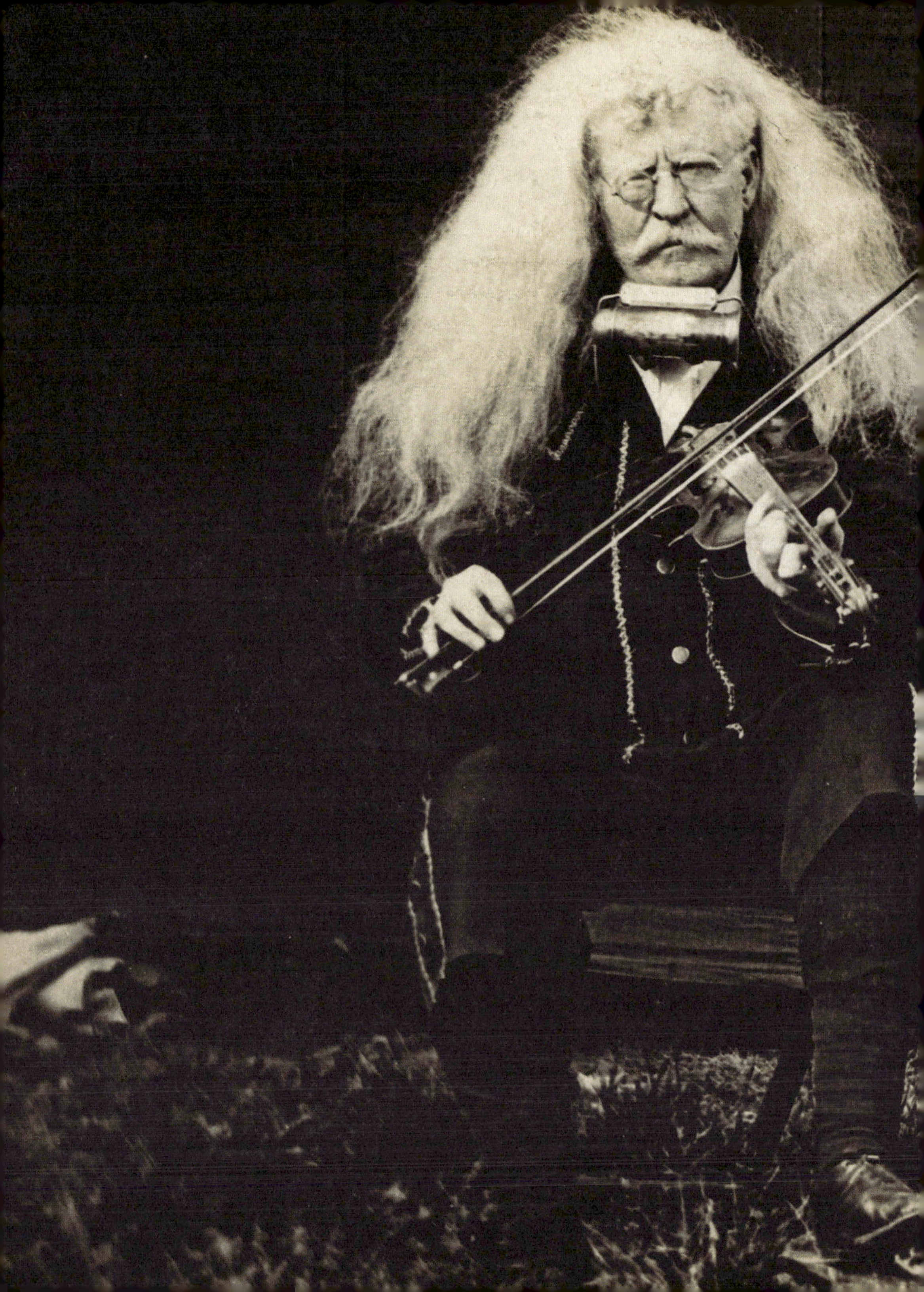

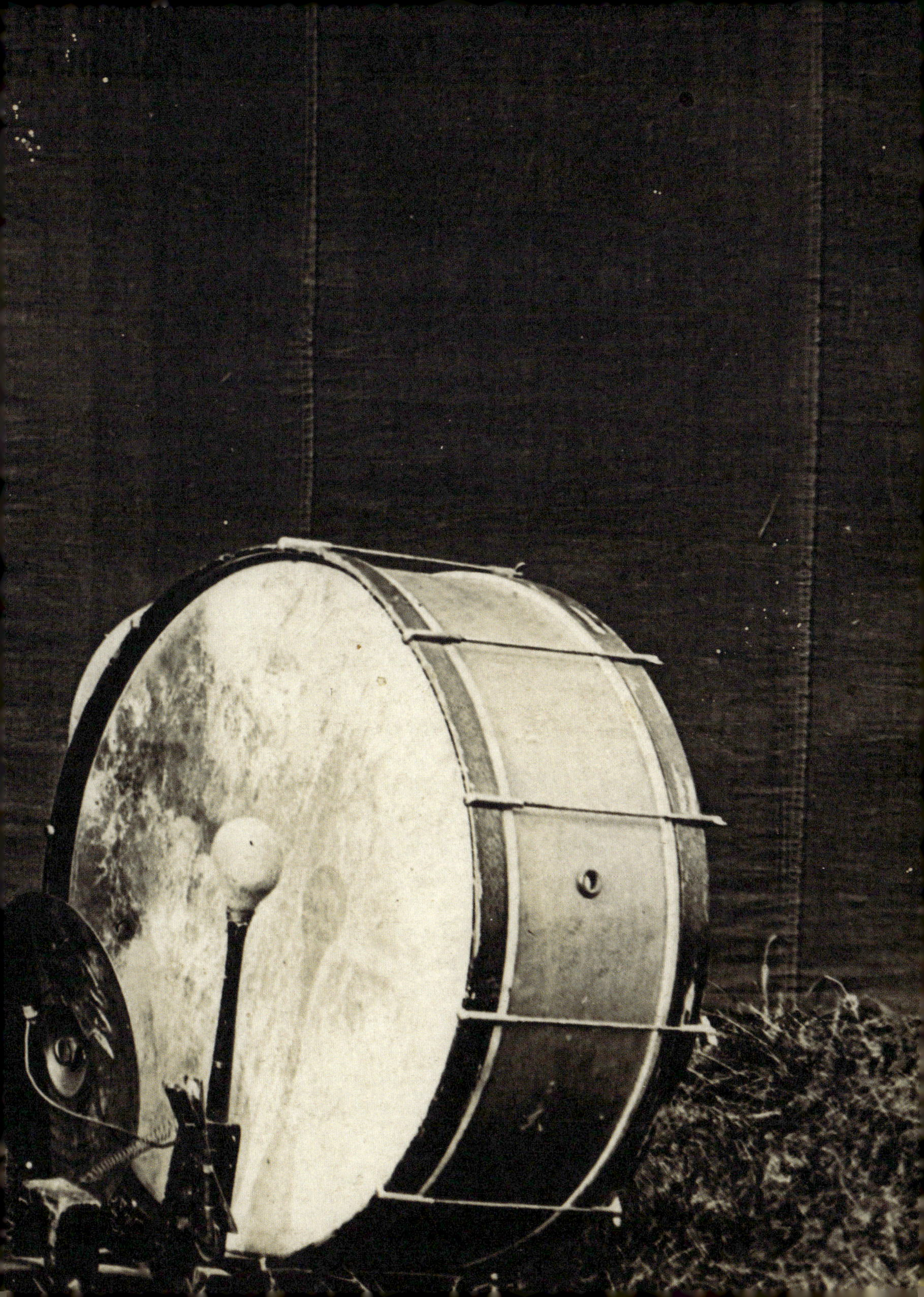

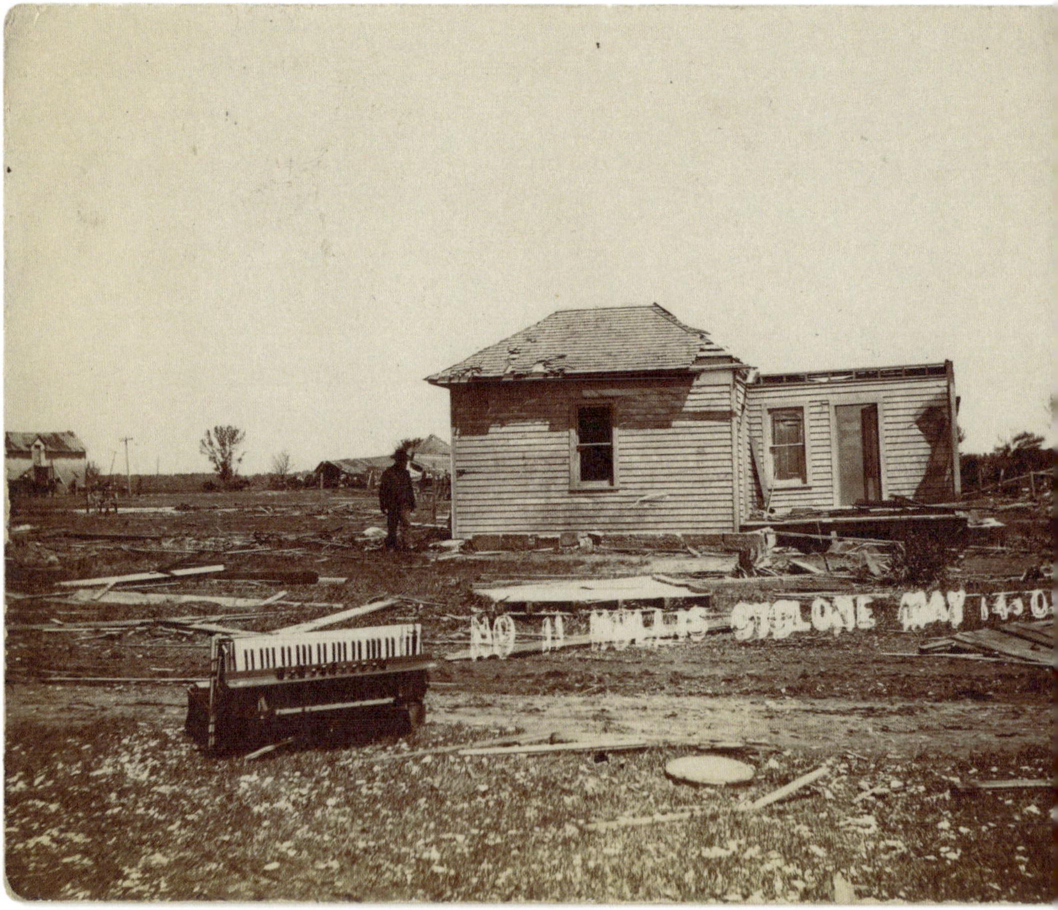

during the rain there is a certain darkness that stretches out all objects. beyond that, its effect on our body forces us to withdraw into ourselves, and this inwardness makes our soul infinitely more sensitive. the very noise rain produces continuously occupies the ear, awakes attentiveness and keeps us on the alert. the brownish hue moisture gives to the walls, the trees, the rocks, adds to the impression these objects make. and the solitude and silence it spreads out around the traveler, but forcing animals and men to be quiet and to seek shelter makes these impressions more distinct. enveloped in his coat, his head covered, and moving along deserted paths, the traveler is struck by everything, and everything is enlarged before his imagination or his eyes. the streams are swollen, the grass is thicker, the stones are more sharply defined: the sky is closer to the earth, and all objects, closed up in this narrow horizon, occupy a greater space and importance.

the notebooks of joseph joubert

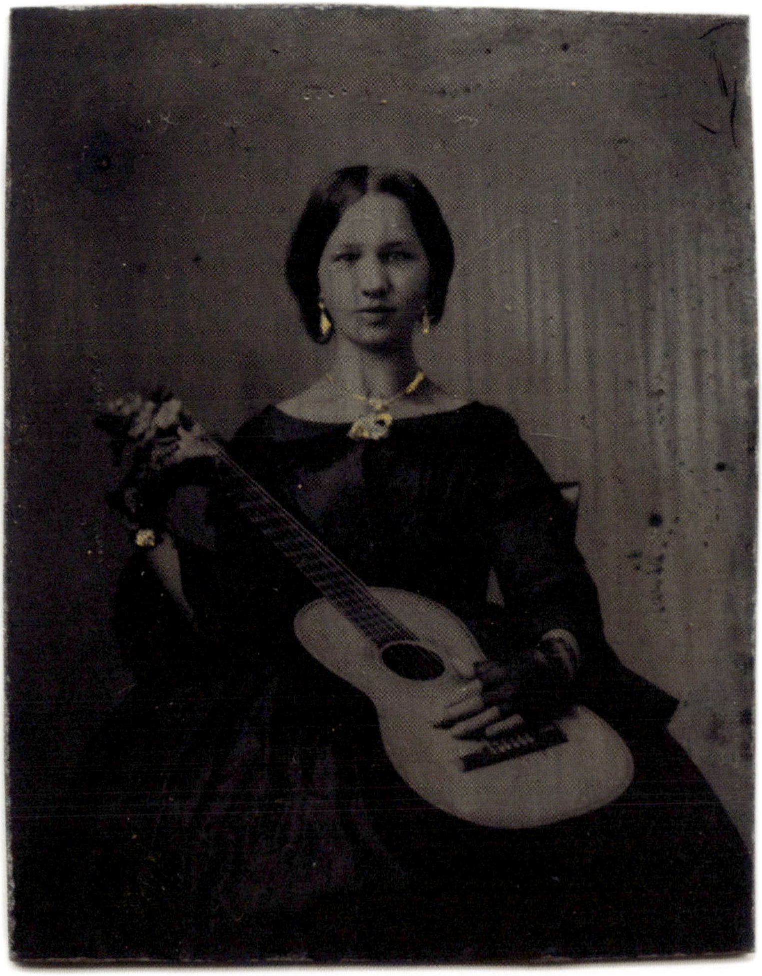

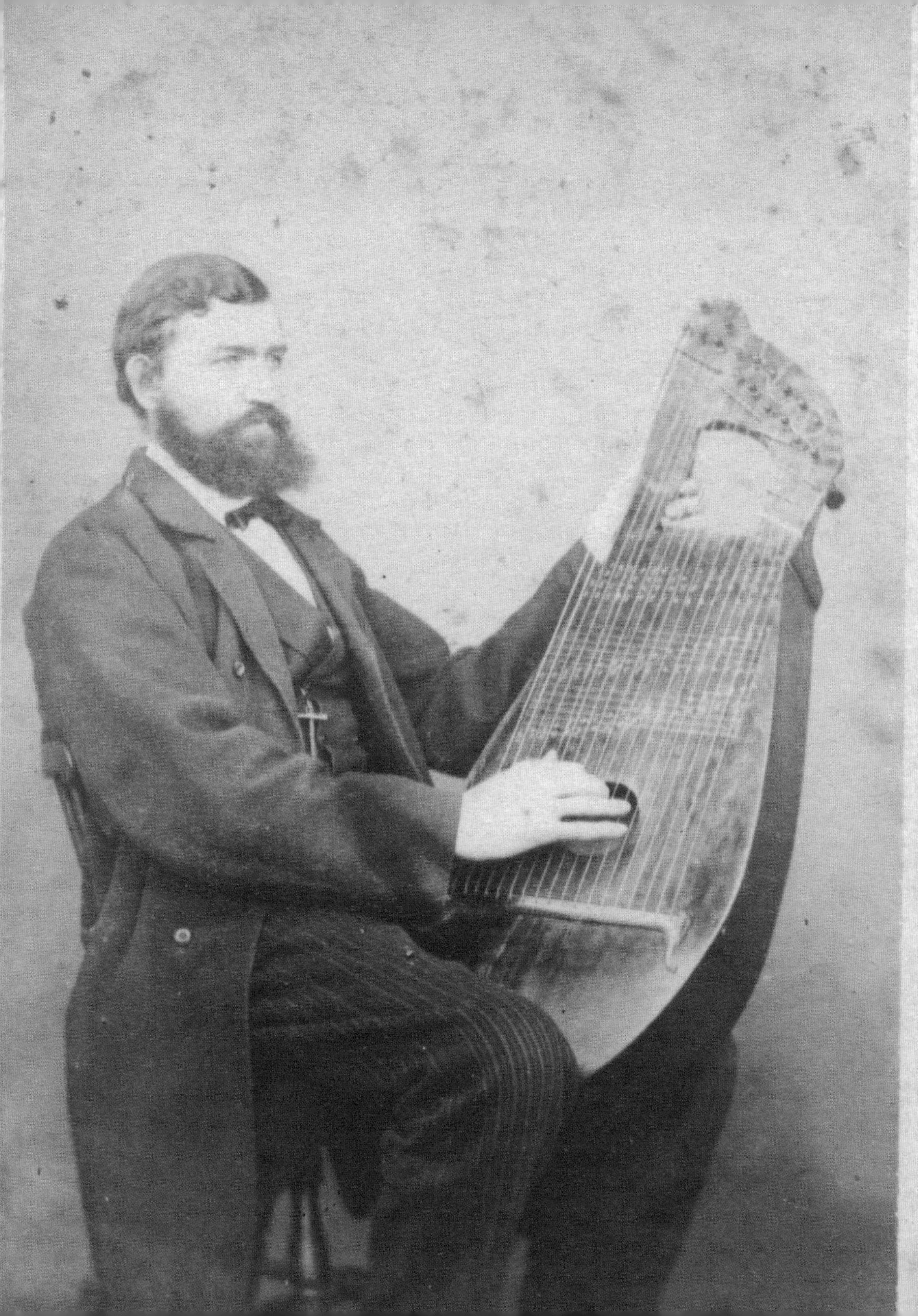

Anderson — Kearney, Neb.

The Empire — 230 S. Market St. Canton, O.

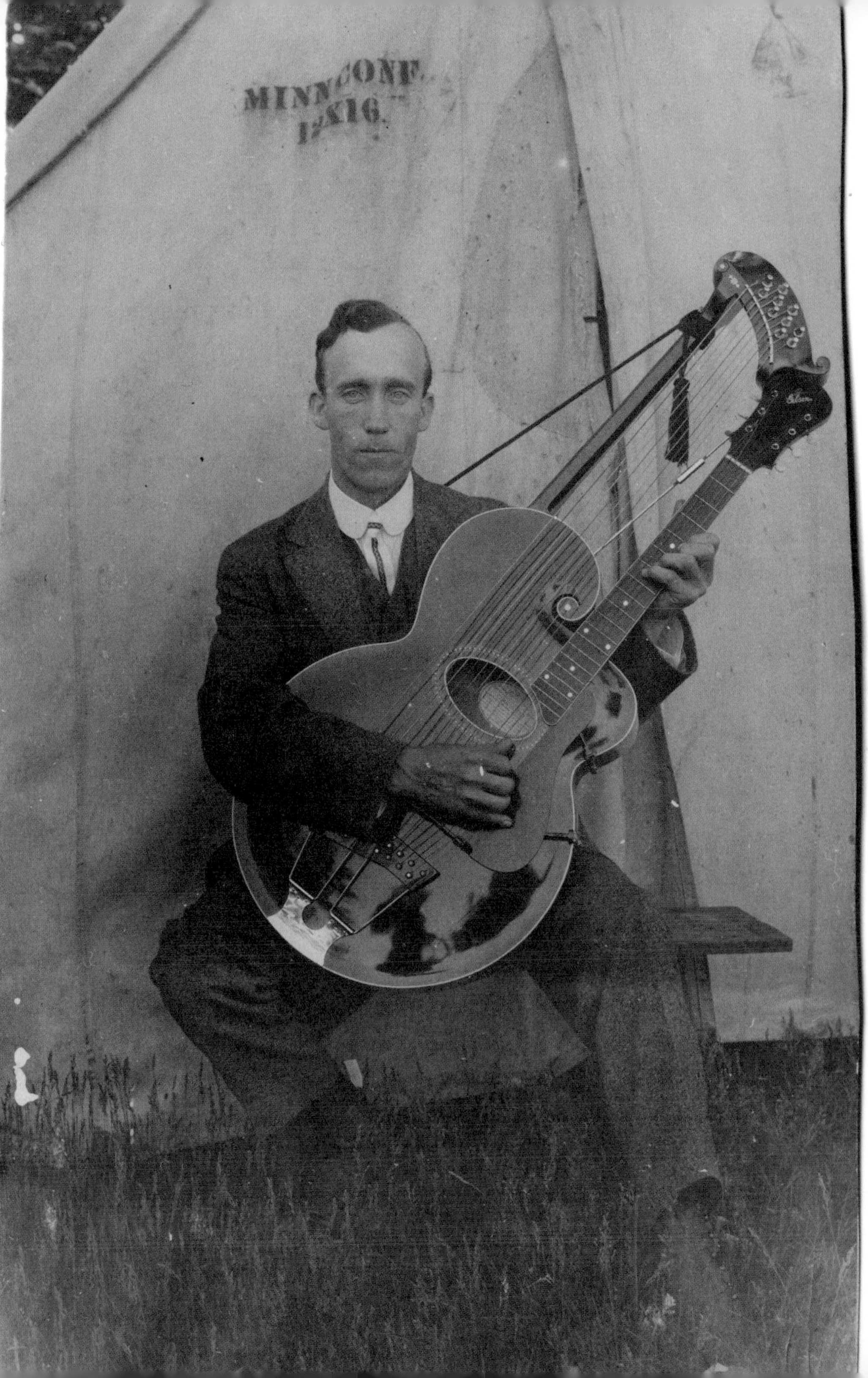
MINN CONF.

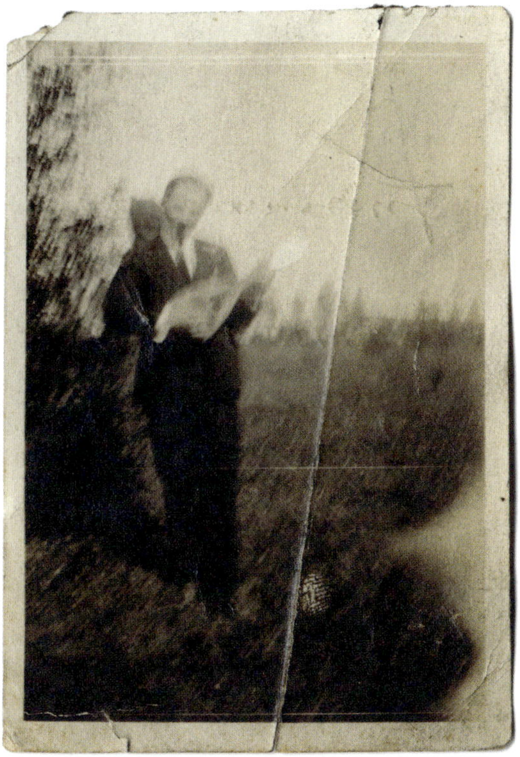

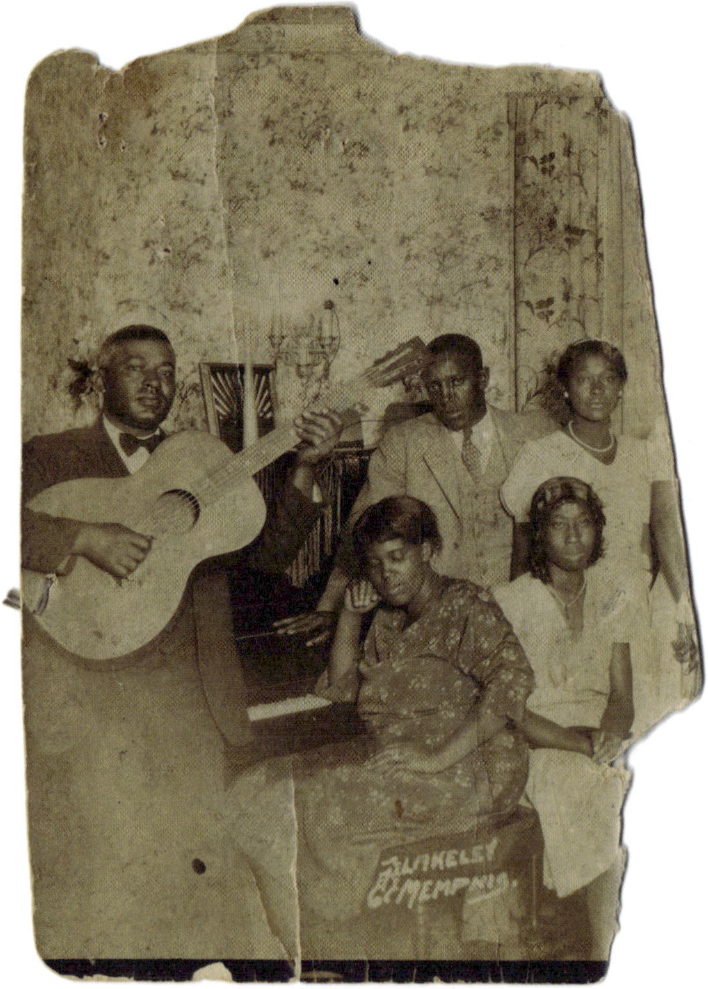
MEMPHIS.

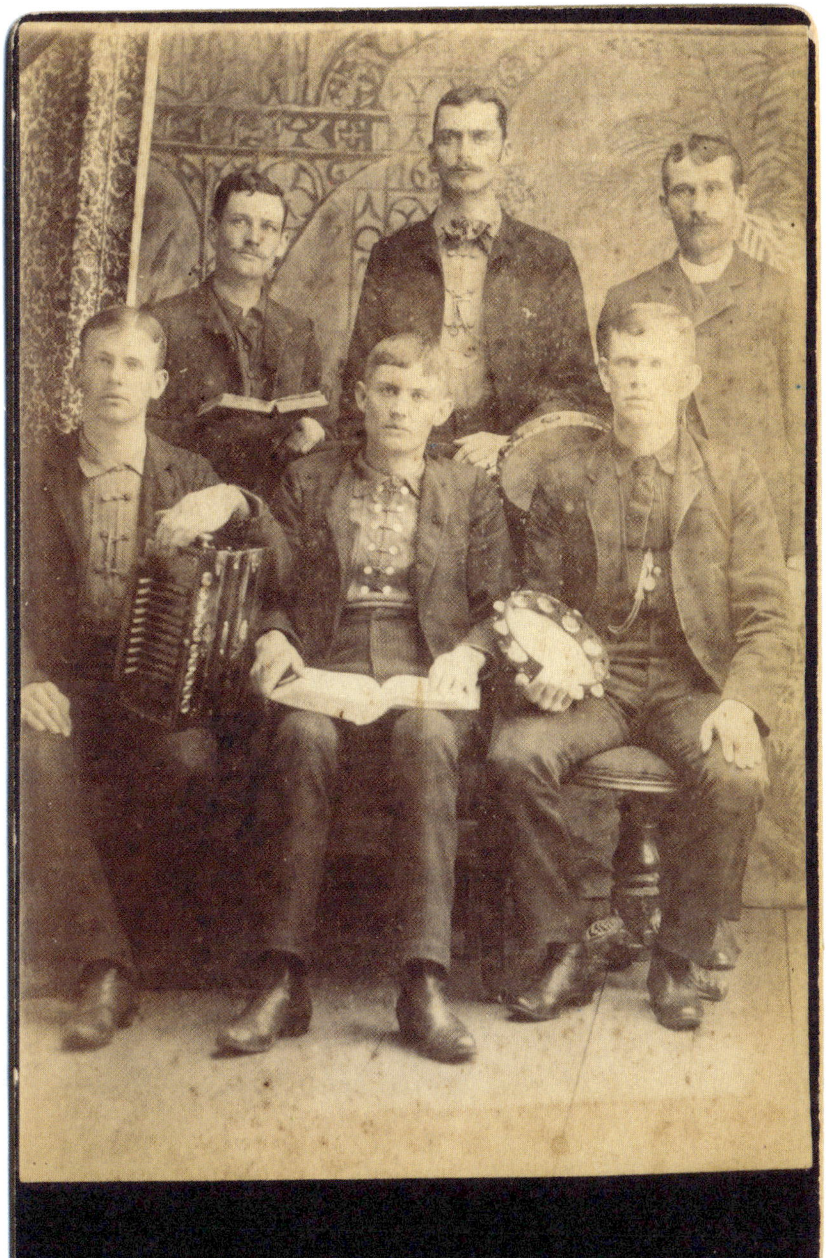

CABINET PORTRAIT

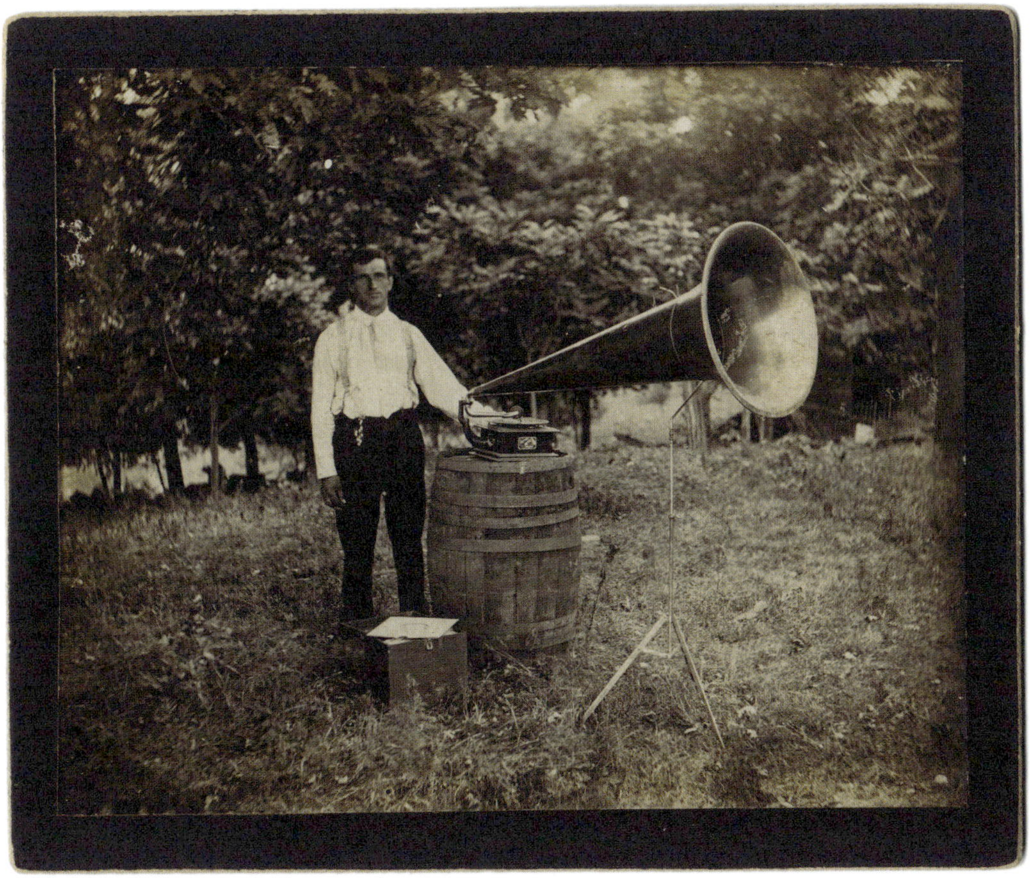

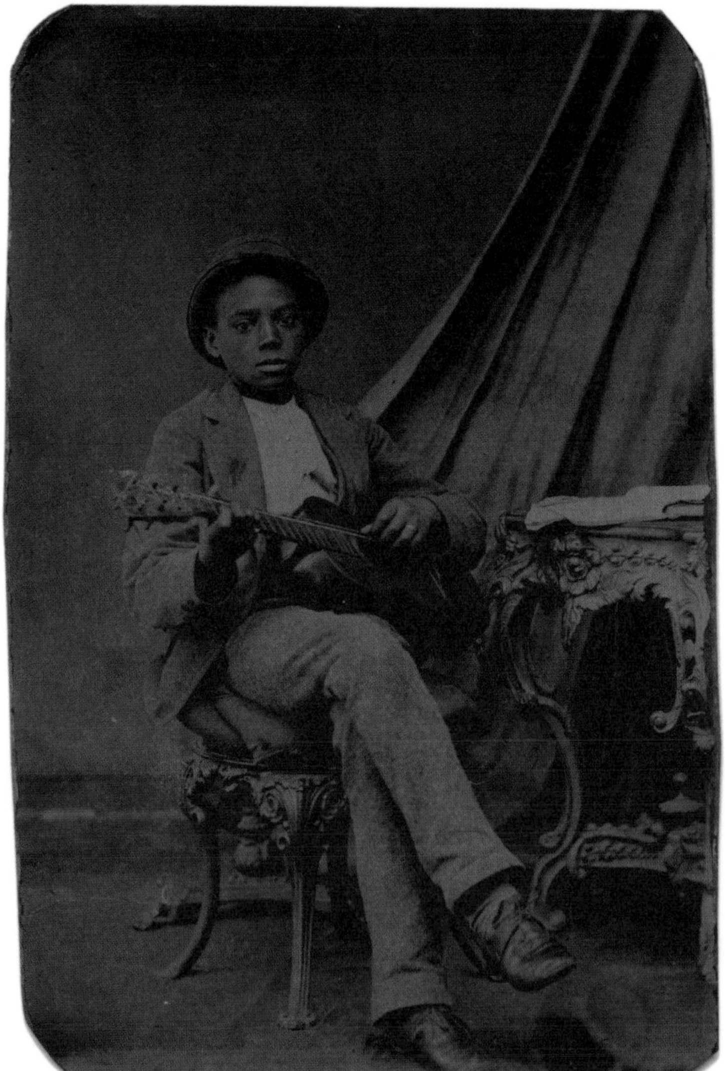

Coules & Westervelt,
North Beach,   Santa Monica, Cal.

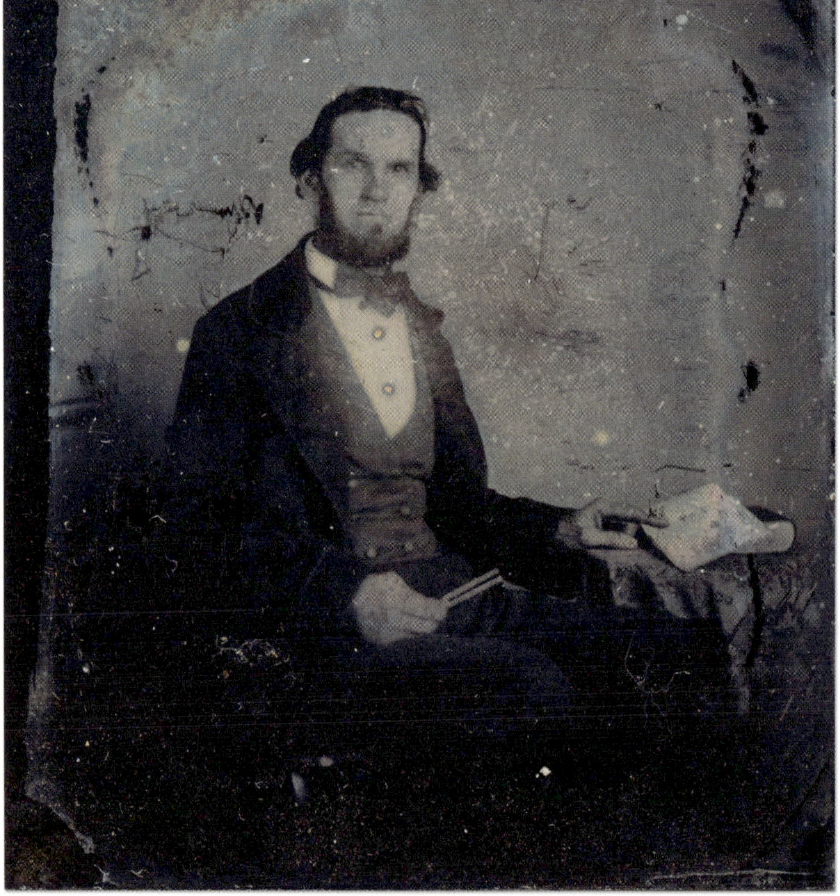

F. W. Schmidt, Fairbury, Neb.

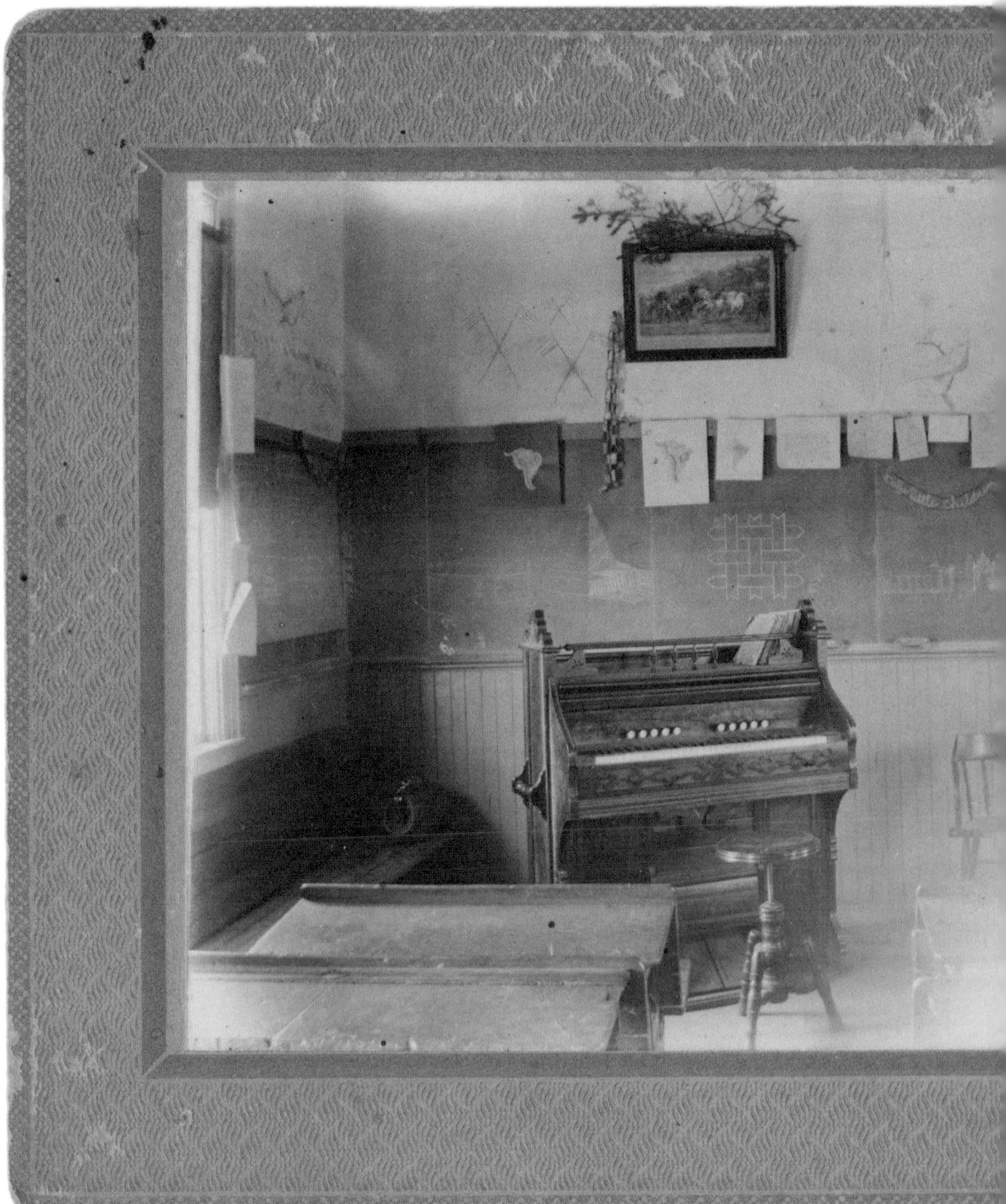

with the onset of summer the cross-marked sheep were herded higher into the mountains. a babbling metallic tinkling, of unknown origin and from an unknown direction, would gradually become audible. floating nearer, it enveloped the listener, giving him an odd tickling sensation in the mouth. then, in a cloud of dust, came flowing a gray, curly, tightly packed mass of sheep rubbing against each other, and the moist, hollow tinkle of the bells, which delighted all of one's senses, mounted, swelled so mysteriously that the dust itself seemed to be ringing as it billowed above the moving backs of the sheep. from time to time one of them would get separated from the rest and trot past, whereupon a shaggy dog would drive it back to the flock; and behind, gently treading, walked the shepherd. then the tintinnabulation would change timber, and once more grow hollower and softer, but for a long time it would hang in the air together with the dust...

vladimir nabokov
podvig

✦ Prof. Mc. Rae, ✦

✤Ontario's Musical Wonder.✤

Crawford
The
Musical
Wonder

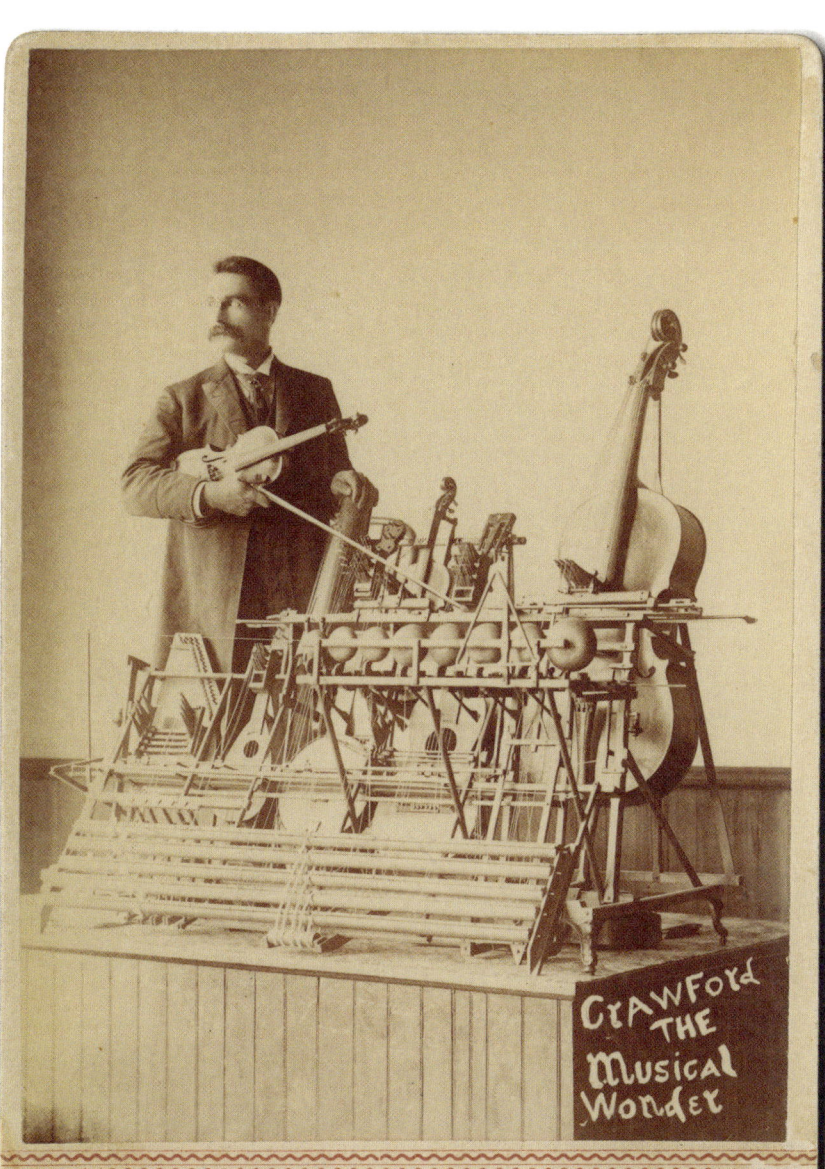

Goble & Wenzel, 114½ South High St., COLUMBUS, O.

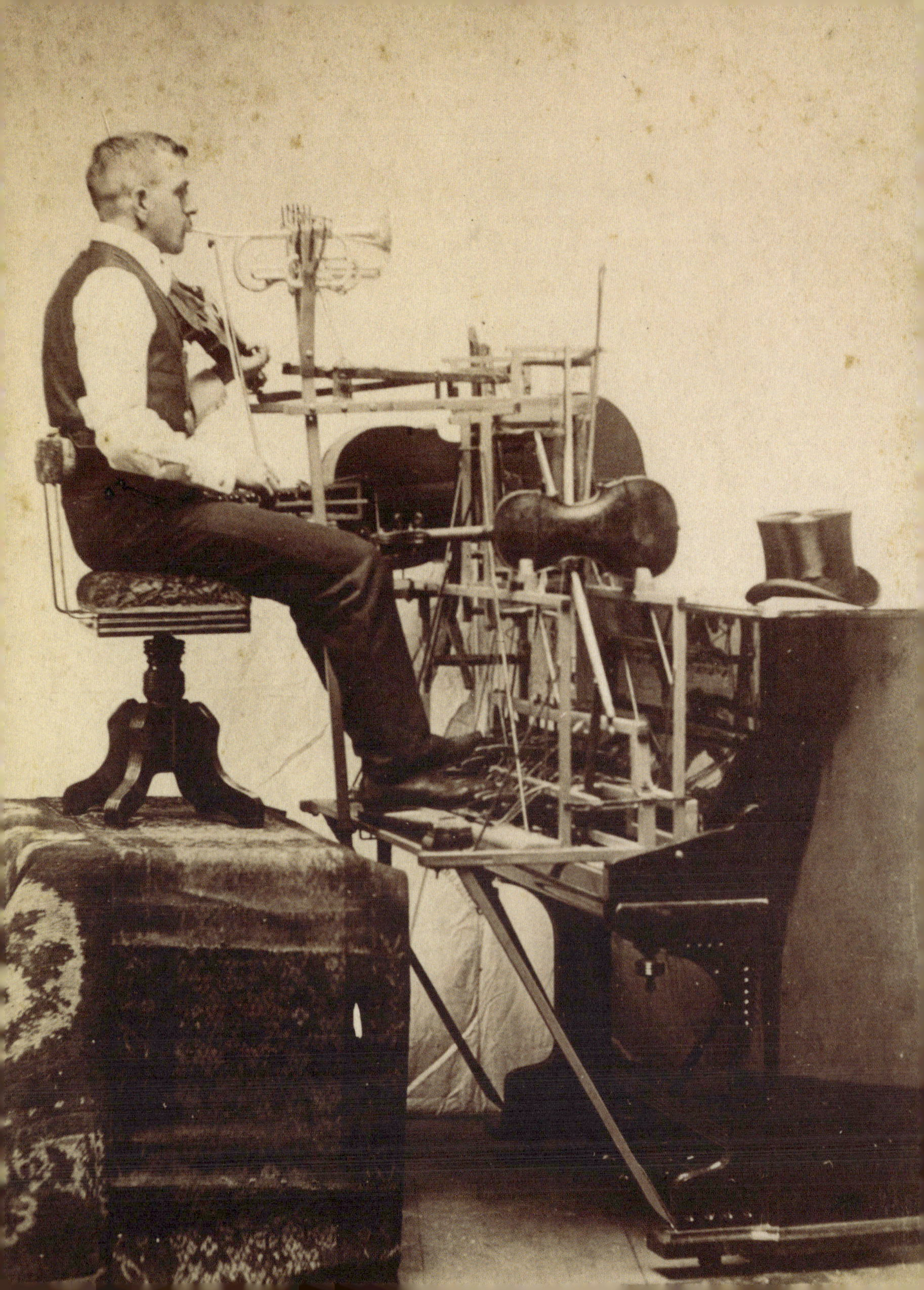

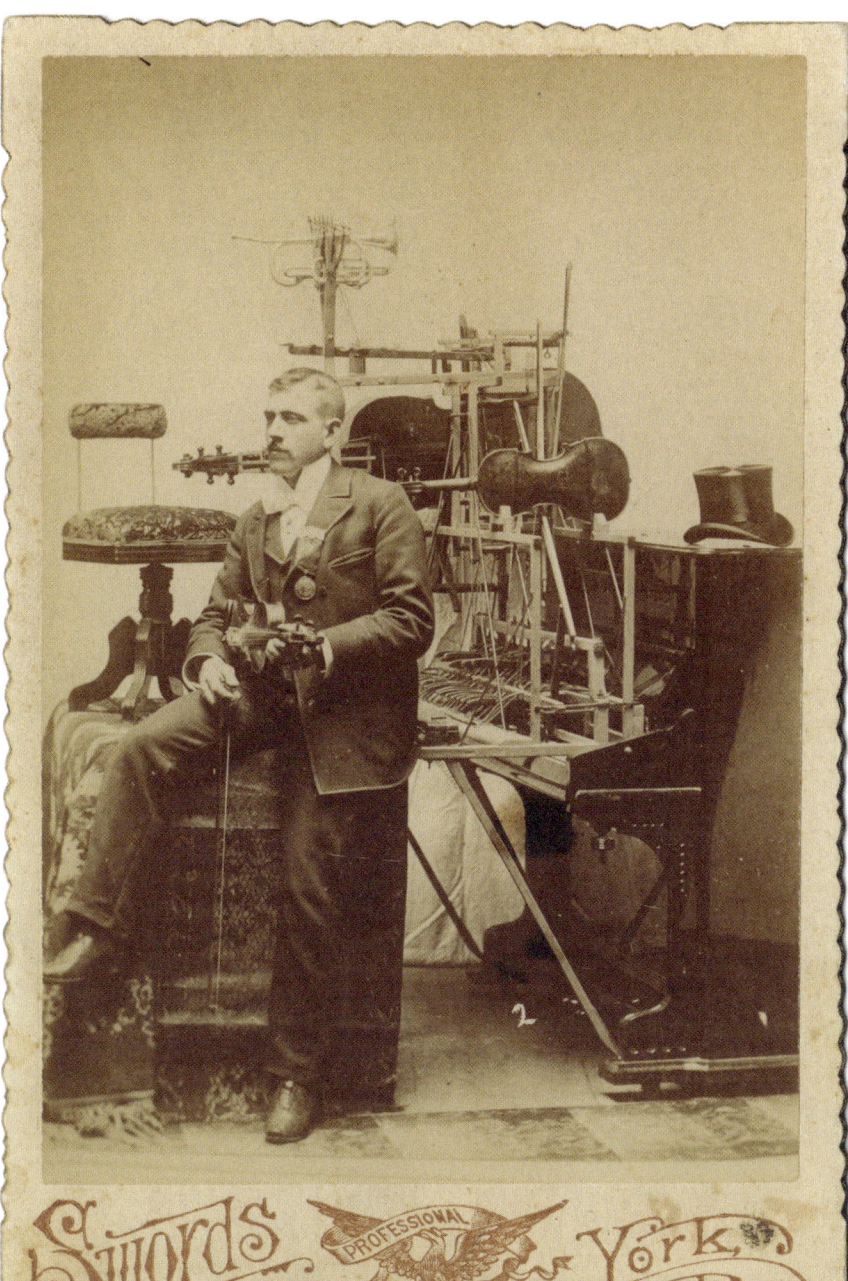

Swords Bros. PROFESSIONAL PHOTOGRAPHERS York, PA.

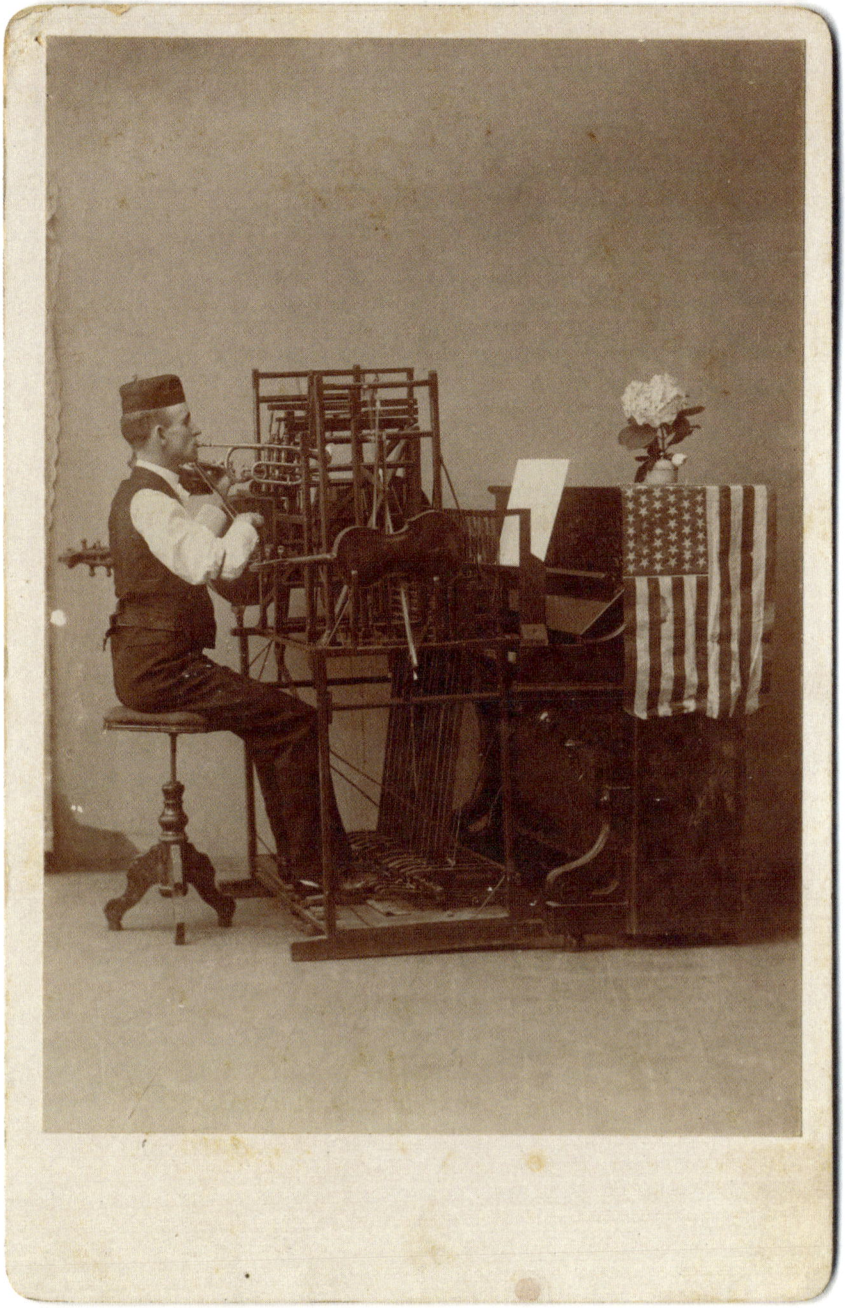

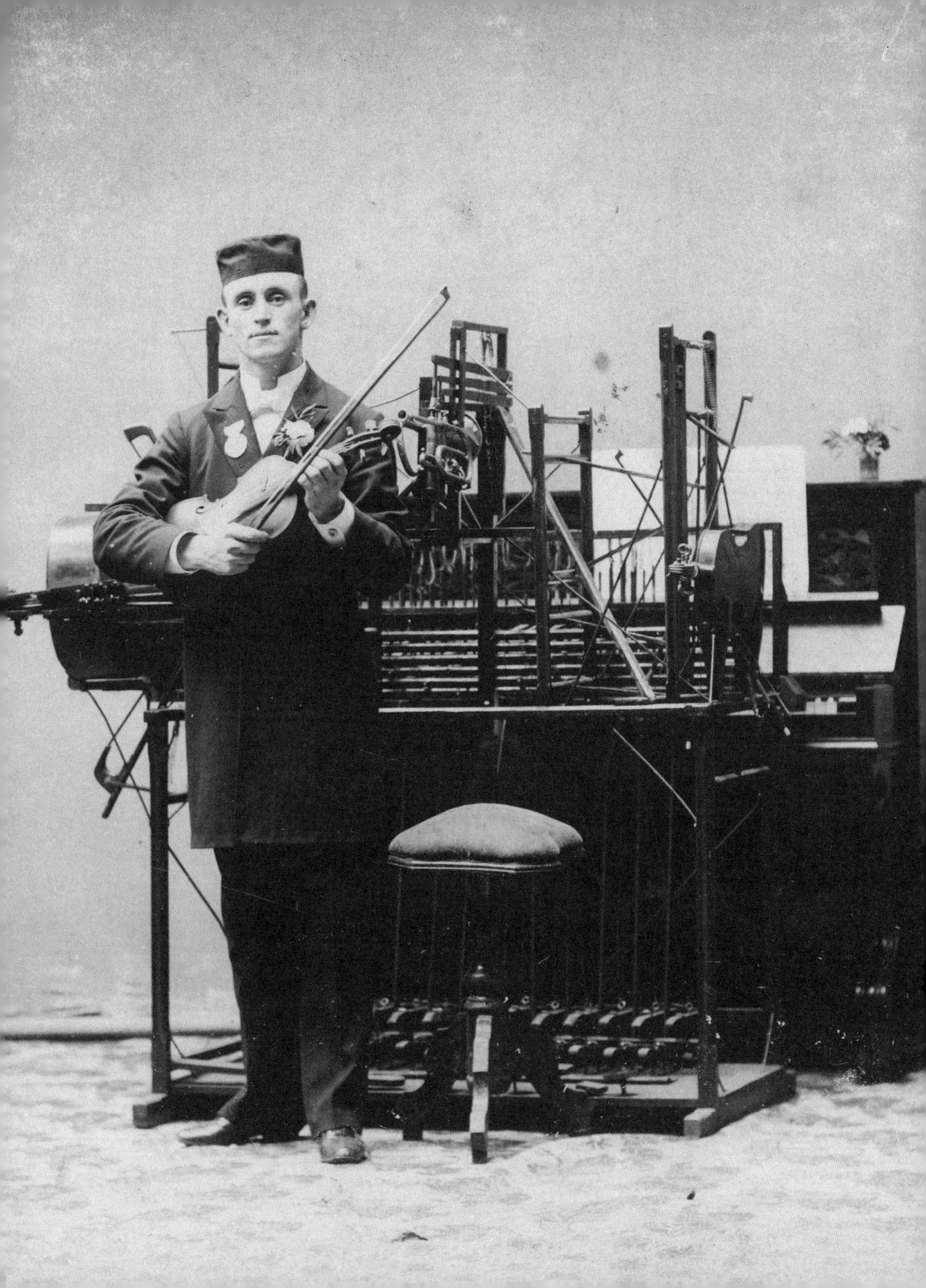

1903

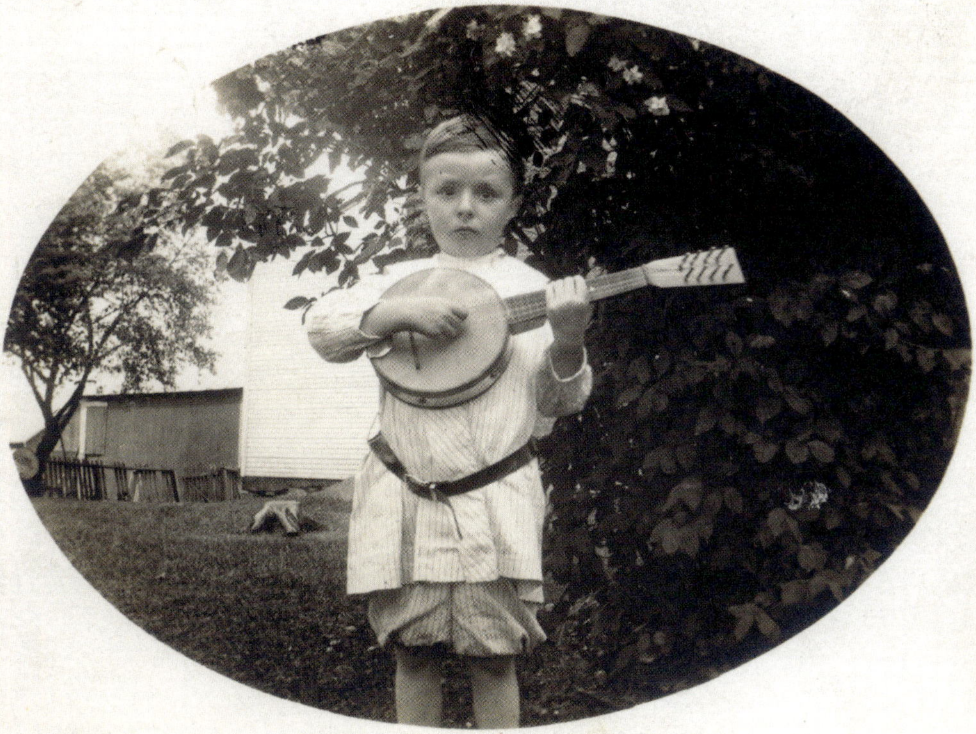

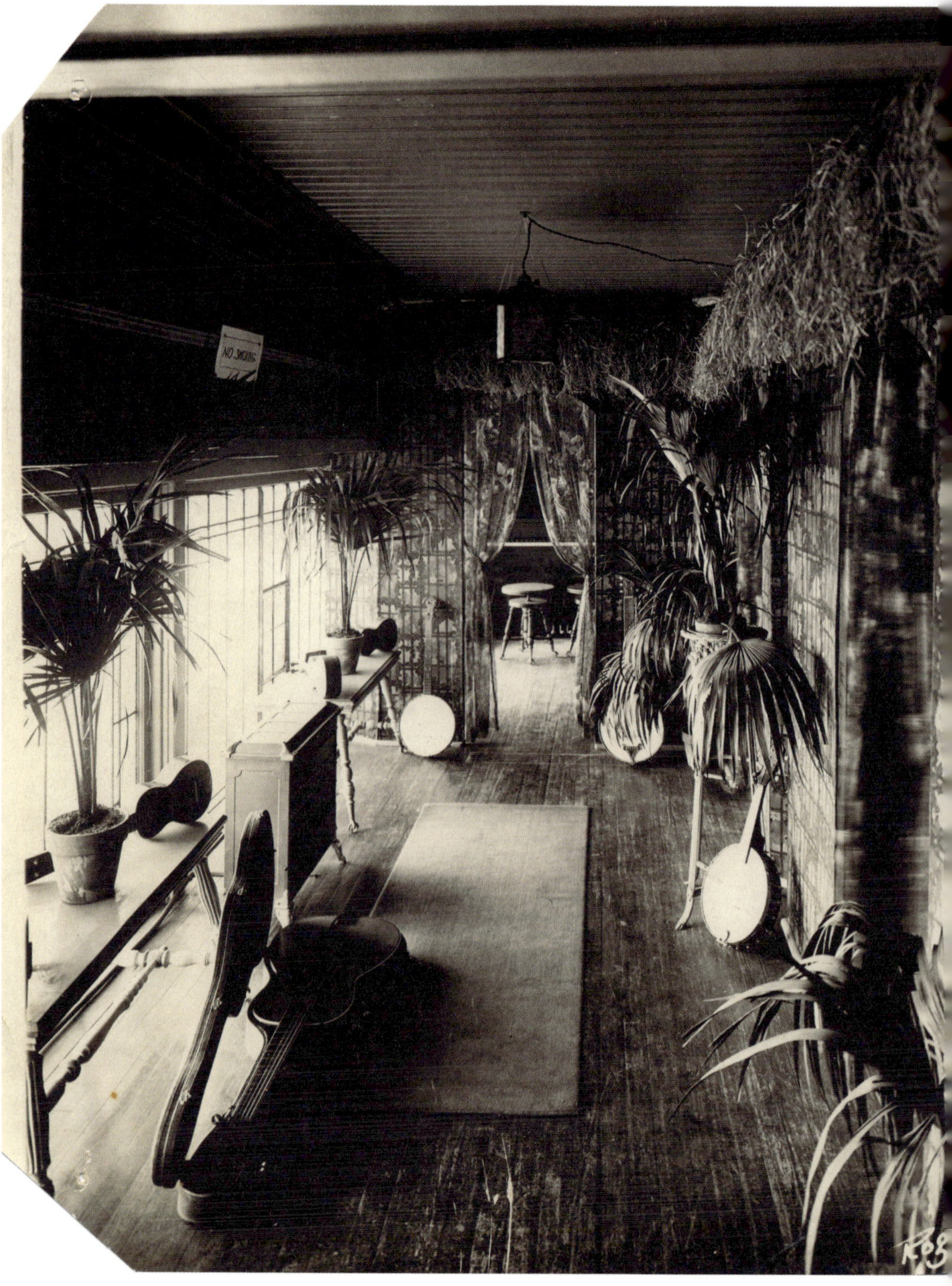
NO SMOKING

*instantly the room was populous with sounds of
melodiousness, and mournfulness, and wonderfulness;
the room swarmed with the unintelligible but delicious
sounds. the sounds seemed waltzing in the room;
the sounds hung pendulous like glittering icicles from
the corners of the room; and fell upon him with a ringing
silveryness; and were drawn up again to the ceiling,
and hung pendulous again, and dropt down upon him
again with the ringing silveryness. fire-flies seemed
buzzing in the sounds; summer-lightnings seemed
vividly yet softly audible in the sounds.*

herman melville
pierre: or, the ambiguities

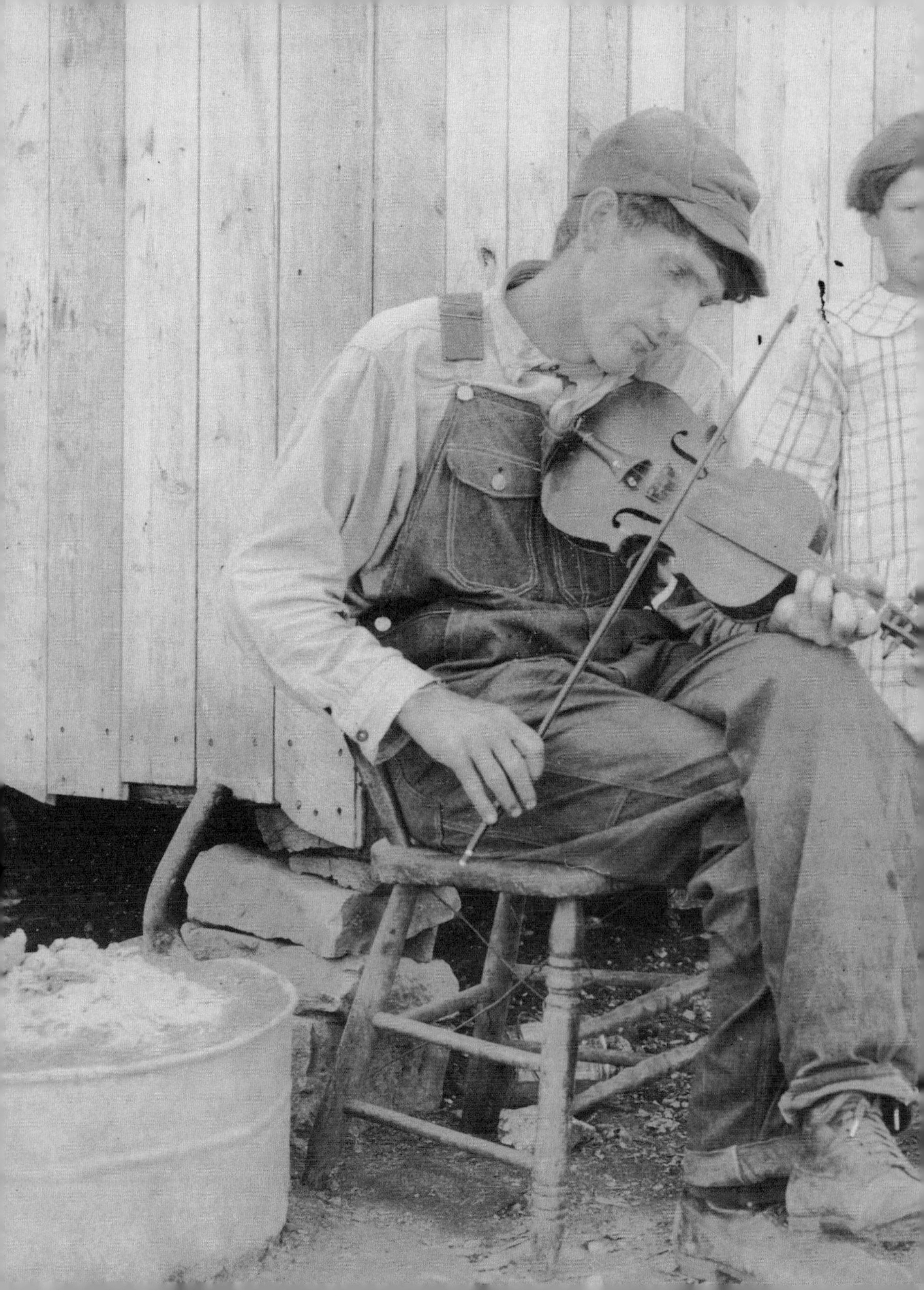

An Ozark Mountain Orchestra
Branson, Mo.

spring had come to the mountain-tracts. it was sunday morning; the weather was mild and calm, but the air somewhat heavy, and the mist lay low on the forest... when he opened the door the fresh smell of the leaves met him; the garden lay dewy and bright in the morning breeze, but from the ravine sounded the roaring of the waterfall, now in lower, then again in louder booms, till all around seemed to tremble... as he went further from the fall, its booming became less awful, and soon it lay over the landscape like the deep tones of an organ.

                                             bjorn bjornstarne
                                             arne

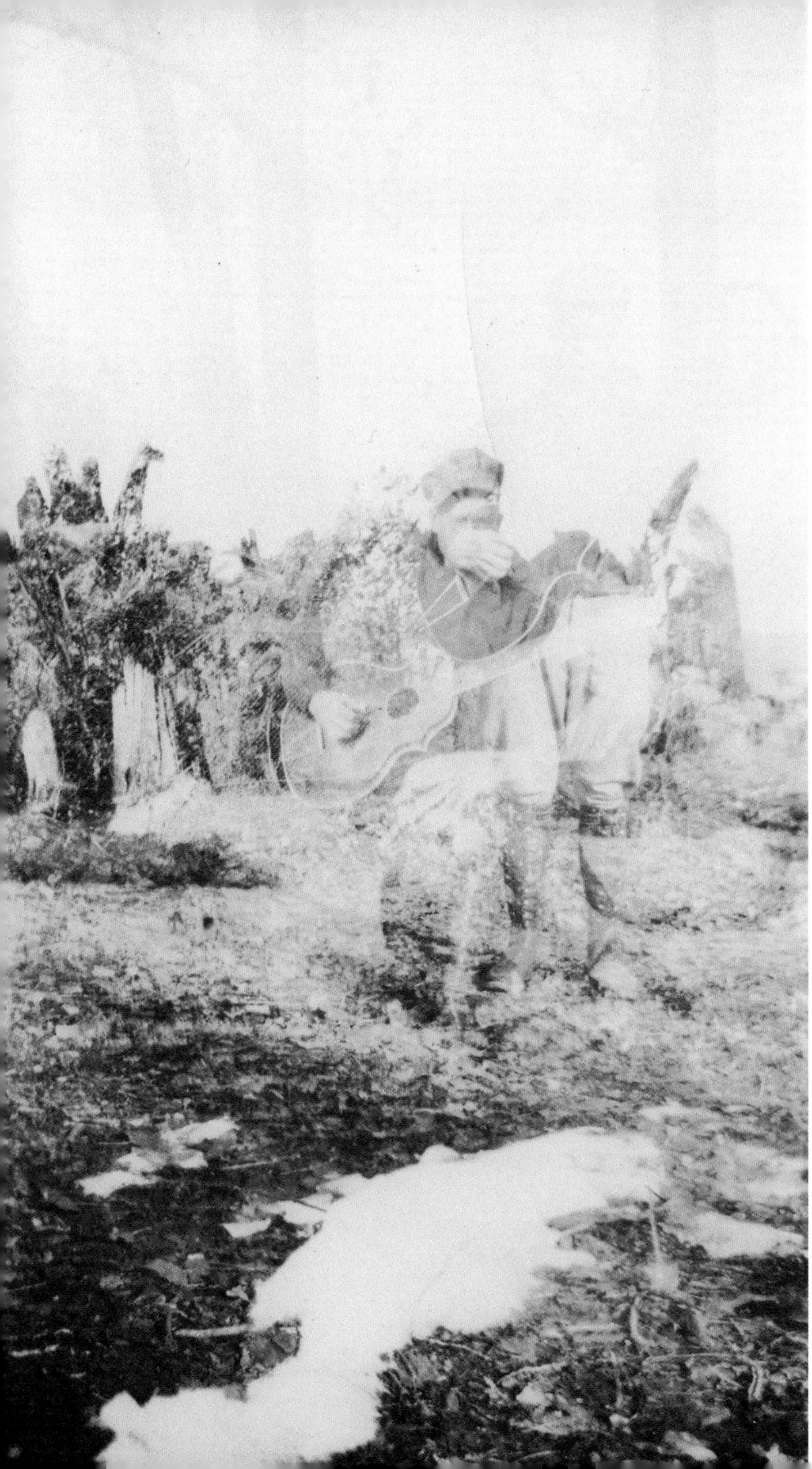

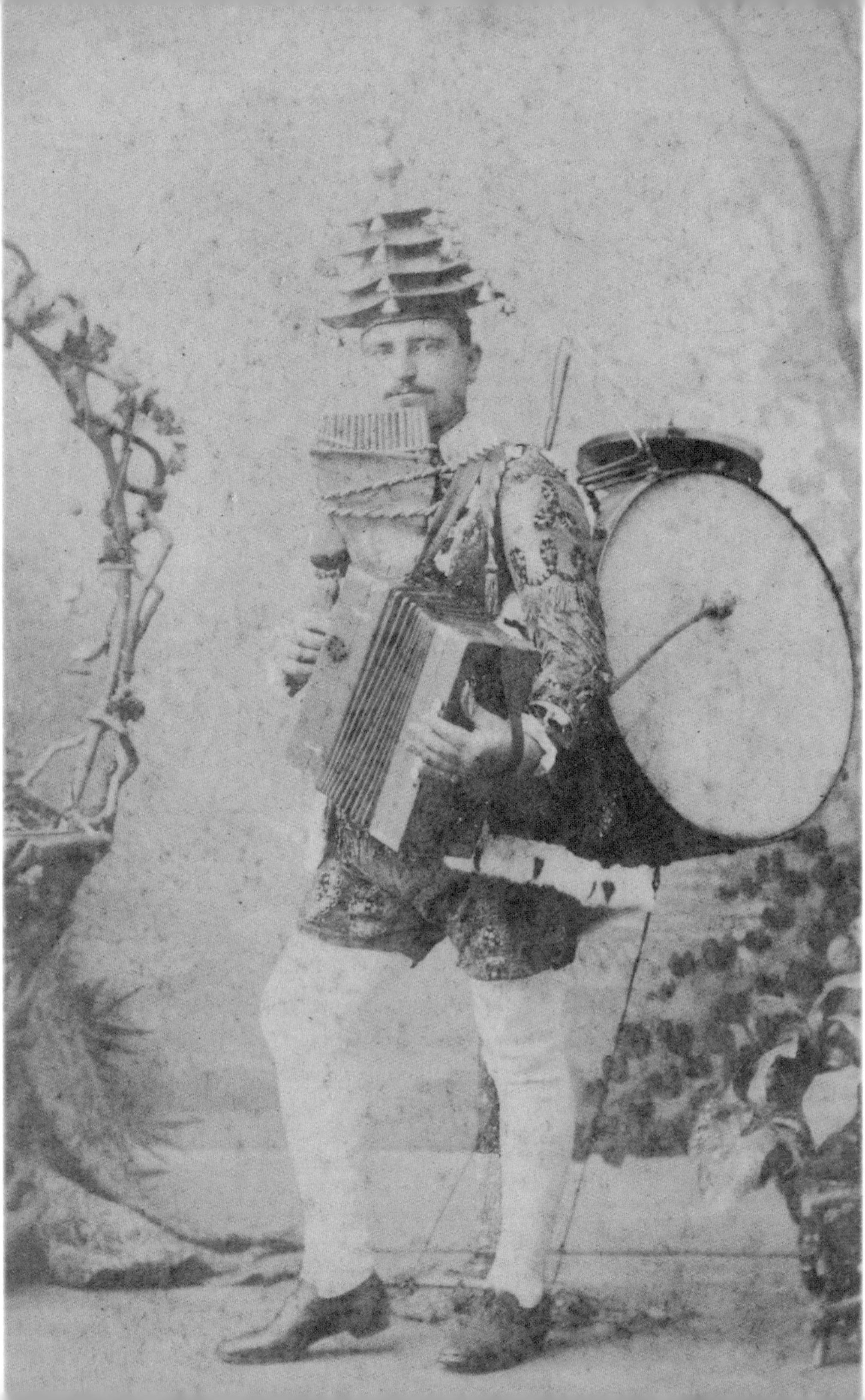

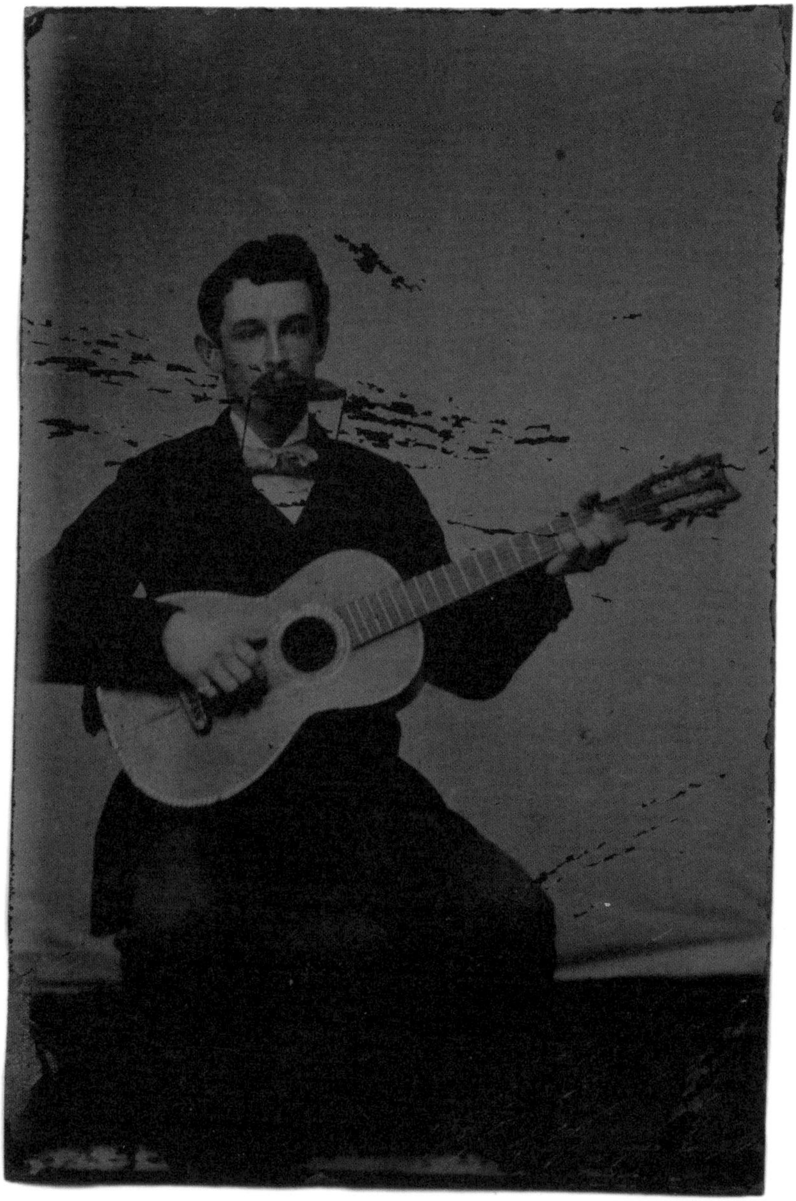

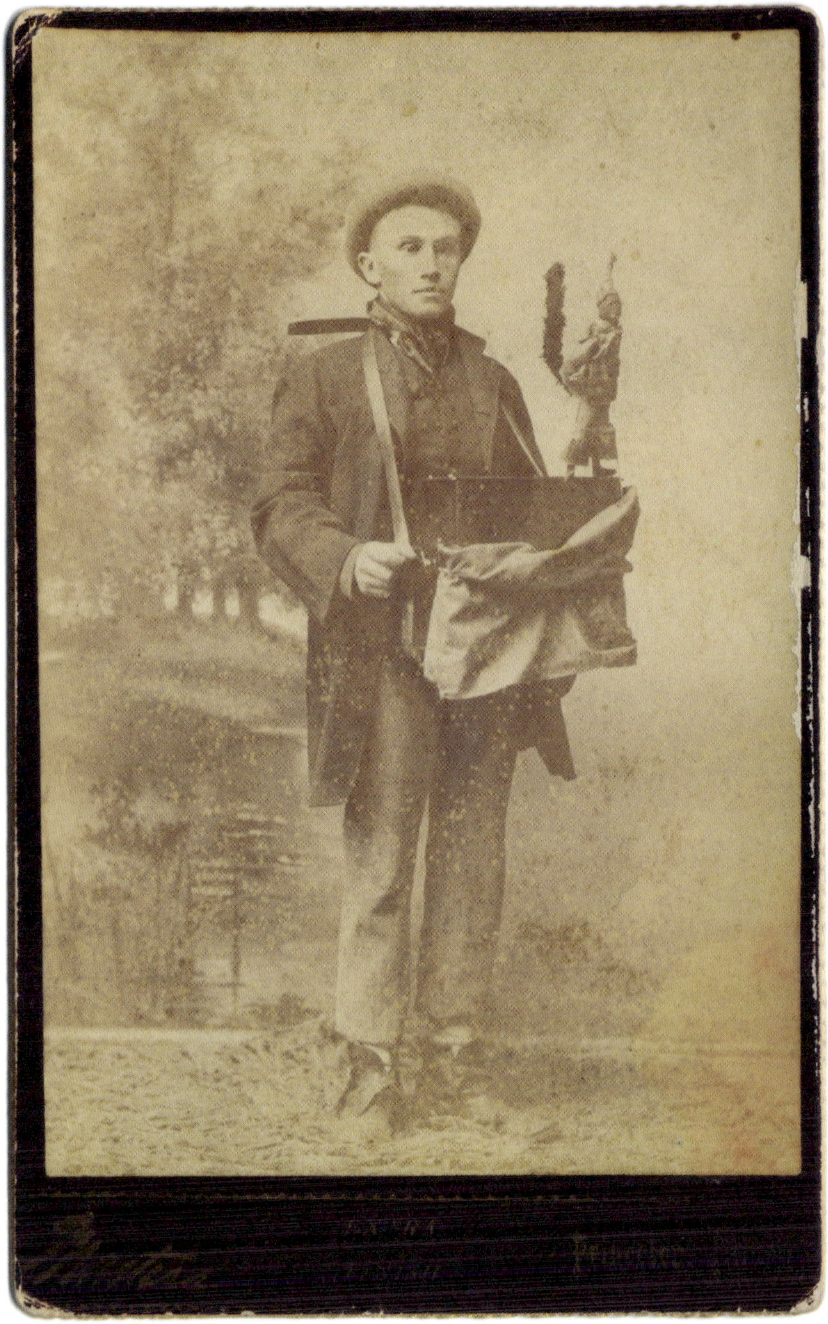

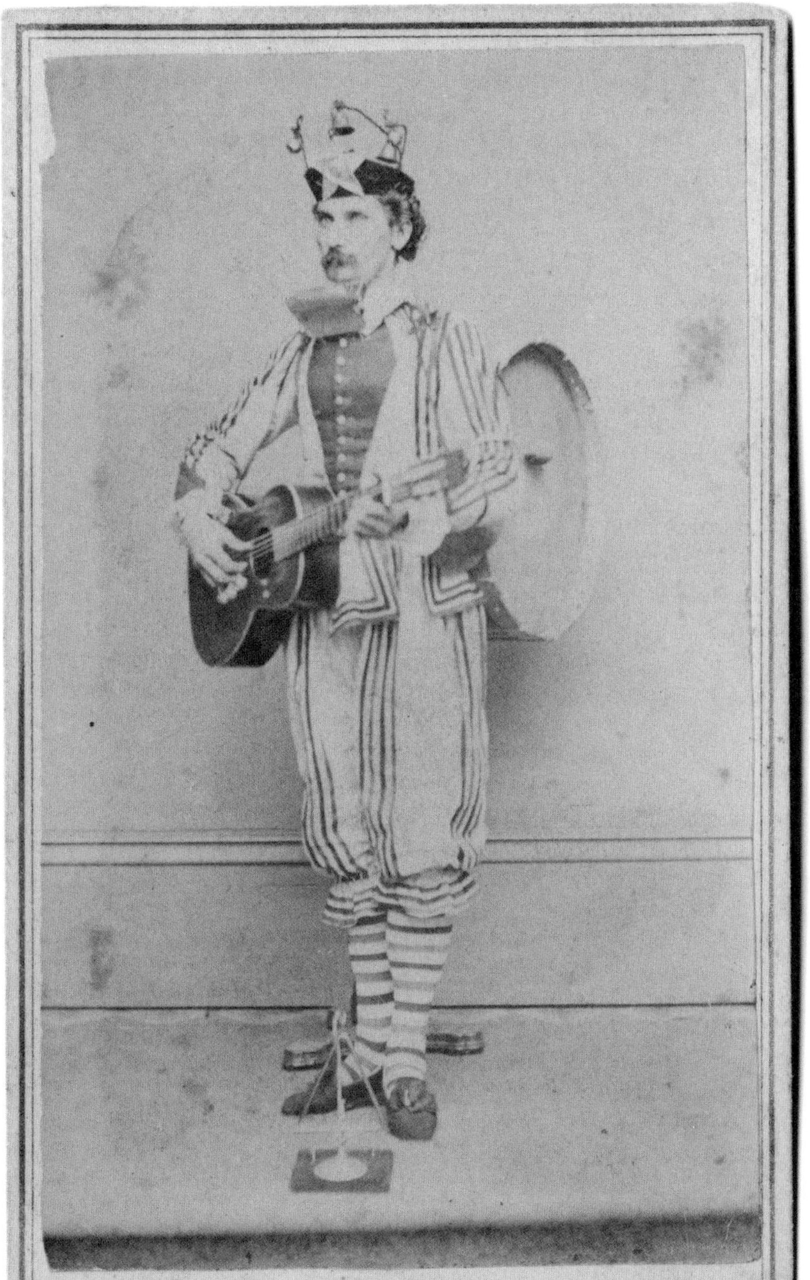

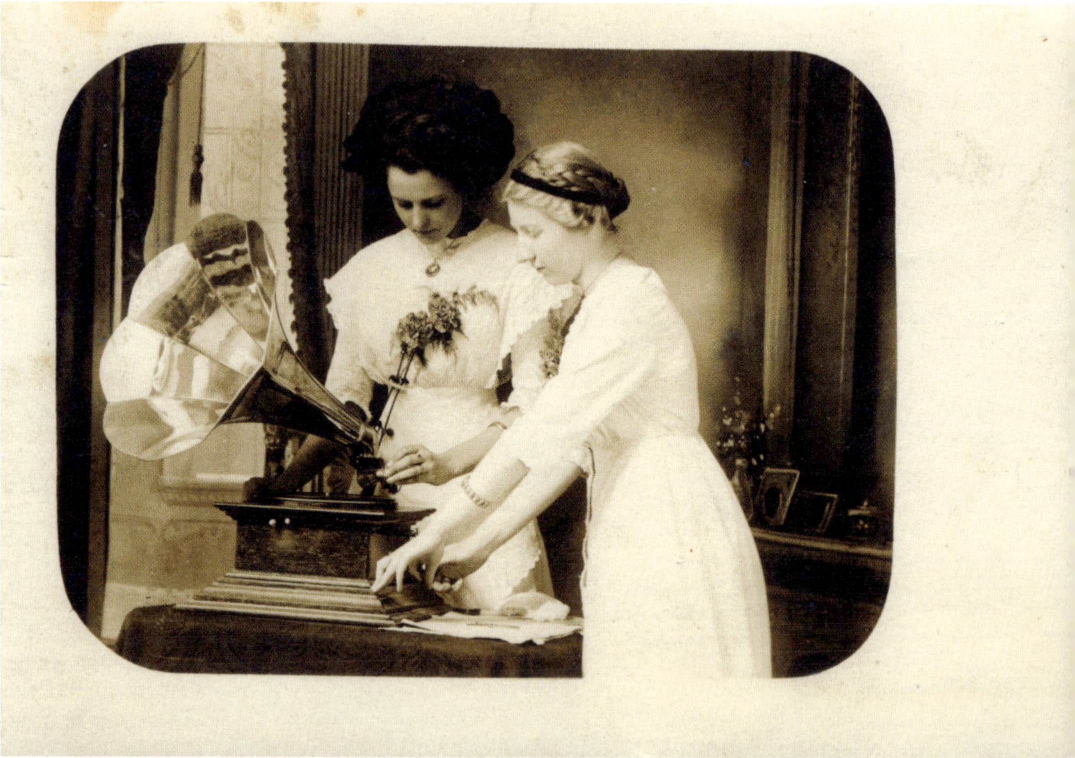

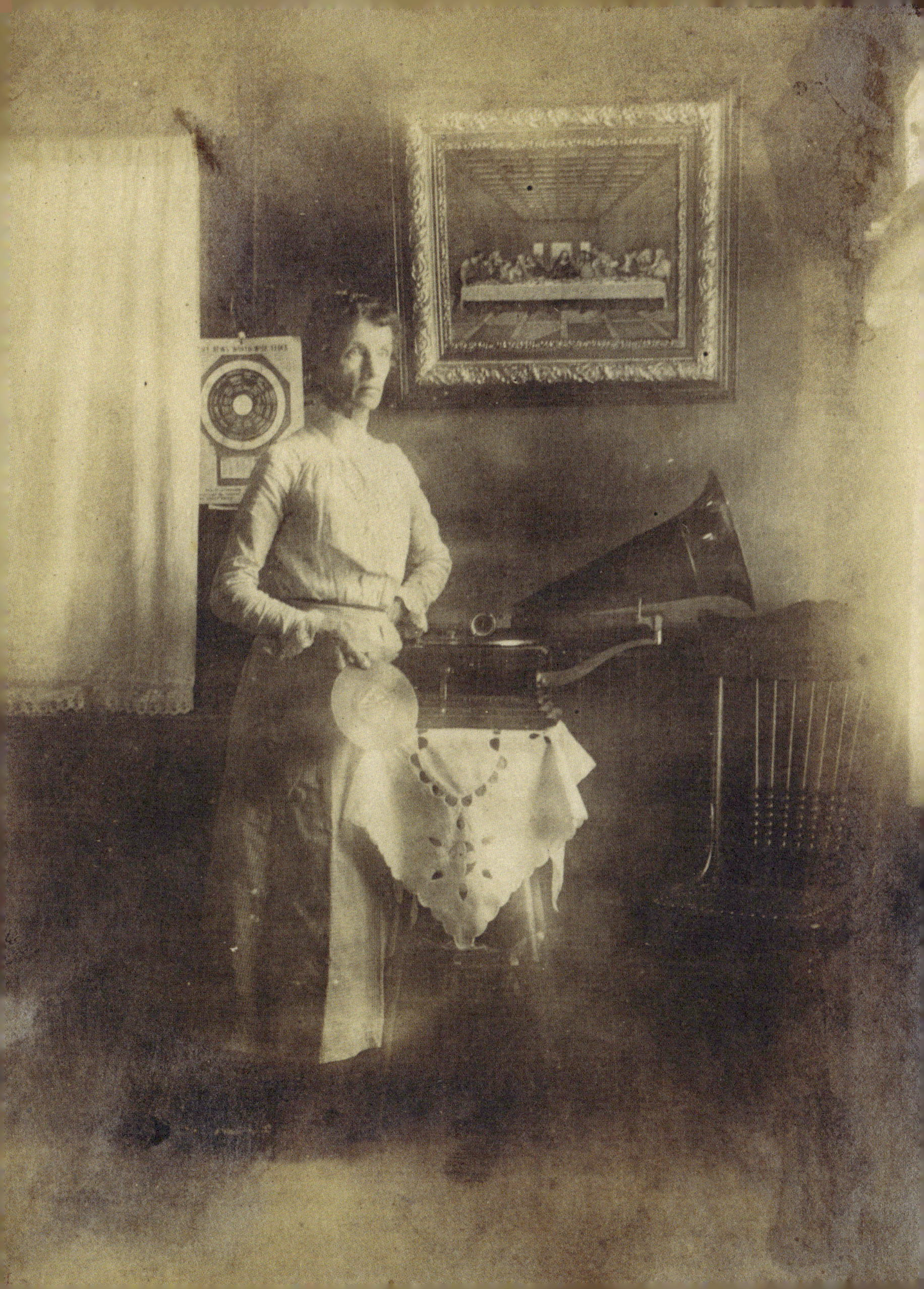

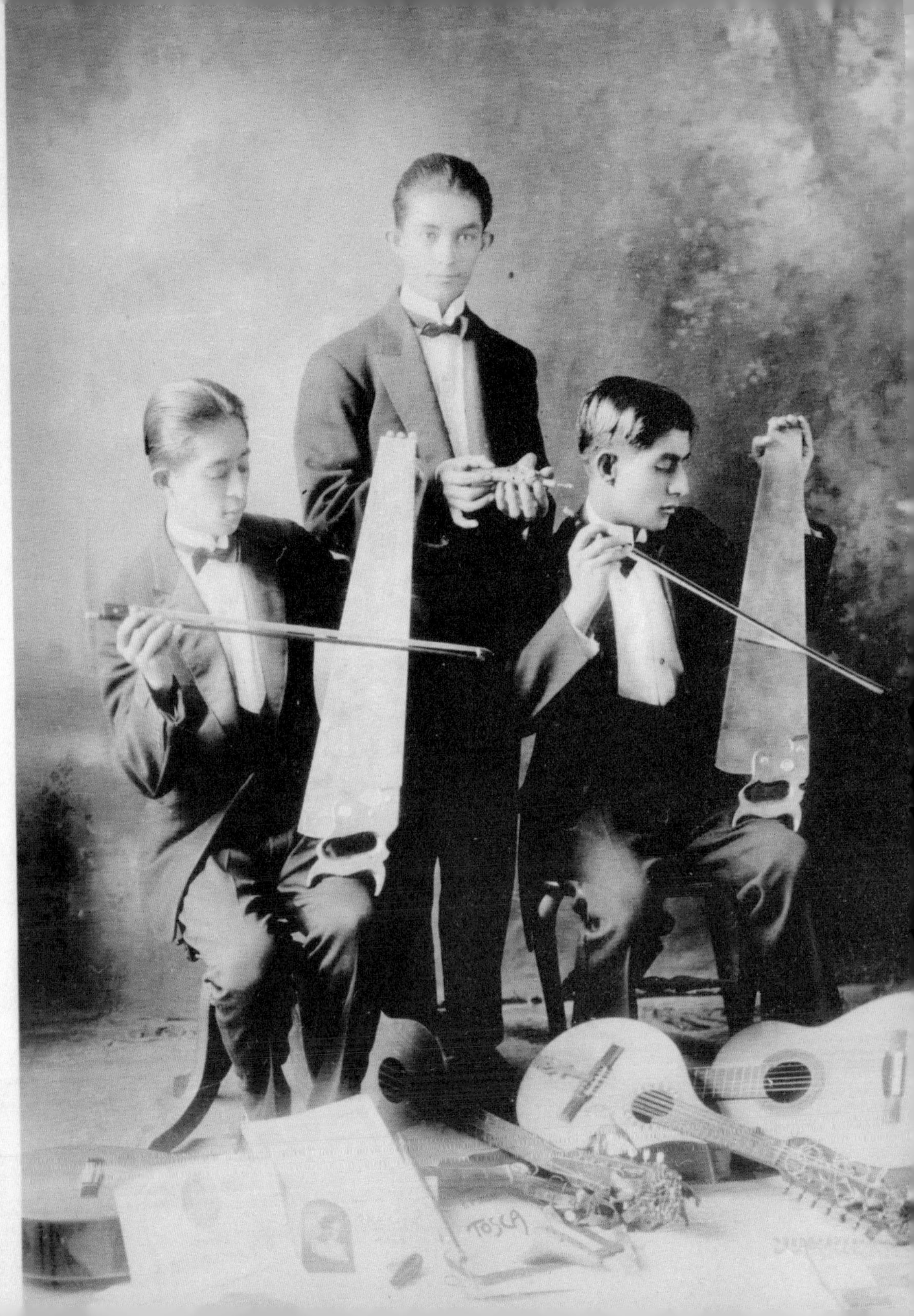
TOSCA

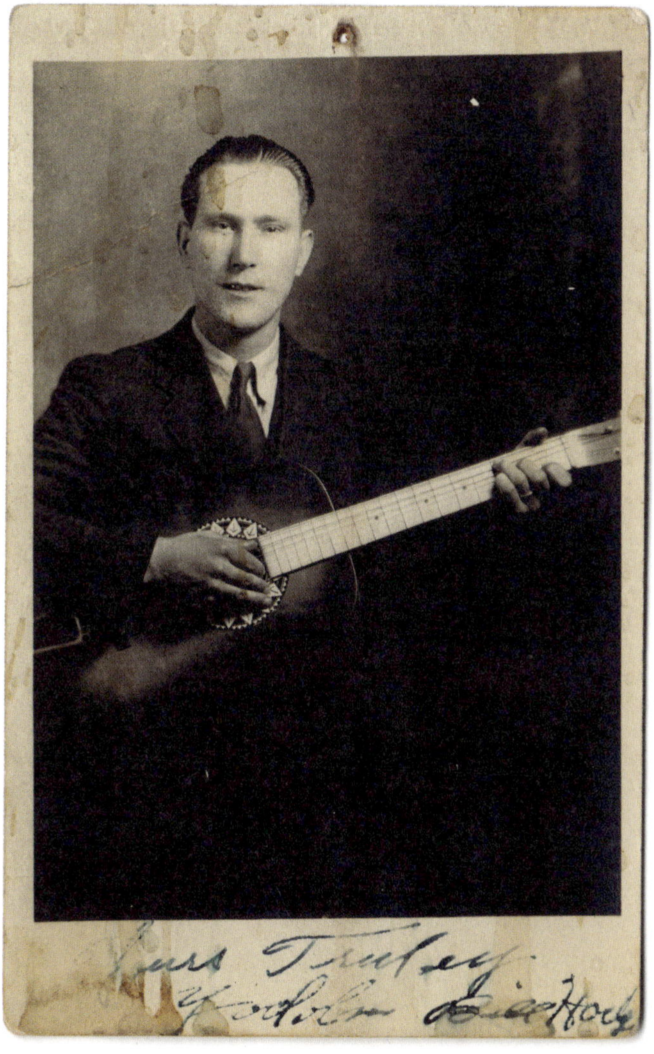

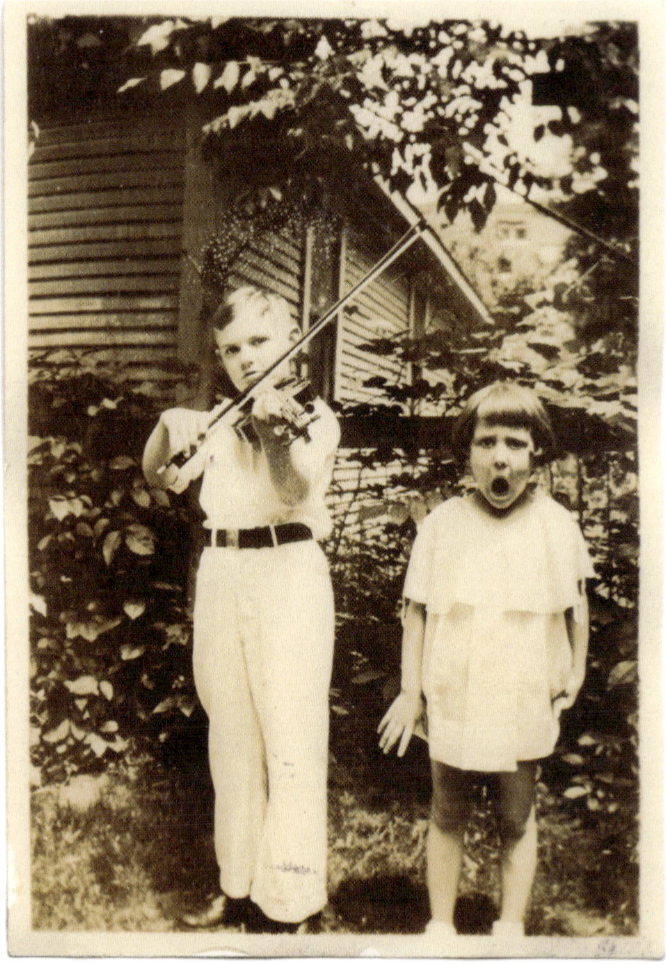

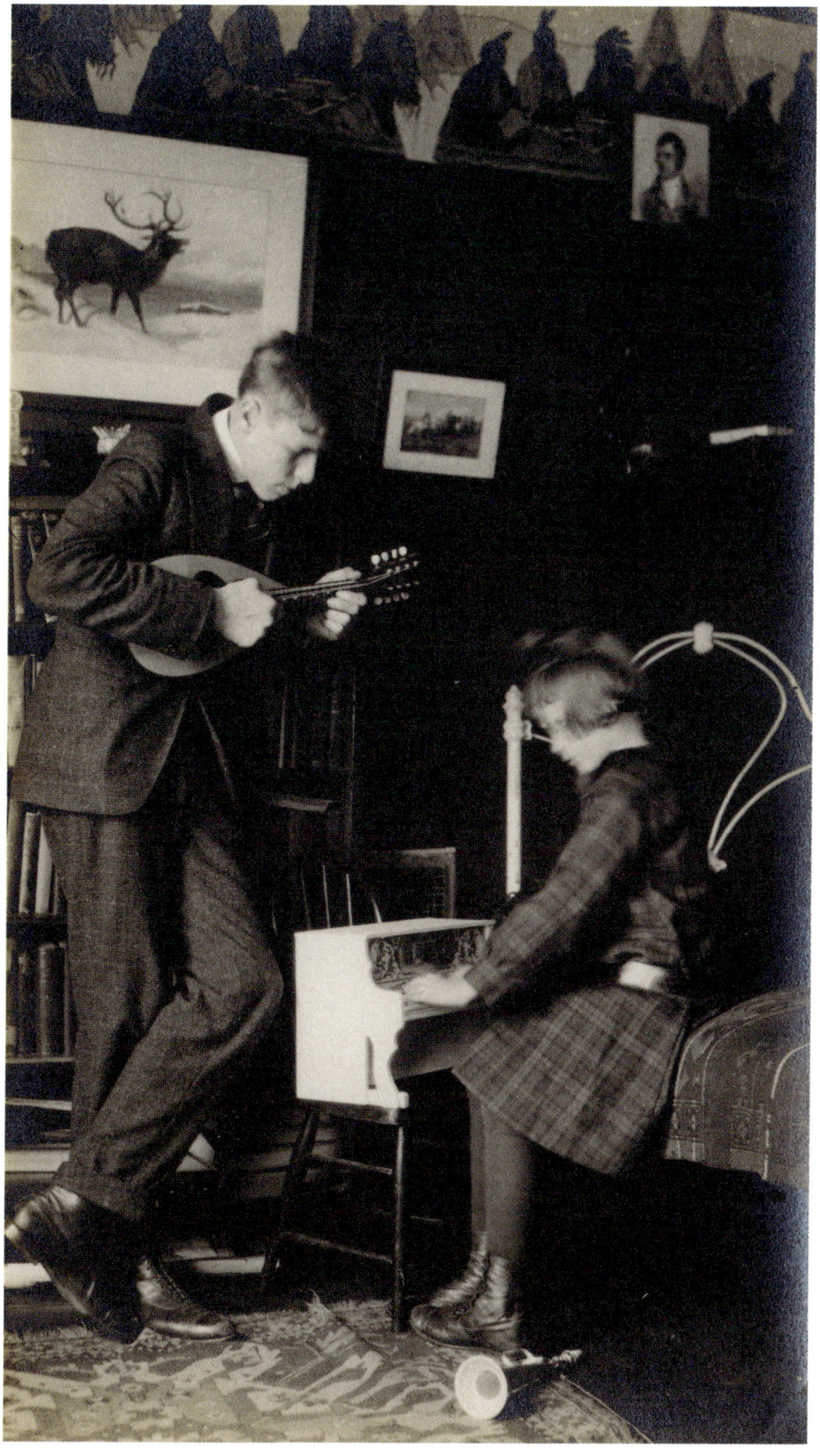

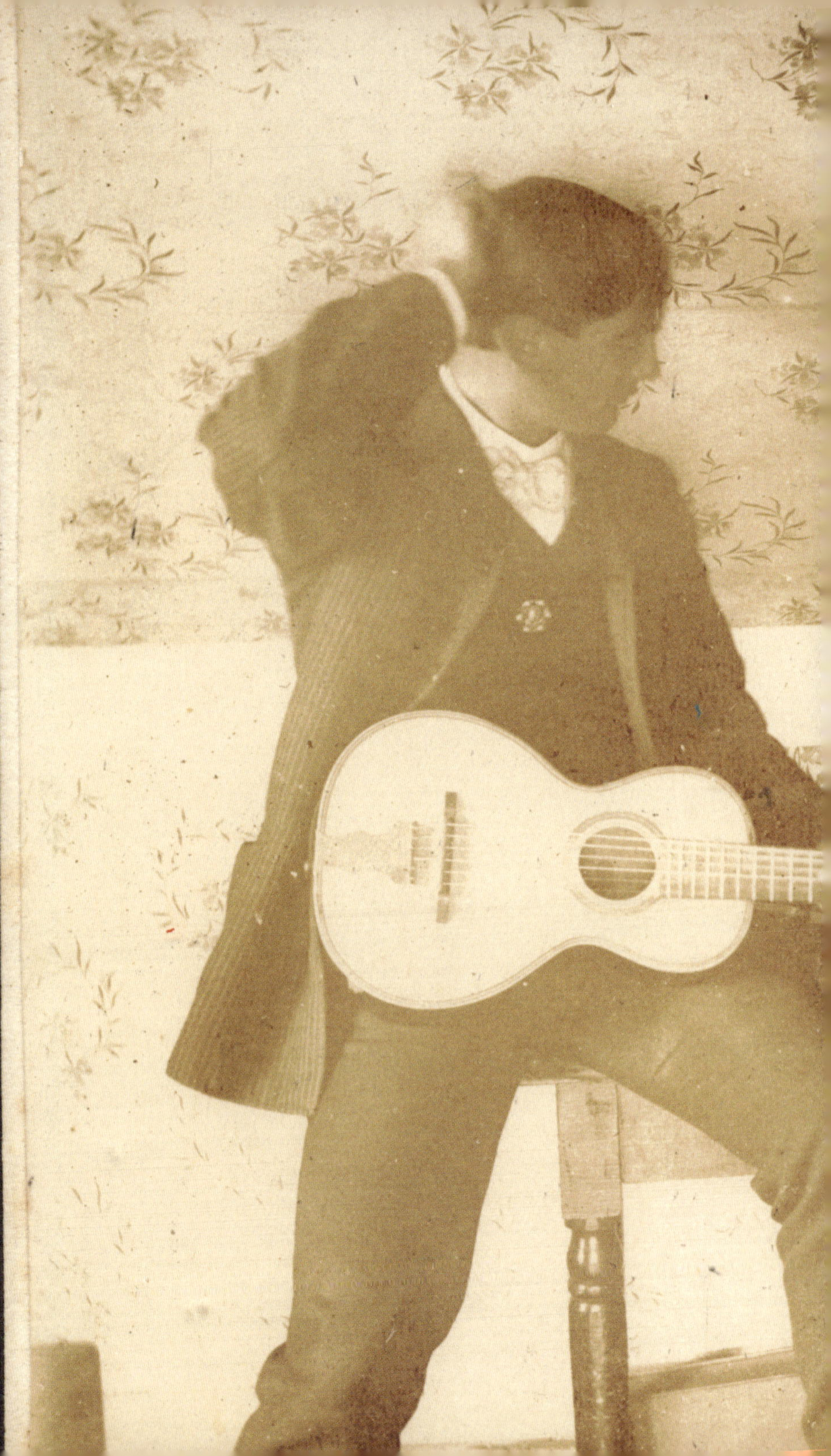

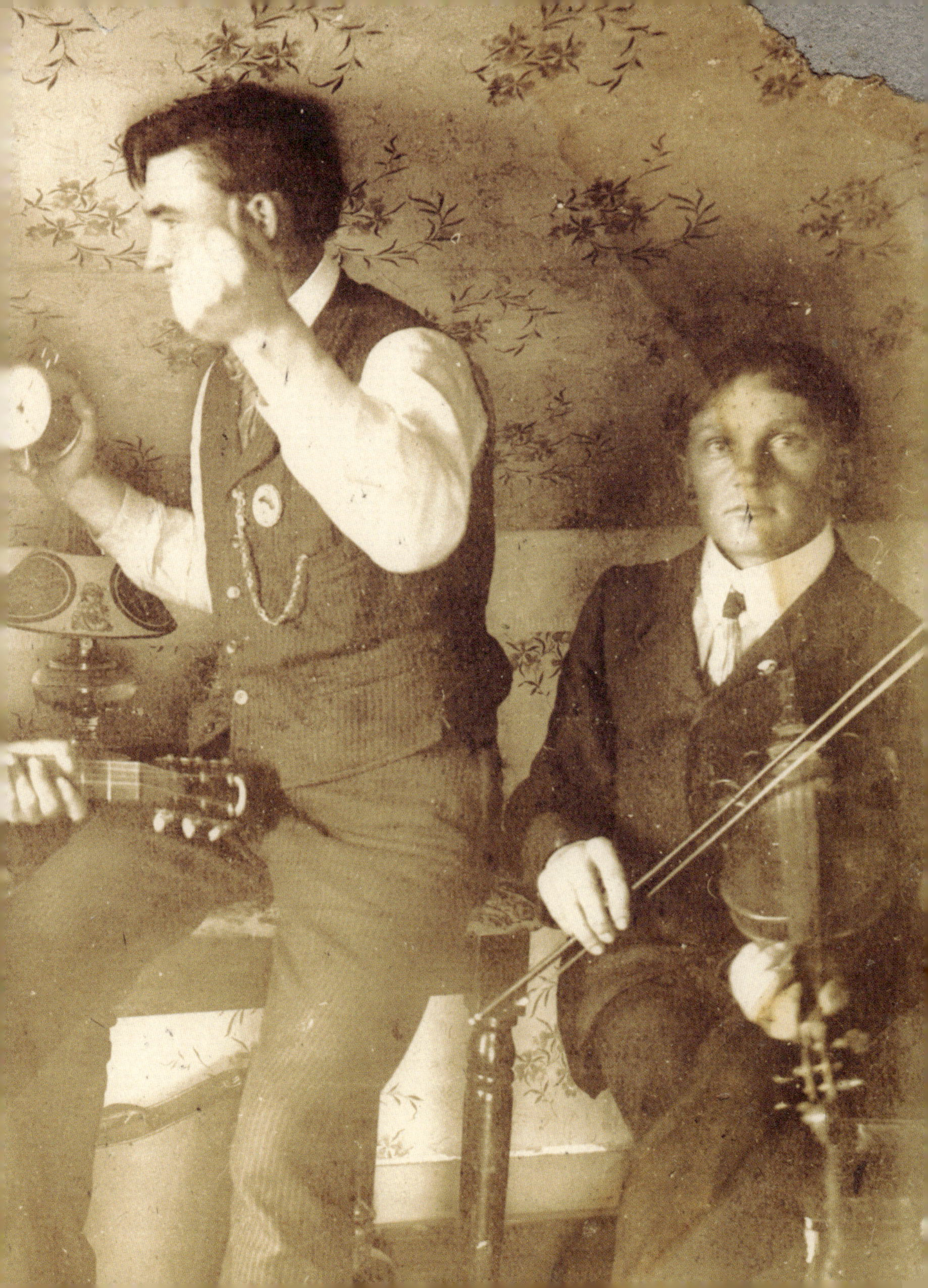

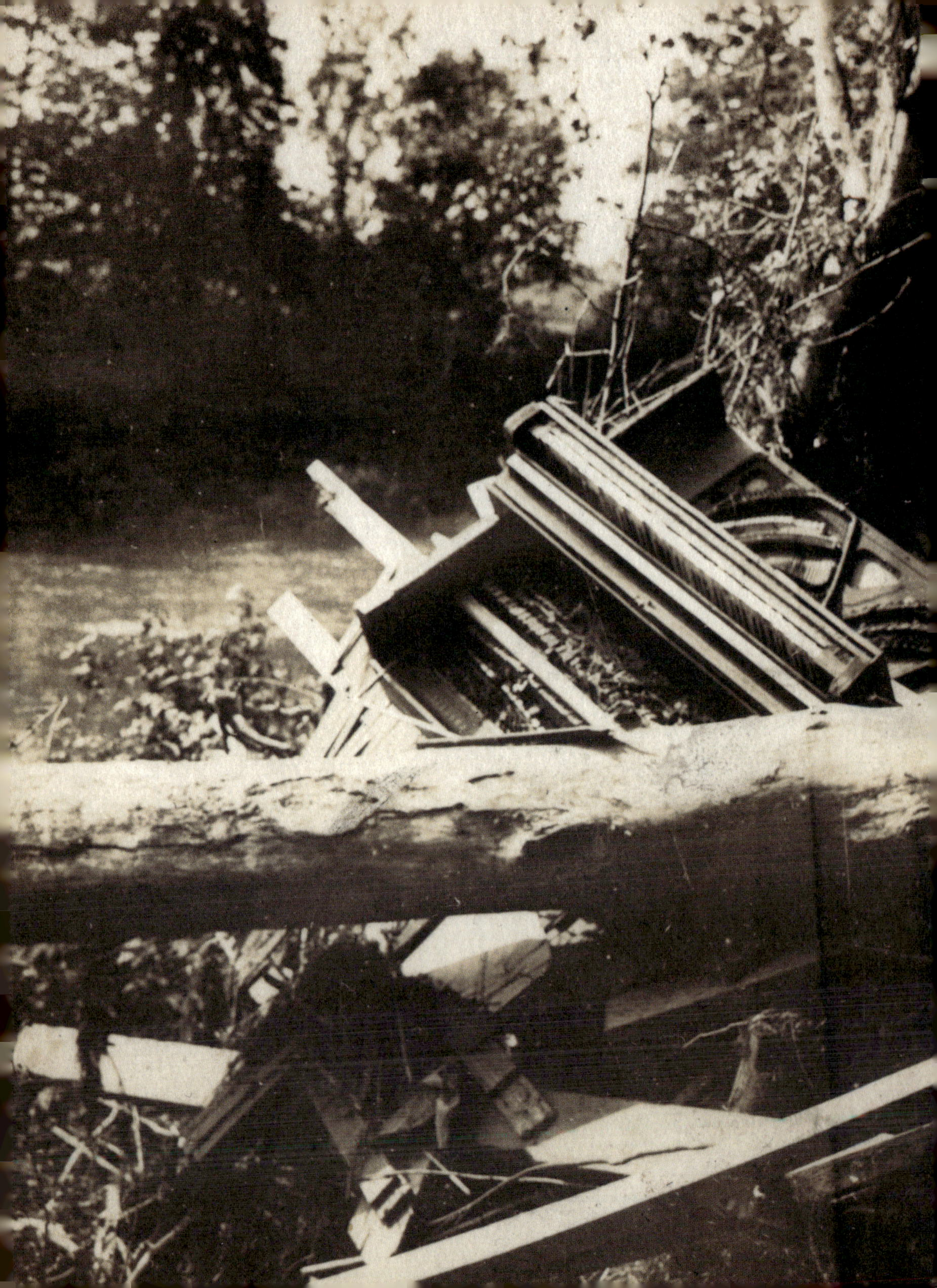

get a radio or a phonograph capable of the most extreme loudness possible, and sit down to listen to a performance of beethoven's seventh symphony or of schubert's c-major symphony. but i don't mean just sit down and listen. i mean this: turn it on as loud as you can get it. then get down on the floor and jam your ear as close into the loudspeaker as you can get it and stay there, breathing as lightly as possible, and not moving, and neither eating nor drinking. concentrate everything you can into your hearing and into your body. you won't hear it nicely. if it hurts you, be glad of it. as near as you will ever get, you are inside the music; not only inside it, you are it; your body is no longer your shape and substance, it is the shape and substance of music.

                                      james agee
                                      let us know praise famous men

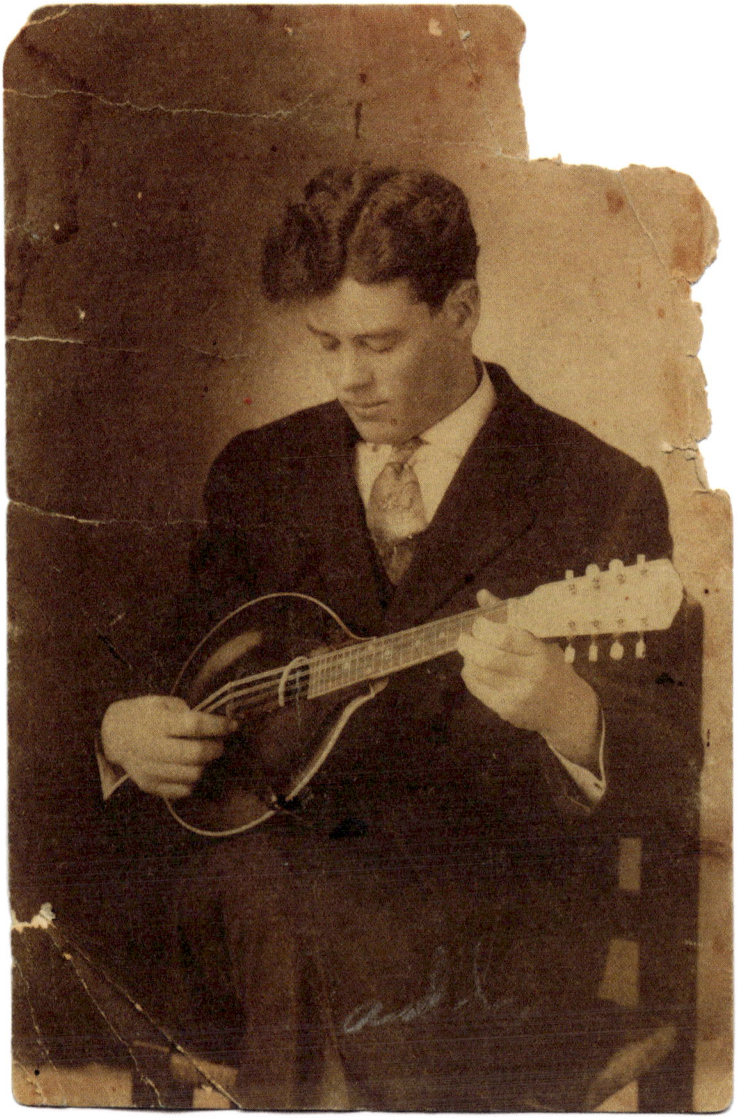

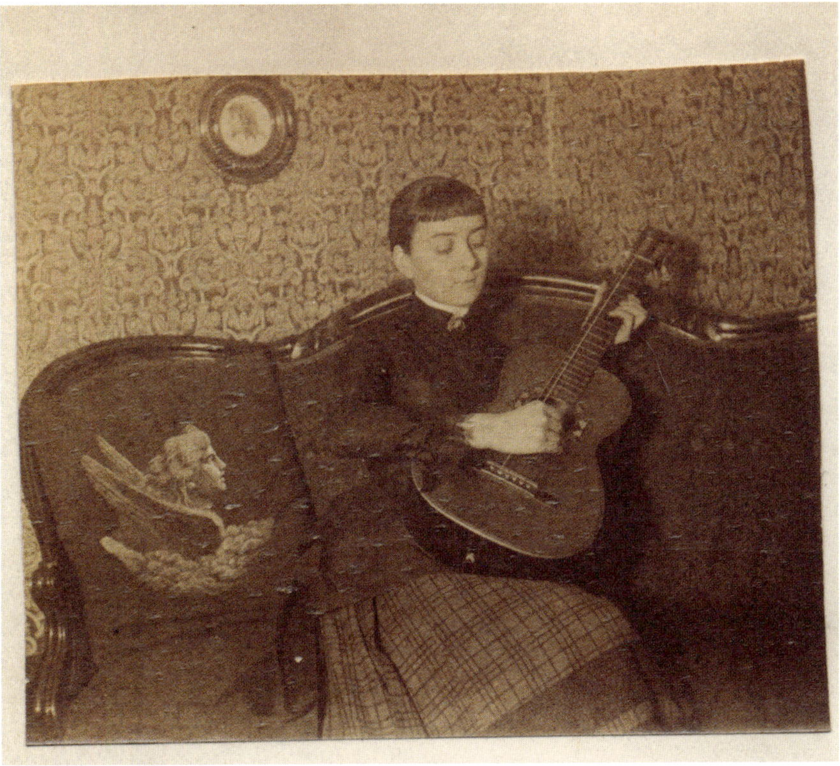

PHONOGRAPHS
DR. DELAVAN.
27
EDISON
RECORDS
December
Now on Sale

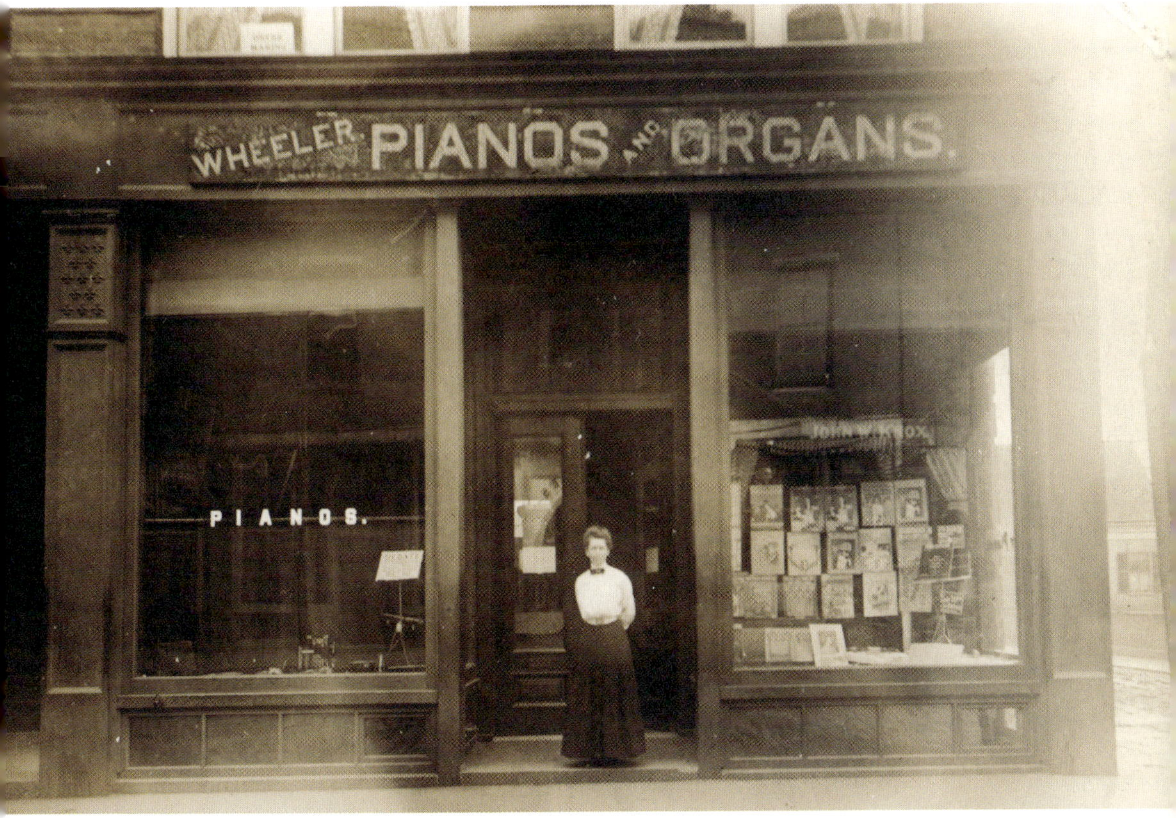
WHEELER.
PIANOS AND ORGANS.
PIANOS.

disc one

wind	hmv weather effects c.1935
john henry	john jacob niles 1940
untitled	anonymous (societe anonyme)
then we'll need that true religion	reverend edward clayborn 1927
in the baggage coach ahead	ernest thompson 1924
blue blazes blues	emery glen 1927
walking on ice	gennett sound effects c.1936
kind lovin' blues	clara smith 1923
if you hadn't gone away	nick lucas 1925
beautiful mansions of gold	anonymous (knight home-recording disc)
i seen my pretty papa standing on a hill	eva parker 1926
the rosary	pale k. lua 1914
mocking bird	gennett sound effects c.1936
froggie went a-courting	bradley kincaid 1928
damfino stump	sylvester weaver 1927
montana call	seger ellis 1931
when they ring the golden bells	alfred g. karnes 1928
mandolin	anonymous (recordio home-recording disc)
the stranger	anonymous (recordio home-recording disc)
brother noah built an ark	ex-governor alf. taylor's old limber quartet 1924
a little love a little kiss	ed lang 1927
canadian geese	standard radio sound effect c.1948
reaching for the moon	roy smeck's trio 1931
i want to go home	roland hayes 1941
the old grey horse	obed pickard of station wsm nashville tennessee 1927

disc two

walking in snow and thin underbrush	gennett sound effects c.1936
rovin' gambler	kelly harrell 1926
i've got to go and leave my daddy behind	sara martin & sylvester weaver 1923
pinin' hawaii for you	frank ferera's hawaiians 1928
going my way	gabriel brown and his guitar 1943
rainfall and thunder (thunder not from life)	gennett sound effects c.1936
it don't do nothing but rain	lew childre 1936
graveyard love	bertha idaho 1928
pretty polly	frank luther 1940
canary birds: several hundred	gennett sound effects c.1936
xango	roland hayes 1941
the girl i left behind me	dick reinhert 1929
yes i know	rev. calbert & sister billie holstein 1928
bib-a-lollie-boo	chubby parker 1927
winnebago love song (duet)	thurlow lieurance & clement barone 1929
my good for nuthin' man	clara smith 1925
stack o' lee blues	sol hoopii's novelty trio 1926
(i'm cryin' 'cause i know i'm) losing you	ukulele ike (cliff edwards) 1927
william & mary	marc williams 1934
way down home	anonymous (recordio home recording disc)
night noises	gennett sound effects c.1936
ya gotta quit kickin' my dog aroun'	gid tanner & his skillet lickers with riley puckett 1926
cripple creek and sourwood mountain	stovepipe no. 1 (sam jones) 1925
cowboy's prayer	goebel reeves 1934
precious memorys (sic)	bill kearney & earl bush (s.o.s. recording and radio service disc, honolulu, november 3, 1955 "to dotty from bill kearney")
o bury me not on the lone prairie	carl t. sprague 1926

anonymous and home recording disc dates are unknown

PHOTOGRAPHIC STOCK HOUSE AND GALLERY
G.W. JORNS 1882
G. W. JORNS.
215

the photographs and recordings reproduced in this book are from my personal collection, which, of course, contains not only music and sound related photographs and old records, but veers off in numerous other directions. things have been plucked from flea markets, auctions, ebay, dealers and friends—and yes, i'm always looking for more.

special thanks to: dan goodsell, my flea market compadre for nearly 20 years, who still makes fun of my looking through boxes of "old timey" records; sari roden for accepting the addiction and ignoring the clutter; steve peters for sending me that cassette of washington phillips years ago; damon cleckler for the harry smith anthology and opening my ears to music i thought i hated. muriel pic for sharing benjamin, warburg, sebald and butterflies; 'ear stone' for the melville quote and continued wing folding; rob millis for sarcasm, enthusiasm, stellar collaboration, and absolutely making this book happen; lance and april ledbetter from dust-to-digital for wanting to publish it; john hubbard for his incredible design; jonathan ward for doing high class transfers of my rare $2 records and for not hating bradley kincaid; to robert jackson, eric rollins, randy jones, patrick jenkins, marc sullo, and everyone else who has given, traded or sold me photographs over the past few years; and lastly to my mother who took me to flea markets when i was a youngster... yes, it is all her fault!

—steve roden, 2011

for more information:
inbetweennoise.blogspot.com
www.inbetweennoise.com

Executive producer: Steven Lance Ledbetter

Produced by Steve Roden and Robert Millis

Original 78s from the collection of Steve Roden

Records transferred by Steve Roden, Jonathan Ward

Audio mastered by Michael Graves, Osiris Studio

Designed by John Hubbard

Original photographs from the collection of Steve Roden

Images scanned by April G. Ledbetter, Steve Roden, Hilary Staff

Color by iocolor, Seattle
Printed in China by C&C Offset Printing Co., Ltd.

Components under license from various sources.
©℗ 2011 Dust-to-Digital / Steve Roden

Dust-to-Digital
PO Box 54743
Atlanta, GA 30308-0743
www.dust-digital.com

ISBN 978-0-9817342-4-8

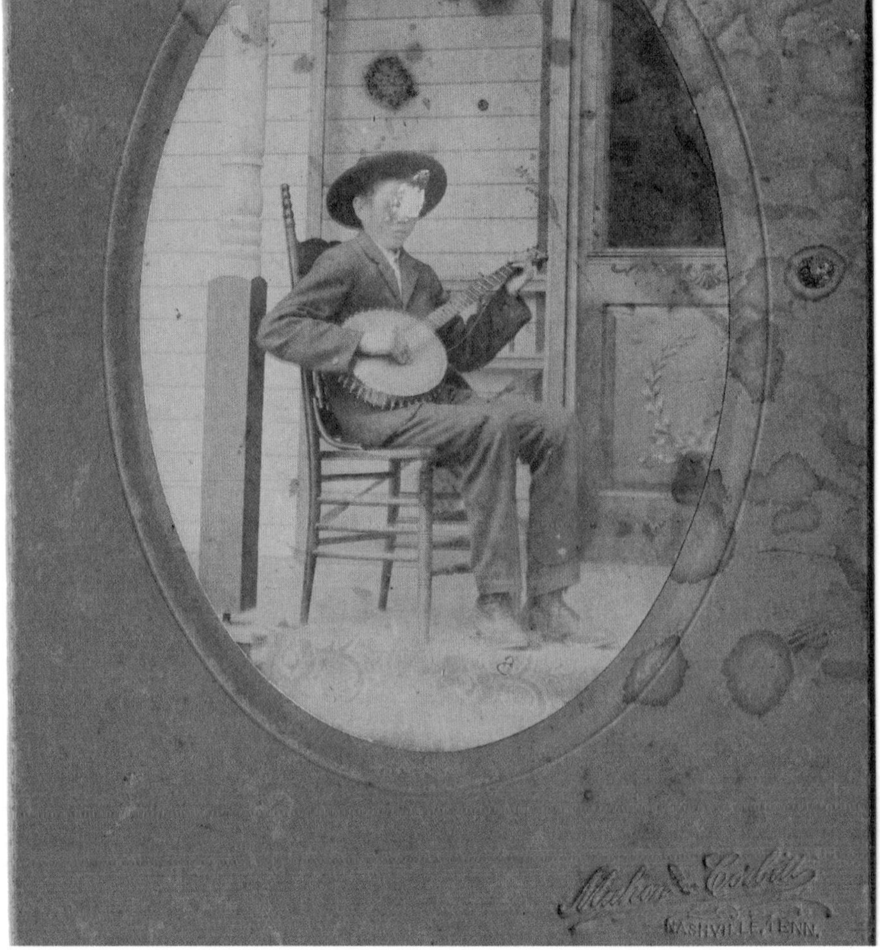
NASHVILLE, TENN.